Kathy's Cookbook
...from Klek to Cleveland

*Kathy McClellan's
Signature Recipes*

© 2010 John A. McClellan
All rights reserved
ISBN 978-1-257-90953-7

Table Of Contents

Acknowledgment *4*

Appetizers & Side Dishes *5*

Breads & Spreads *29*

Breakfast *57*

Cakes *67*

Canning Recipes *97*

Cookies *105*

Christmas *150*

Easter *161*

New Year's Day *167*

Saint Patrick's Day *170*

Thanksgiving *175*

Main Course Dishes *186*

Miscellaneous *260*

Muffins & Stuff *275*

Pies *286*

Salads, Fruits & Vegetables *296*

Sandwiches *334*

Scones *349*

Snacks & Desserts *357*

Soups *408*

Acknowledgment

This cookbook is both inspired by and dedicated to my mother, Kathy A. McClellan. Although she didn't always use recipes, I used to help out in the kitchen, and with my wife's help, I've tried my best to reproduce many of her signature dishes.

Several of my great-grandmother's recipes are included as well. In fact, quite a few are typical of the Donauschwäbische region where she was born (Klek, Banat).

I hope you enjoy this cookbook as much as I enjoyed making it!

John A. McClellan
March 31st, 2010
Cleveland, Ohio

Appetizers & Side Dishes

Cheese Spaetzle

1 (16 ounce) package spaetzle
3 tablespoons melted butter
½ pound bacon
2 medium onions, thinly sliced
8 ounces mushrooms, sliced
3 cloves garlic, minced
Salt and freshly ground black pepper, to taste
2 cups shredded muenster cheese

Bring a large pot of water to boil. Prepare spaetzle according to package directions. Drain, and return spaetzle to pot. Add melted butter, and stir briefly.

Preheat oven to 350 degrees F.

In a medium saucepan, sauté bacon until crisp. Remove bacon, and set aside to drain on paper towel. Reserve approximately 2 tablespoons bacon fat, and discard the rest.

Add onions, and sauté in bacon fat for 3 to 4 minutes. Add mushrooms, garlic, salt, and freshly ground black pepper; and cook for another 2 to 3 minutes. Combine onions with spaetzle, and toss lightly.

Crumble bacon over top, and transfer spaetzle to a greased 9 x 13 inch baking dish. Top with shredded muenster cheese, cover with foil, and bake for 20 minutes, or until cheese has melted. Carefully remove foil, and let stand at least 15 minutes before serving.

Chicken Puffs

1 cup unbleached flour
½ cup "goldfish" cheddar cheese crackers, *finely ground*
1 teaspoon parsley
½ teaspoon dill
¼ teaspoon ground ancho chili pepper
¼ teaspoon salt
¼ teaspoon freshly ground black pepper
½ cup vegetable oil
1 cup chicken broth
4 eggs
1½ cups cooked chicken breast, finely chopped
1/3 cup slivered almonds, chopped

Preheat oven to 450 degrees F.

In a medium mixing bowl, use a whisk to combine the flour, cheddar cheese crackers, parsley, dill, ancho chili pepper, salt, and black pepper.

In a medium saucepan, bring vegetable oil and chicken broth to boil over medium heat. Then, add flour mixture, and stir until a smooth ball forms. Remove from the heat, and let stand for approximately 5 minutes.

Add eggs, one at a time, and beat until smooth. Add chicken breast and slivered almonds, and drop by heaping teaspoonful onto greased baking sheet.

Bake for 12 to 14 minutes, or until golden brown.

Chicken Salad Casserole

"This is one of my great-grandmother's recipes. It's a great way to make use of leftover chicken!"

2 tablespoons extra-virgin olive oil
1 small onion, finely chopped
1 medium celery stalk, finely chopped
1 small red bell pepper, chopped
Salt and freshly ground pepper, to taste
1 pound cooked chicken breast, cubed
1 teaspoon parsley
2 tablespoons fresh lemon juice
¾ cup mayonnaise
¼ cup sour cream
½ cup grated jack or white cheddar cheese
½ cup slivered almonds, toasted
2/3 cup finely crushed potato chips

Preheat oven to 375 degrees F.

In a large heavy skillet, heat the olive oil over medium high heat. Add onion, celery, red bell pepper, salt, and pepper. Sauté until tender, about 3 to 5 minutes.

In a large mixing bowl, combine chicken, onion mixture, parsley, lemon juice, mayonnaise, sour cream, cheese, and almonds.

Place chicken salad in a greased 8 x 8 inch baking dish. Sprinkle crushed potato chips on top, and bake for 20 minutes, or until bubbly. Serve immediately with toasted pita chips.

Spicy Chicken Wings

"My mom's chicken wings were much more flavorful than traditional buffalo-style wings; always well received at pot luck gatherings."

4 pounds chicken wings or small chicken legs
1 (18 ounce) bottle kraft original barbecue sauce
1 tablespoon cajun seasoning
½ teaspoon cayenne pepper
¼ teaspoon salt
1 teaspoon freshly ground black pepper
3 tablespoons worcestershire sauce
1 teaspoon hot sauce
1 teaspoon chipotle pepper sauce
1 medium onion, cut in half and thinly sliced
2 cloves garlic, minced

Preheat oven to 350 degrees F.

Rinse the chicken wings with cold water, and pat them dry with a paper towel. Place the wings on an ungreased baking sheet, and bake for 30 minutes.

In a medium mixing bowl, use a whisk to combine the barbecue sauce, cajun seasoning, cayenne pepper, salt, black pepper, worcestershire sauce, hot sauce, and chipotle pepper sauce. Add the onion and garlic, and set aside.

Place the chicken wings in a 3½ quart slow cooker and add the barbecue sauce. Cover, and cook on 'low' for 3½ to 4 hours.

Colcannon

"Colcannon is a traditional Irish dish made from mashed potatoes, onions, carrots, and cabbage. It's a great addition to any holiday meal."

6 medium potatoes, cooked, peeled and mashed
1/3 cup milk
1/3 cup butter
¼ teaspoon salt
1/8 teaspoon freshly ground black pepper
2 tablespoons vegetable oil
1 small onion, cut in half and thinly sliced
2 cloves garlic, minced
1 carrot, *very thinly sliced*
Salt, and freshly ground black pepper, to taste
3 cups cabbage, *finely shredded*

In a large pot, combine potatoes, 1 teaspoon salt, and just enough cold water to cover the potatoes. Bring to a boil over high heat. Then reduce the heat to medium low, and simmer until fork tender, about 45 minutes. Peel the potatoes. Mash the potatoes with a potato masher while they're still warm, gradually adding the milk, butter, salt, and pepper. Set aside.

In a large heavy skillet, heat the vegetable oil over medium low heat. Sauté the onion, garlic, carrot, salt, and pepper; about 3 to 5 minutes. Then, add the shredded cabbage, and cook approximately 5 to 7 minutes longer, stirring occasionally. Cover, reduce heat to low, and let cook for an additional 10 minutes. Add vegetables to potatoes, and mix well.

Corn Pudding with Cheese

3 eggs
3 tablespoons unbleached flour
1 tablespoon sugar
½ teaspoon freshly ground black pepper
1 (16 ounce) can cream style corn
2 cups frozen whole kernel corn, thawed
1 cup white cheddar cheese, shredded
1/3 cup milk
1 tablespoon butter, melted
¼ teaspoon paprika

Preheat oven to 350 degrees F.

In a medium mixing bowl, beat eggs, flour, sugar, and black pepper together. Stir in cream corn, whole kernel corn, white cheddar cheese, and milk. Mix well.

Pour mixture into a greased 8 inch square baking dish. Top with melted butter, and sprinkle with paprika.

Bake for 55 minutes, and let stand for 10 minutes before serving.

George's Favorite Corn Pudding

"My mom made a few different kinds of corn pudding, but this is my dad's favorite."

3 eggs
2 cups milk
2 teaspoons baking powder
1 teaspoon salt
¼ teaspoon pepper
¾ cup yellow cornmeal
1 cup boiling water
¼ cup butter, softened
1 (8 ounce) package frozen corn, thawed
2 tablespoons melted butter

Preheat oven to 375 degrees F.

In a medium mixing bowl, beat eggs, milk, baking powder, salt, and pepper. Set aside.

In a separate mixing bowl, use a whisk to combine cornmeal, boiling water, and butter. Add egg mixture, and mix-in corn.

In a 1½ quart baking dish, add melted butter and cornmeal mixture.

Bake for 10 minutes at 375 degrees F. Then, reduce heat to 350 degrees F, and bake for an additional 30 to 35 minutes, or until golden brown.

Deviled Eggs

12 eggs, hard boiled, cooled, and peeled
1/2 cup mayonnaise
2 teaspoons dijon mustard
2 teaspoons cider vinegar
2 teaspoons parsley
Salt and freshly ground black pepper, to taste
Paprika

Place eggs in a medium saucepan and add cold water, at least an inch above the egg shells. Cover, and bring to a boil. As soon as the water comes to a full boil, remove from heat and let stand in hot water for 10 to 12 minutes. Drain water. Then, cover with cold water and ice cubes. Let stand in cold water until completely cooled. Peel and chop the eggs.

Cut eggs in half, lengthwise. Remove yolks, and place yolks in small mixing bowl.

Mash yolks with a fork, and mix in the mayonnaise, dijon mustard, cider vinegar, parsley, salt, and pepper, to form a smooth paste.

Fill the egg whites with the yolk mixture, and sprinkle with paprika. Refrigerate.

Duchess Potatoes

"Inspired by the late, great Fant's Steakhouse of Richmond Heights. The owner, Dana Fant, had a slightly different method for preparing duchess potatoes. Instead of using a pastry bag to form rosettes, she preferred to use a rubber spatula to fill small stoneware baking dishes. Duchess Potatoes were an exceptionally popular side dish at the steakhouse."

5 medium yukon gold potatoes
¼ cup butter
¼ cup sour cream
2 tablespoons grated cheddar cheese
1 egg
½ teaspoon salt
¼ teaspoon white pepper
2 teaspoons paprika

In a large pot, combine potatoes, 1 teaspoon salt, and just enough cold water to cover the potatoes. Bring to a boil over high heat. Then reduce the heat to medium low, and simmer until fork tender, about 45 minutes.

Peel the potatoes. Mash the potatoes with a potato masher *while they're still warm*. Now, using an electric mixer, beat-in the butter, sour cream, cheddar cheese, egg, salt, and white pepper; until smooth.

Using a rubber spatula, fill several small (*1 cup*) stoneware baking dishes with the potato mixture*. Place on a baking sheet, cover loosely with plastic wrap, and *refrigerate overnight*.

Preheat oven to 400 degrees F.

Sprinkle with paprika, and bake for 25 to 30 minutes, or until edges begin to brown.

*Alternately, transfer to a pastry bag fitted with a large tip, and pipe into rosettes on a greased baking sheet.

Five Layer Guacamole Dip

1 (16 ounce) can refried beans
1 teaspoon cumin
1 clove garlic, minced
3 avocados, peeled and mashed
1 teaspoon salt
1 tablespoon lemon juice
2 medium tomatoes, chopped
1 cup sour cream
1½ cups kalamata olives, pitted and chopped

To make the first layer, in a small sauce pan, over a medium flame, heat the refried beans. When heated throughout, add cumin and garlic. Mix well, and spread refried bean mixture into an 8 inch square baking dish.

To make the second layer, in a medium bowl, combine the mashed avocados, salt, and lemon juice. Spread avocado mixture on top of refried bean mixture.

To make the third layer, chop tomatoes, and sprinkle on top of avocado mixture.

To make the fourth layer, spread sour cream on top of the chopped tomatoes.

To make the fifth layer, spread chopped kalamata olives on top of the sour cream.

Ham Roll Ups

"Ham roll ups make a great appetizer for New Year's Eve or Super Bowl Sunday. They need to be prepared in advance and chilled though. My mom learned how to make these from her cousin, Paula, when my parents were living in Germany."

2 pounds smoked ham, thinly sliced
1 (10 ounce) package frozen peas, thawed
½ small red onion, diced
1 stalk celery, finely chopped
1 egg, hard boiled and chopped
2 tablespoons sour cream
¼ cup miracle whip
1 teaspoon dill
Salt and pepper to taste

Place eggs in a medium saucepan and add cold water, at least an inch above the egg shells. Cover, and bring to a boil. As soon as the water comes to a full boil, remove from heat and let stand in hot water for 10 to 12 minutes. Drain water. Then, cover with cold water and ice cubes. Let stand in cold water until completely cooled. Peel and chop the eggs.

In a medium mixing bowl, combine the peas, onion, celery, egg, sour cream, miracle whip, dill, salt, and pepper.

Spread the mixture onto the sliced ham. Tightly roll the slices, and secure each roll up with a toothpick. Refrigerate, for at least 1 hour.

Hush Puppies

"We used to take family vacations at the Colony IV Motel, on the Outer Banks of North Carolina. In fact, we all loved the hush puppies that Tale of the Whale, The Wharf, and Port O' Call served. Not exactly health food, but neither is salt water taffy, right?"

2 cups finely ground corn meal
1 tablespoon brown sugar
2 teaspoons baking soda
1 teaspoon salt
½ small onion, minced
1 egg
1 cup buttermilk
4 to 5 tablespoons cold water

In a small mixing bowl, combine onion, and buttermilk, and beat until frothy.

In a separate, medium mixing bowl, combine corn meal, brown sugar, soda and salt.

Add onion, and egg mixture to corn meal mixture, and stir lightly to mix. Now, add just enough cold water until the dough hold its shape in the spoon, and can be handled easily.

Pour a generous amount of oil into a large saucepan, about 2 inches. Heat the oil 360 to 370 degrees F, and drop dough by spoonful into hot oil. Fry until sides are golden brown, turning occasionally, about 3 to 5 minutes.

Trina's Nachos Grande

"'Trina' was one of my mom's nicknames. Although she didn't eat a lot of fast food, this is our take on one of her favorites, Nachos BellGrande!"

½ pound lean ground beef
1 medium onion, chopped
2 cloves garlic, minced
½ teaspoon oregano
½ teaspoon parsley
½ teaspoon thyme
½ teaspoon ground cumin
¼ teaspoon chipotle powder
Salt and freshly ground black pepper, to taste
1 can refried beans
1 large bag tortilla chips
1½ cup grated jack or white cheddar cheese
1 tomato, diced
1 cup sour cream

Preheat the oven to 350 degrees F.

In a medium saucepan, brown the ground beef, and drain the fat. Then, add the onion, garlic, oregano, parsley, thyme, ground cumin, chipotle powder, salt, and pepper. Cook over medium heat, *stirring frequently*, until onions are tender.

In a separate, small saucepan, cook the refried beans over low heat, until smooth enough to easily spread onto tortilla chips.

Arrange the tortilla chips in single layer on a lightly greased baking pan, overlapping chips if necessary. Top with refried beans, seasoned ground beef, and grated cheese.

Bake for 5 to 10 minutes, or until cheese has completely melted. Remove from oven, and top nachos with diced tomato and sour cream. Serve immediately.

Pigs in a Blanket

1 pound Hillshire Farm smoked sausage
2 (8 ounce) cans Pillsbury crescents
1 (18 ounce) bottle Kraft hickory smoked barbecue sauce

Preheat oven to 400 degrees F.

Quarter the sausage lengthwise. Then, cut into 2 inch pieces. Roll each piece of sausage in crescent dough, and place on an *ungreased* baking sheet.

Bake for 10 to 12 minutes, or until the dough is golden brown. Serve immediately, with Kraft hickory smoke barbecue sauce.

Potato Pancakes

2 tablespoons butter
3 medium onions, cut in half and thinly sliced
2 medium apples, peeled, cored, and sliced
1 tablespoon brown sugar
1 tablespoon cider vinegar
Salt and freshly ground black pepper, to taste
1 (6 ounce) package Hungry Jack potato pancake mix
2 cups water
Vegetable oil, for pan frying
½ cup sour cream

In a large nonstick skillet, melt the butter over medium-high flame. Add the onions and apples, and cook for 12 to 15 minutes, or until tender and golden brown. Add the brown sugar, cider vinegar, salt, and freshly ground black pepper. Cover, and set aside.

In a medium mixing bowl, use a whisk to combine the potato pancake mix and water. Let stand for 10 minutes, to thicken.

In a large nonstick skillet, heat approximately ½ inch of vegetable oil over a medium-high flame. Then, drop about ¼ cup of batter into the skillet, flattening with the back of a wooden spoon. Make 2 or 3 more pancakes, evenly spaced apart.

Using a spatula, cook the pancakes until brown on both sides; about 2 to 3 minutes on each side. Place on paper towels to drain, and repeat with remaining batter.

To serve, top potato pancakes with caramelized onions and apples, and a generous portion of sour cream.

Saffron Rice

½ teaspoon saffron threads
2 tablespoons boiling water
¼ cup vegetable oil
1 medium onion, cut in half and thinly sliced
1 cinnamon stick, splintered
4 cardamom pods or ½ teaspoon of ground cardamom
1 tablespoon cumin seeds or ½ teaspoon ground cumin
4 whole cloves
4 bay leaves
1 teaspoon salt
2 cups long-grain white rice
4 cups chicken stock

In a small bowl, combine the saffron threads and boiling water. Set aside to soak.

In a large pot or dutch oven, heat the vegetable oil over a medium-high flame. Sauté the onion for 3 to 5 minutes, or until tender. Add the cinnamon stick, cardamom pods, cumin seeds, whole cloves, bay leaves, and salt. Cook for another 3 minutes. Then, add the rice, and cook for approximately 1 minute, *stirring regularly*; until translucent.

Add the saffron threads (*including 2 tablespoons water*) and chicken stock. Bring to a boil. Then, reduce heat to low, and simmer for 8 to 10 minutes. Cover, and cook until water is fully absorbed, about 15 minutes more. Remove pan from heat, and let stand for an additional 15 minutes.

Fresh Tomato Salsa

6 medium tomatoes, chopped
1 teaspoon salt
1 small red onion, finely chopped
2 cloves garlic, minced
1 jalapeno pepper, seeded and finely chopped
½ bunch cilantro, finely chopped
¼ teaspoon freshly ground black pepper
1 teaspoon lemon juice

In a strainer, combine the chopped tomatoes and salt. Let stand for approximately 30 minutes. Then, be sure to drain any excess liquid.

Now, in a large bowl, combine the red onion, garlic, jalapeno pepper, cilantro, freshly ground black pepper, and lemon juice. Mix well.

Sauerkraut

1 (16 ounce) can of sauerkraut, drained and rinsed
½ (12 ounce) bottle of beer
1 medium onion, cut in half and thinly sliced
4 slices bacon, chopped
1 teaspoon caraway seeds
½ teaspoon paprika

Preheat oven to 350 degrees F.

Place the sauerkraut, beer, onion, bacon, caraway seeds, and paprika in a greased 8 x 8 inch baking dish. Toss gently.

Cover, and bake for 40 to 45 minutes; until heated throughout.*

An even better approach would be to use a slow cooker. To do so, place combined ingredients in a 3½ quart slow cooker, cover, and cook on 'high' for approximately 4 hours.

Scalloped Potatoes

2 tablespoons vegetable oil
2 medium onions, very thinly sliced
3 cloves garlic, minced
1 teaspoon thyme
½ teaspoon nutmeg
Salt and freshly ground black pepper, to taste
1½ cups heavy cream
3 pounds yukon gold potatoes, *peeled and sliced about ¼ inch thick*
½ cup freshly grated parmesan cheese

Preheat the oven to 375 degrees F.

In a medium saucepan, heat vegetable oil over medium-high heat. Sauté onions for 2 to 3 minutes. Add garlic, thyme, nutmeg, salt, pepper, and heavy cream. Cook for an additional 2 to 3 minutes.

Arrange a layer of sliced potatoes in a greased 9 x 9 inch baking dish, slightly overlapping them. Alternate layers of potatoes, heavy cream mixture, and freshly grated parmesan cheese. Cover with foil, and bake for 40 minutes. Then, carefully remove foil, and bake for an additional 10 minutes.

Soft Pretzels

1 package quick-rise yeast
2¾ cups warm water, *divided*
1 tablespoon sugar
½ teaspoon salt
2 cups unbleached flour
2 tablespoons baking soda
Coarsely ground salt, to taste
2 tablespoons sweet cream butter, melted

Dissolve quick-rise yeast in *¾ cup warm water*. Add sugar and salt. Stir to dissolve. Then, gradually add flour, and knead dough until smooth and elastic. Place in a greased bowl, cover loosely with greased plastic wrap, and *set aside to rise for at least 30 minutes*. Meanwhile, in a separate mixing bowl, dissolve baking soda in *2 cups warm water*.

After dough has risen, pinch off a ball of pretzel dough about the size of a baseball. Roll the dough to about a ½ inch thickness, forming a 24 to 28 inch rope. Bend the rope into a 'U' shape, and cross one end of the rope over the other end. Twist the cross ends, fold the ends backward, and open the ends slightly to form a pretzel shape by pressing the ends firmly into the dough.

Dip the pretzel in baking soda solution, and place on greased baking sheet. *Allow the pretzels to rise again, for another 30 minutes.*

Preheat oven to 450 degrees F.

Bake for 10 minutes, or until golden. Then, brush with melted butter, sprinkle with coarsely ground salt, and serve immediately.

Tabouleh

1 cup bulgar wheat
1 cup boiling water
1 tablespoon fresh lemon juice
2 tablespoons extra-virgin olive oil
1 small onion, cut in half and thinly sliced
2 cloves garlic, minced
¼ cup fresh mint *or basil* leaves, chopped
1 small bunch fresh parsley, chopped
2 medium tomatoes, chopped
1 (15 ounce) can garbanzo beans, *drained and rinsed*
¼ cup kalamata olives, pitted and chopped
Salt and freshly ground black pepper, to taste
1 cup feta cheese, crumbled

In a large mixing bowl, use a whisk to combine the bulgar wheat, boiling water, fresh lemon juice, and olive oil. *Let stand for 1 hour.* Then, add the onion, garlic, mint, parsley, tomatoes, garbanzo beans, kalamata olives, salt, and freshly ground black pepper. Cover loosely with plastic wrap, and *refrigerate for at least 2 hours.* Serve on a bed of leaf lettuce and top with crumbled feta cheese.

Tomatillo Salsa

8 tomatillos, husked, rinsed, and quartered
1 jalapeno pepper, seeded and finely chopped
1 medium onion, finely chopped
6 cloves garlic, minced
2 teaspoons salt
¼ cup chicken broth
1 bunch fresh cilantro, finely chopped
2 teaspoons lemon juice

Bring a large pot of water to boil. Add the tomatillos, jalapeno pepper, onion, garlic, and salt. Reduce heat and let simmer for 5 to 10 minutes, or until the tomatillos are tender. Drain. Add the chicken broth, cilantro, and lemon juice, and using a handheld blender, puree.

Zucchini & Potato Pancakes

"This is my mom's recipe for zucchini and potato pancakes; another great seasonal dish. These pancakes are savory and should be eaten as a side dish, not with apple sauce."

2 to 3 small zucchini, shredded
1 large potato, peeled and shredded
½ medium onion, finely chopped
1 (10 ounce) packages frozen chopped spinach, *thawed and drained*
1 teaspoon dill, *optional*
1 egg
½ cup unbleached flour
Salt and freshly ground black pepper, to taste

In a medium mixing bowl, combine the zucchini, potato, onion, spinach, dill, egg, flour, salt, and freshly ground black pepper.

Heat a non-stick griddle over medium-high heat, and use a paper towel to lightly coat the griddle with vegetable oil. Then, using a ladle, pour about ¼ cup of batter onto the griddle. Make 1 or 2 more pancakes, evenly spaced apart.

Cook for about 5 to 6 minutes per side, using a spatula to turn the pancake over, and gently press down to flatten the pancake. Both sides should be golden brown.

Repeat with the remaining batter, adding more vegetable oil to the griddle as needed. Serve hot, with a generous portion of sour cream.

Breads & Spreads

Bacon Bread

½ pound bacon or ham scraps, chopped
1 package quick-rise yeast
¼ cup warm water
3¼ cups unbleached flour
1 teaspoon salt
1 tablespoon sugar
1 cups milk

Sauté the bacon in a heavy skillet. Remove, and set aside to drain on a paper towel. *Reserve approximately 3 tablespoons of bacon fat*, and discard the rest.

In a small bowl, dissolve the quick-rise yeast in ¼ cup of warm water; with a pinch of sugar. Let stand for 5 minutes.

Now, in a large mixing bowl, combine the flour, salt, and sugar. Gradually add the milk and bacon fat, until a dough forms. Add the chopped bacon, and mix just enough to blend well.

Knead the dough until smooth, place in a greased bowl, cover loosely with plastic wrap, and *let rise in warm place until double in size, about 1 hour*

If necessary, remove the air pockets by working the dough with your hands. Shape into a loaf, and place in a greased bread loaf pan. *Let rise in warm place until the dough fills the bread pan, about 30 minutes.*

Preheat oven to 375 degrees F.

Bake for 30 to 35 minutes, or until golden brown. Immediately remove from pan, brush with melted butter, and serve.

Banana Bread

"I can't remember my mother ever making a special trip to the grocery store to buy ingredients for banana bread. She'd be more likely to come across some over-ripe bananas in the discount bin, and purchase them with the intent of making banana bread."

2/3 cup vegetable oil
1 cup brown sugar
2 eggs
½ teaspoon vanilla extract
1 cup ripe, mashed bananas (about 3 bananas)
2 cups unbleached flour
½ teaspoon baking powder
1 teaspoon baking soda
½ teaspoon salt
½ cup chopped walnuts

Preheat oven at 325 degrees F and coat the inside of a bread loaf pan with shortening.

In a medium mixing bowl, combine the vegetable oil and brown sugar. Add the eggs, vanilla extract, and mashed bananas, and mix well.

In a separate bowl, combine the flour, baking powder, baking soda, and salt. Now, gradually add the flour mixture to the egg mixture and fold in the chopped walnuts.

Pour the batter into the bread loaf pan, and bake for 60 to 70 minutes, or until a toothpick inserted into the center of the bread is clean when removed.

Granny's Homemade Biscuits

"This is my great-grandmother's homemade biscuit recipe. No need to for bisquick here!"

Mix Ingredients:

2¼ cups unbleached flour
1 tablespoon baking powder
1 teaspoon salt
½ cup butter, softened

In a medium mixing bowl, combine flour, baking powder, and salt. Then cut-in butter using a pastry blender, until mixture resembles coarse crumbs. Cover with plastic wrap, and store in refrigerator until ready to use.

Biscuit Ingredients:

2½ cups biscuit mix
½ cup milk
¼ cup melted butter

Preheat oven to 450 degrees F.

In a medium mixing bowl, combine the biscuit mix and milk, and knead the dough for 2 or 3 minutes, or until smooth.

Now, on a lightly floured work surface, roll-out the dough to about a ½ inch thickness, and cut biscuit rounds using a small, floured drinking glass or cookie cutter (*approximately 2 inches in diameter*).

Place on lightly greased baking sheet, and bake for 12 to 15 minutes; until golden brown. *Brush with melted butter*, and serve with jam.

Brown Bread

2 cups whole-wheat flour
2 cups unbleached white flour
½ cup toasted wheat germ
2 teaspoons salt
2 teaspoons brown sugar
1 teaspoon baking soda
½ teaspoon cream of tartar
½ cup butter, cut into small pieces
2 cups buttermilk

Preheat oven to 400 degrees F. Then, grease and flour a 9 inch round baking pan.

In a large mixing bowl, use a whisk to combine the wheat flour, white flour, wheat germ, salt, brown sugar, baking soda, and cream of tartar. Then cut in the butter, until the mixture resembles coarse meal. Gradually add the buttermilk, stirring all the while, until a thick dough forms.

On a lightly floured work surface, knead the dough until smooth, adding just enough flour to keep it from sticking. Shape the dough into a large round bun, and place in a greased 9 inch round baking pan. Pat the dough gently, ensuring that it touches the sides of the pan. Using a sharp knife, make the sign of the cross in the top of the dough, about ½ inch deep.

Bake for 30 to 40 minutes, or until a toothpick inserted into the center of the bread is clean when removed.

Cheese Biscuits

"These biscuits are very filling. Usually, one or two are more than enough, especially if you serve them as an accompaniment to a hearty soup or stew. We like to use muenster or white cheddar cheese, but you can use whatever cheese you like."

Biscuit Ingredients:
2 cups unbleached flour
1 tablespoon baking powder
1 teaspoon salt
2 tablespoons shortening
2/3 cup milk
¾ cup shredded muenster or white cheddar cheese

Garlic Butter Ingredients:
¼ cup butter, softened
2 teaspoons extra-virgin olive oil
2 cloves garlic, minced
½ teaspoon parsley
¼ teaspoon freshly ground black pepper

Preheat oven to 450 degrees F.

To prepare the biscuits, in a medium mixing bowl, combine the flour, baking powder, and salt. Then, cut-in the shortening (*mixture should resemble coarse crumbs*). Add the milk and cheese, and knead until a soft dough forms. Drop by large wooden spoon (*about ¼ cup at a time*) onto a *greased* baking sheet. Bake for 8 to 10 minutes, or until golden brown.

To prepare the garlic butter, in a small mixing bowl, beat the butter, olive oil, garlic, parsley, and black pepper until light and fluffy. Brush hot biscuits with melted garlic butter, and serve immediately.

Cornbread

1½ cups unbleached flour
1¼ cups yellow cornmeal
¼ cup brown sugar
½ teaspoon baking powder
½ teaspoon baking soda
½ teaspoon salt
2 eggs
½ cup vegetable oil
1 cup buttermilk
1 cup frozen corn, thawed

Preheat oven to 350 degrees F.

In a large mixing bowl, combine flour, cornmeal, brown sugar, baking powder, baking soda, and salt.

In a separate, small mixing bowl, beat eggs, vegetable oil, and milk. Add egg mixture and corn to flour mixture. Mix well.

Pour batter into greased and floured bread loaf pan. Then, bake for 1 hour, or until a toothpick inserted into the center of the bread is clean when removed.

Cornmeal Rolls

"Ohio has a considerable Amish population and cornmeal appears to be very common among the Amish. This recipe was inspired by one of my mother's many, many trips to Sugarcreek."

2 cups milk
½ cup cornmeal
½ cup vegetable oil
½ cup brown sugar
1 teaspoon salt
1 package quick-rise yeast
¼ cup warm water
2 eggs
4½ cups unbleached flour

In a medium saucepan, heat the milk, cornmeal, vegetable oil, brown sugar, and salt over a medium flame, stirring frequently. When slightly thickened, remove from heat and set aside to cool.

Dissolve the quick-rise yeast in ¼ cup warm water. Let stand for 5 minutes. Then, in a medium mixing bowl, combine the cornmeal mixture, quick-rise yeast, and eggs. Place in a greased bowl, and *let rise for 2 hours.*

Add enough flour (about 4½ cups) to make a soft dough. Knead the dough until smooth, and somewhat sticky. Place the dough in a greased bowl, and *let rise for 1 hour.*

Once more, knead the dough. Shape the dough into dinner rolls (about 1 inch in diameter) and place the rolls next to each other; in 2 lightly greased 9 inch round cake pans.

Let rise for 1 hour. Preheat oven to 375 degrees F. Bake for 15 to 25 minutes.

Date Bread

1 cup chopped dates
1 cup boiling water
2 cups unbleached flour
1 teaspoon baking soda
½ teaspoon salt
1 tablespoon butter
1 cup brown sugar
1 egg
½ cup chopped walnuts

Preheat oven to 375 degrees F. Grease and flour a bread loaf pan.

In a small mixing bowl, combine chopped dates and boiling water. Set aside.

In a separate, medium mixing bowl, use a whisk to combine the flour, baking soda, and salt.

In a large mixing bowl, beat the butter, brown sugar, egg, and date/water mixture. Add the flour mixture and chopped walnuts to the egg mixture, and blend well.

Pour batter into greased, floured bread loaf pan. Then, bake for 50 to 60 minutes, or until a toothpick inserted into the center of the bread is clean when removed.

Eggplant Caviar

"In case you're wondering, the seeds in this dish (also known as poor man's caviar) are supposed to resemble caviar eggs. Hence, the name."

2 medium eggplants, peeled and quartered
3 cloves garlic, minced
½ bunch fresh parsley
¼ teaspoon freshly ground black pepper
½ teaspoon salt
½ cup extra-virgin olive oil
2 tablespoons lemon juice

Preheat oven to 350 degrees F.

Brush the eggplant with olive oil, and roast at 350 degrees F for 30 minutes, or until soft. Set aside, and let cool. *If you prefer, you can grill the eggplant instead.*

Combine the eggplant, garlic, parsley, black pepper, salt, olive oil, and lemon juice in a food processor and grind into a paste.

Serve as a spread, with freshly baked bread.

Eggplant Spread

1 2/3 cups vegetable oil
6 medium onions, cut in half and thinly sliced
2 red bell peppers, thinly sliced
6 cloves garlic, minced
6 medium eggplants, roasted, peeled, and chopped
2½ tablespoons v*egeta** or vegetable soup base
1½ teaspoons freshly ground black pepper
2 (14.5 ounce) cans tomato sauce

Preheat oven o 350 degrees F.

In a large dutch oven, heat the vegetable oil over a medium-high flame. Sauté the onions for 3 minutes. Then, add the red bell peppers, and cook for an additional 5 to 7 minutes, or until tender. Add the garlic, chopped eggplant, vegeta, and freshly ground black pepper, and cook for an additional 3 to 5 minutes.

Bake for 1½ hours. Add the tomato sauce, and bake for an additional 30 minutes. Serve as a spread, with freshly baked bread.

*Vegeta is condiment produced by Podravka, a company from Koprivnica, Croatia. It was first sold in Yugoslavia in 1959 (as "Vegeta 40") and contains salt, dehydrated vegetables (carrot, parsnip, onions, celery, parsley leaves), monosodium glutamate, disodium inosinate, sugar, spices, cornstarch, and riboflavin.

Fried Dough (Krapfen)

"Krapfen is essentially a Swabian fried yeast cake, similar to a jelly-filled donut, covered with powdered sugar. My grandmother once told me that my great-grandmother served krapfen as a depression-era meal, braided in the shape of a figure eight."

1 cup milk
1 teaspoon salt
2 tablespoons sugar
1/3 cup butter
2 packages quick-rise yeast
½ cup warm water
3½ cups unbleached flour
Vegetable oil, for pan frying
¼ cup powdered sugar
½ cup raspberry preserves

In a small saucepan, combine milk, salt, sugar and butter. Heat over medium flame until butter melts and sugar dissolves. *Let cool to room temperature.*

Dissolve quick-rise yeast in ½ cup warm water. Let stand for approximately 5 minutes. Once milk has cooled to room temperature, add yeast mixture, and transfer to a large mixing bowl. Gradually add flour (*about ½ cup at a time*), and use a dough hook to form a soft dough.

On a lightly floured work surface, knead dough until smooth and elastic. Place dough in greased bowl, cover loosely with plastic wrap, and let rise in warm place, about 30 minutes.

On a lightly floured work surface, roll-out dough to about a ½ inch thickness, and cut rounds using a small, floured drinking glass or cookie cutter (*approximately 2 inches in diameter*).

Heat vegetable oil in large skillet, over medium flame. Fry dough for 1 to 2 minutes on each side, or until golden brown. Let drain on paper towels.

Garnish with powdered sugar, and top with raspberry preserves while still warm. Serve immediately.

Garlic Butter

¼ cup butter, softened
1 teaspoon extra-virgin olive oil
2 cloves garlic, minced
¼ teaspoon parsley
½ teaspoon salt
¼ teaspoon freshly ground black pepper

In a small mixing bowl, cream the butter, olive oil, garlic, parsley, salt, and black pepper. *Chill for at least 2 hours before serving.*

Monkey Bread

"This is my mom's monkey bread recipe. It's savory (not sweet) and is made with 1 inch balls of dough covered in olive oil and parmesan cheese, and baked in a bundt pan. It must be served hot, pulled apart, and eaten by hand, much like a young child or 'little monkey' would."

1 package quick-rise yeast
1 teaspoon sugar
¼ cup lukewarm milk
3 cups unbleached flour
½ teaspoon salt
1 tablespoon oregano
1 teaspoon basil
¾ cup + 2 tablespoons lukewarm water
2 tablespoons + 1/3 cup extra-virgin olive oil
1 cup freshly grated parmesan cheese

Dissolve quick-rise yeast and sugar in lukewarm milk. Let stand 5 minutes.

In a medium mixing bowl, combine flour, salt, oregano, and basil. Add yeast mixture, lukewarm water, and 2 tablespoons extra-virgin olive oil. Mix just enough to blend well. Knead the dough until smooth and elastic, place in a greased bowl, cover with plastic wrap, and *let rise for 1 hour.*

Shape dough into 1 inch balls. Then, roll the dough in remaining 1/3 cup olive oil and grated parmesan cheese. Arrange in a well-greased 9 inch bundt pan, forming multiple layers. Pour remaining olive oil over top, and sprinkle with remaining parmesan cheese. *Cover loosely with plastic wrap, and let rise for 1 hour.*

Preheat oven to 350 degrees F. Bake for 30 to 35 minutes, or until golden brown.

Kalamata Olive Bread

"There used to be a restaurant called 'Villa De Este' on Murray Hill, in Little Italy. In addition Italian fare, they served quite a few items that were influenced by Greek cuisine, including olive bread. I'm pretty sure that's what inspired my mom to refine her own recipe."

2 tablespoons extra-virgin olive oil
1 medium onion, chopped
1 clove garlic, chopped
1 cup whole wheat flour
3 cups unbleached white flour
1 tablespoon baking powder
1 teaspoon salt
1 cup water
¼ cup extra-virgin olive oil
1 teaspoon thyme
1 teaspoon rosemary
1 cup Kalamata olives, pitted and chopped
2 tablespoons milk

In a medium skillet, heat 2 tablespoons extra-virgin olive oil over medium-low heat. Sauté the onion and garlic until tender, about 5 to 7 minutes. Set aside to cool.

Preheat oven to 400 degrees F.

In a medium mixing bowl, combine the whole wheat flour, unbleached white flour, baking powder, and salt. Add the sautéed onion and garlic, water, ¼ cup extra-virgin olive oil, thyme, rosemary, and Kalamata olives. Mix until well blended.

On a lightly floured, wooden cutting board, knead the dough for approximately 3 to 5 minutes. Shape into loaf and place in greased bread pan.

Bake for 60 to 70 minutes, or until golden brown. As soon as the bread is ready, remove from oven and brush with milk. Set aside to cool.

Poppy Seed Bread

Bread Ingredients:
1½ cups unbleached flour
1 teaspoon baking powder
¼ teaspoon salt
½ cup vegetable oil, plus 1 tablespoon
1 cup brown sugar
1 teaspoon almond extract*
1 teaspoon vanilla extract
2 eggs
¾ cup milk
2 tablespoons poppy seeds
1 teaspoon lemon juice

Syrup Ingredients:
2/3 cup brown sugar
¼ cup water
½ teaspoon vanilla
Juice of ½ lemon

Preheat oven to 350 degrees F.

To make the bread, in a medium mixing bowl, use a whisk to combine the flour, baking powder, and salt.

In a separate mixing bowl, combine vegetable oil and sugar. Add almond extract, vanilla extract, and eggs. Then, gradually mix-in the flour mixture alternately with the milk. *Mix just enough to blend well*. Stir-in the poppy seeds, and lemon juice.

Pour batter into greased bread loaf pan. Then, bake for 55 to 60 minutes, or until a toothpick inserted into the center of the bread is clean when removed.

To make the syrup, in a medium saucepan, combine brown sugar, water, vanilla, and lemon juice. Bring to a boil over medium high heat. Once the brown sugar has completely dissolved, remove from heat and let cool before using.

Once the bread has cooled completely, lightly prick with a toothpick. Then, w*hile still in the bread pan*, drizzle syrup over top and allow the poppy seed bread to absorb the syrup before serving.

* You may also substitute 1 tablespoon grated lemon peel if you prefer.

Three Hour Potato Rolls

"My great-grandmother's potato roll recipe; another great way to make use of leftover mashed potatoes."

1 package quick-rise yeast
½ cup lukewarm water
5 cups unbleached flour, divided
2 eggs
1 cup mashed potatoes, about 3 medium potatoes
1/3 cup sugar
2 teaspoons salt
¾ cup butter, *softened*
1 cup warm milk

Dissolve quick-rise yeast in lukewarm water. Let stand for approximately 5 minutes.

In a medium mixing bowl, combine *1 cup flour*, eggs, mashed potatoes, sugar, and salt. Cut in the butter, and add the yeast mixture. *Cover loosely with a clean kitchen towel or dish cloth, and let rise in a warm place for 2 hours.*

Gradually add the remaining 4 cups of flour, and add the milk, *a little at a time. Cover, and let rise in a warm place for 1 hour.*

Lightly oil a muffin tin, or if you prefer, use a nonstick spray. Then, form the dough into 2 to 3 inch balls (about 1/3 cup each), place in muffin tins, and *let rise for 30 minutes.*

Preheat oven to 375 degrees F.

Bake for 25 to 30 minutes, or until golden brown. Remove from muffin tin, brush with melted butter, and serve immediately.

Pumpernickel

"Pumpernickel is a traditional German bread made from coarse rye flour. This recipe, however, is a classic American rye, made from a combination of wheat and rye flour."

1 cup water
2 tablespoons molasses
2 tablespoons butter
1 package quick-rise yeast
2 tablespoons cocoa powder
1 tablespoon brown sugar
1½ teaspoons caraway seed
½ teaspoon salt
1½ cups coarse rye flour or rye meal
1½ cups unbleached white flour

In a small saucepan, combine water, molasses, and butter. Heat over low flame until butter melts. *Let cool to room temperature.*

In large mixing bowl, use a whisk to combine yeast, cocoa powder, brown sugar, caraway seed, salt, and rye flour.

Once molasses mixture has cooled to room temperature, blend into yeast mixture. Gradually add white flour (*about ½ cup at a time*) to form a soft dough.

On a lightly floured work surface, knead dough until smooth and elastic. Place dough in greased bowl, cover loosely with plastic wrap, and *let rise in warm place until double in size, about 1 hour.*

Punch down dough to remove air bubbles if necessary. Shape into a loaf, and place in a greased bread loaf pan. *Let rise in warm place until dough fills pan and tops of loaf is about 1 inch above pan edge, about 1 hour.*

Preheat oven to 375 degrees F.

Bake for 20 minutes. Then, cover loosely with foil, and bake for an additional 15 minutes. Remove from pan immediately. Brush with melted butter, and serve.

Pumpkin Bread

"I remember my mother baking pumpkin bread every autumn. When I was a kid, she bought fresh pumpkin from the market to make toasted pumpkin seeds and pumpkin bread, but after a while it became a bit of a nuisance. This is a simplified version of the pumpkin bread my mother used to make. After all, there's something to be said for convenience."

3 cups unbleached flour
½ teaspoon baking powder
2 teaspoons baking soda
1 teaspoon cinnamon
½ teaspoon ground nutmeg
¼ teaspoon ground cloves
½ teaspoon salt
3 eggs
2 cups brown sugar
1 cup vegetable oil
1 (16 ounce) can pumpkin

Preheat oven at 350 degrees F. Coat the inside of two bread loaf pans with shortening.

In a medium mixing bowl, use a whisk to combine the flour, baking powder, baking soda, cinnamon, nutmeg, ground cloves, and salt.

In a separate, large mixing bowl, beat eggs, brown sugar, vegetable oil, and pumpkin. Add the flour mixture to the egg mixture, and blend well.

Divide the batter evenly into two bread loaf pans, and bake for 65 to 75 minutes, or until a toothpick inserted into the center of the bread is clean when removed.

Raisin Bread

¾ cup sun dried raisins
3 tablespoons butter, softened
¾ cup brown sugar
½ teaspoon vanilla extract
1 cup milk
3 eggs
3 cups unbleached flour
1 tablespoon baking powder
½ teaspoon nutmeg
½ teaspoon cinnamon
1 teaspoon salt

Preheat oven to 350 degrees F. Then, grease and flour a bread loaf pan.

In a small bowl, combine raisins with about ½ cup water, and set aside to soak.

In a medium mixing bowl, beat butter, brown sugar, vanilla extract, milk, eggs, and *drained* raisins. Gradually add flour, baking powder, nutmeg, cinnamon, and salt. Blend well.

Pour batter into greased and floured bread loaf pan. Bake for 45 to 50 minutes, or until a toothpick inserted into the center of the bread is clean when removed.

Rye Bread

"This rye bread recipe makes use of mixed grains. Although much denser than white bread, it's noticeably lighter than most rye breads containing only rye flour. If you prefer, you can add a tablespoon of caraway seed as well."

1 package quick-rise yeast
¼ cup warm water
1 tablespoon butter
1 tablespoon sugar
¼ cup molasses
1¾ cups coarse rye flour or rye meal
1¼ cups unbleached white flour
½ teaspoon salt
¾ cup warm milk

In a small bowl, dissolve quick-rise yeast in warm water. Let stand for 5 minutes.

In a medium mixing bowl, combine butter, sugar, and molasses.

In a separate mixing bowl, use a whisk to combine rye flour, white flour, and salt. Add yeast mixture and milk, *a little at a time*.

On a lightly floured work surface, knead dough until smooth and elastic. Place dough in greased bowl, cover loosely with plastic wrap, and *let rise in warm place until double in size, about 1 hour.*

Punch down dough to remove air bubbles if necessary. Shape into a loaf, and place in a greased bread loaf pan. *Let rise in warm place until dough fills pan and top of loaf is about 1 inch above pan edge, about 1 hour.*

Preheat oven to 375 degrees F.

Bake for 30 to 35 minutes. Remove from pan immediately, brush with melted butter, and serve.

Soda Bread

2 cups whole-wheat flour
2 cups unbleached flour
¼ cup brown sugar
1 teaspoon salt
1 teaspoon baking powder
1 teaspoon baking soda
½ cup shortening
1 1/3 cups buttermilk
1 egg
1 cup raisins
1 tablespoon butter, melted

Preheat oven to 350 degrees F.

In a small bowl, combine raisins with about 1 cup water, and set aside to soak.

In a large mixing bowl, combine the whole wheat flour, unbleached flour, brown sugar, salt, baking powder, and baking soda. Cut-in shortening, until mixture resembles fine crumbs.

In a small bowl, combine buttermilk, egg, and *drained* raisins. Gradually add to flour mixture, mixing just enough to moisten. Do not over-mix!

On a lightly floured work surface, knead dough until smooth. Shape the dough into a large round bun, and place in a greased 9 inch round baking pan. Pat the dough gently, ensuring that it touches the sides of the pan. Using a sharp knife, make the sign of the cross in the top of the dough, about ½ inch deep.

Bake for 50 minutes, or until a toothpick inserted into the center is clean when removed. Brush top of bread with melted butter, and serve warm.

Sunflower Seed Rolls

2½ cups unbleached flour
¾ cup rye flour
1 package quick-rise yeast
1 teaspoon sugar
1 teaspoon salt
1½ cups lukewarm water
½ cup sourdough
1/3 cup sunflower seeds, toasted

In a medium mixing bowl, combine flour and yeast. Add sugar, salt, water and sourdough. Knead the dough until smooth. Gradually, work-in the sunflower seeds, reserving about 1 tablespoon for garnish.

Place dough in mixing bowl, cover bowl with greased plastic wrap, and let rise for about 1 hour.

Remove from mixing bowl and knead dough on lightly floured work surface. Then, roll into a thick sausage shape, cut into 12 to 14 pieces, and shape into rolls.

Preheat oven to 425 degrees F.

Place rolls on a greased baking sheet, brush with water, and sprinkle reserved sunflower seeds on top, pressing slightly. Once again, let rise for about 1 hour.

Bake for 30 minutes.

Tapenade

1 pound kalamata olives, pitted and chopped
½ cup capers
½ cup extra-virgin olive oil
1 teaspoon red wine vinegar
1 tablespoon dry red wine
1 tablespoon fresh oregano, chopped
3 tablespoons parsley, chopped
1 teaspoon dijon mustard
2 anchovy fillets
2 cloves garlic, minced
Juice of ½ lemon

Combine the olives, capers, olive oil, vinegar, red wine, oregano, parsley, mustard, anchovy fillets, garlic, and lemon juice in a food processor and grind into a paste.

Serve as a spread, with freshly baked bread.

Tomato Butter

"This recipe's inspired by a terrific Italian restaurant we used to go to, named Molinari's. I haven't been there in quite a while, but they used to serve fresh bread with sun dried tomato butter before the meal. Simple, yet completely delectable. Here's Silvia's take on it..."

1 cup butter
¼ cup fresh parsley, chopped
1 clove garlic, minced
¼ cup sun dried tomatoes, chopped
1 tablespoon tomato paste
Salt and pepper to taste

In a small mixing bowl, cream butter. Mix in parsley, garlic, sun dried tomatoes, and tomato paste. Chill for at least 2 hours before serving.

White Bread

"This is one of my great-grandmother's classic white bread recipes, and is another family favorite. It's best when eaten fresh from the oven, with a bit of butter and jam. It's also delicious with soup. In fact, I could probably eat half a loaf all by myself."

5½ to 6 cups unbleached flour
3 tablespoons sugar
2 teaspoons salt
2 packages quick-rise yeast
2 cups water
¼ cup vegetable oil

In large mixing bowl, combine 2 cups flour, sugar, salt and yeast. Mix well.

In a small saucepan, heat water and oil until almost boiling.

Gradually add water and oil to flour mixture, and beat 3 to 5 minutes. Stir-in additional 2½ to 3 cups flour; until dough pulls away from sides of bowl.

On a lightly floured work surface, knead dough for approximately 10 minutes, or until dough is smooth and elastic.

Place dough in greased bowl, cover loosely with plastic wrap, and let rise in warm place until double in size, about 1 to 1½ hours.

Punch down dough to remove air bubbles if necessary. Then, divide dough into 2 equal parts. Let stand, covered with inverted bowls, for 15 minutes.

Remove air pockets by working dough with hands. Shape into loaves, and place in two greased bread loaf pans. Let rise in warm place until dough fills pans and tops of loaves are about 1 inch above pan edges, about 1 hour.

Preheat oven to 375 degrees F.

Bake for 45 to 55 minutes, or until golden brown. Remove from pans, brush with melted butter, and serve immediately.

Aunt Dorothy's Yeast Dough

"A basic recipe for making homemade bread, dinner rolls, and pizza."

¼ cup warm water
1 package quick-rise yeast
3 cups unbleached flour
1 teaspoon salt
2 tablespoons sugar
¾ cup butter, softened
¼ cup milk
1 egg

In a small bowl, dissolve quick-rise yeast in warm water. Let stand for 5 minutes.

In a large mixing bowl, use a whisk to combine the flour, salt, and sugar. Then cut in the butter using a pastry blender, until mixture resembles coarse meal. Add milk, egg, and yeast mixture, stirring all the while until a dough forms.

Place dough in a floured bowl, and cover loosely with plastic wrap. Set aside, and allow to double in size. Approximately 1½ to 2 hours.

Zucchini Bread

"My mother always had a large vegetable garden, and Zucchini did extremely well for her. Sometimes it seemed as though it produced more than she could ever possibly know what to do with, but she'd always find a use for it. Zucchini bread was one of many late summer treats. My mom also shared this recipe with my great-grandmother, who typically added ½ cup chopped walnuts."

3 cups unbleached flour
1 teaspoon baking powder
1 teaspoon baking soda
1 teaspoon salt
1 tablespoon cinnamon
3 eggs
1¾ cup brown sugar
1 cup vegetable oil
2 cups grated zucchini
Zest of one lemon
2 teaspoons vanilla

Preheat oven at 350 degrees F. Coat the inside of two bread loaf pans with shortening or butter.

In a medium mixing bowl, use a whisk to combine the flour, baking powder, baking soda, salt, and cinnamon.

In a separate, large mixing bowl, beat eggs, brown sugar, vegetable oil, grated zucchini, lemon zest, and vanilla. Add the flour mixture to the egg mixture, and blend well.

Divide the batter evenly into two bread loaf pans, and bake for 50 minutes, or until a toothpick inserted into the center of the bread is clean when removed.

Breakfast

Blueberry Pancakes

"Be sure to pick plenty of blueberries this summer at your local farmer's market, so that you can freeze them and enjoy blueberry pancakes year round. Secor's Market, in Perry, is our favorite."

Blueberry Sauce Ingredients:
¼ cup water
1 teaspoon cornstarch
3 cups blueberries
¼ cup sugar
1 tablespoon lemon juice

Blueberry Pancake Ingredients:
2 eggs
3 tablespoons sugar
1 tablespoon baking powder
½ teaspoon baking soda
½ teaspoon salt
½ cup whole wheat flour
1 cup unbleached white flour
¼ cup melted butter
1¾ cups buttermilk
2 cups blueberries

To prepare the blueberry sauce, in a medium saucepan, combine the water, cornstarch, blueberries, and sugar. Bring to a boil over medium heat, stirring occasionally. Then, reduce the heat to low and let simmer for 2 minutes. Remove from heat, and add lemon juice.

To prepare the pancakes, in a medium mixing bowl, combine the eggs, sugar, baking powder, baking soda, and salt. Add the wheat flour, white flour, and melted butter; alternately with the buttermilk (*a little at a time*). Now, add the blueberries, mixing just enough to blend. *Do not over-mix!*

Heat a non-stick griddle over medium high heat, and use a paper towel to lightly coat the griddle with vegetable oil. Then, using a ladle, pour about ¼ cup of batter onto the griddle. Make 1 or 2 more pancakes, evenly spaced apart.

Cook until the top of the pancake begins to bubble and the underside is golden brown. Use a spatula to turn the pancake over, and cook until brown on both sides, about 2 minutes per side. Repeat with remaining batter, adding more vegetable oil to the griddle as needed. Top with blueberry sauce, and serve immediately.

French Toast

"Using a whole-grain bread to make French Toast is a must. Not only is it better for you, it also adds a great deal of flavor. Personally, I prefer Brownberry's 'Health Nut' whole-grain bread."

4 eggs
1/3 cup milk
½ teaspoon vanilla extract
¼ teaspoon cinnamon
1/8 teaspoon nutmeg
Vegetable oil, for pan frying
8 slices whole-grain bread

In a medium mixing bowl, use a whisk to combine the eggs, milk, vanilla extract, cinnamon, and nutmeg.

Heat approximately ½ inch of vegetable oil in a large skillet, over a medium flame.

Dip each slice of whole-grain bread in the egg mixture, and fry until golden brown, approximately 1½ to 2 minutes on each side. Let drain on paper towels, and serve with *pure maple syrup*.

Muesli

"German for 'mixture,' muesli is made of oats, nuts, seeds, and dried fruits. It's usually eaten for breakfast, and is preferably served with milk, honey, and fresh fruit. I used to make my own, but haven't for quite some time now. Not sure why, but the recipe follows. My great-grandfather, John Kleindienst, liked muesli quite a bit as well."

4 cups rolled oats
1 cup raw walnuts, chopped
1 cup raw almonds, chopped
½ cup raw sunflower seeds
1 cup raw cashews, chopped
½ cup raw brazil nuts or raw hazelnuts, chopped
1 cup sundried raisins
1 cup chopped dates
1 cup dried cranberries
½ cup brown sugar, *optional*

In a large mixing bowl combine the oats, walnuts, almonds, sunflower seeds, cashews, brazil nuts, raisins, dates, cranberries, and brown sugar. Mix well, and store in an airtight container.

Oatmeal

2 cups old-fashioned rolled oats
½ teaspoon cinnamon
¼ teaspoon nutmeg, *optional*
1/8 teaspoon salt
4 cups milk
¼ cup pure maple syrup

In a medium saucepan, use a whisk to combine the oats, cinnamon, nutmeg, and salt. Add the milk, and bring to a boil. Then, reduce the heat to low and cook, uncovered, for approximately 5 minutes; stirring occasionally. When the oats have absorbed most of the liquid, remove from heat, stir-in the maple syrup, and let stand for approximately 10 minutes before serving.

Kalamata Omelette

1 medium onion, minced
½ cup cherry tomatoes, quartered
1/3 cup kalamata olives, pitted and finely chopped
½ cup crumbled feta cheese
2 tablespoons butter
6 eggs
Salt and freshly ground black pepper, to taste
1/3 cup fresh parsley, chopped

In a medium mixing bowl, combine onion, cherry tomatoes, kalamata olives, and feta cheese. Set aside.

In a medium non-stick skillet, melt *1 tablespoon* butter over medium-low heat.

In a separate mixing bowl, whisk eggs thoroughly, and season with salt and freshly ground black pepper.

Pour *half* of the egg mixture into the skillet, being careful to coat the entire skillet. Then, spoon *half* of the onion, garlic, cherry tomatoes, kalamata olives, and feta cheese mixture onto *half* the omelette.

Cook until the eggs begin to set, approximately 2 to 3 minutes. *Do not stir!* Gently fold the omelette over the filling, and cook for an additional 2 minutes, or until the eggs are light brown on the bottom. *Repeat with remaining ingredients to make the second omelette.*

To serve, place the omelette on a serving plate and garnish with fresh parsley.

Makes two omelettes.

Palatschinken

"Palatschinken (pfannkuchen, blintzes…) are thin, crepe-like pancakes filled with different types of fillings, typically eaten for lunch or dinner. Though, I prefer to have them for breakfast. My great grandmother used to make them all the time, usually with a cottage cheese filling. If you prefer, you can use ricotta cheese for this recipe instead."

Cottage Cheese Filling Ingredients:
1/3 cup sugar
¼ cup butter
2 eggs
½ teaspoon vanilla extract
Zest of ½ lemon
1/8 teaspoon salt
8 ounces small curd cottage cheese
1/3 cup sour cream
1/3 cup raisins

Pancake Ingredients:
3 eggs
1 tablespoon butter, melted
1 cup milk
½ cup water
1 teaspoon sugar
¼ teaspoon salt
1 cup unbleached flour
¼ cup vegetable oil, *for pan frying*

Glaze/Topping Ingredients:
1 egg
1/3 cup sugar
1½ cups heavy cream

In a small bowl, combine raisins with about 1/3 cup dark rum, and set aside to soak. *Now, to make the cottage cheese filling*, in medium mixing bowl, beat sugar and butter until light and fluffy. Add eggs, vanilla extract, lemon zest, and salt. Beat until well incorporated. Then, add cottage cheese, sour cream, and *drained* raisins. Mix just enough to combine. *Then, refrigerate for 2 hours, or overnight.*

To make the pancakes; in a medium mixing bowl, use a whisk to combine eggs, butter, milk, water, sugar, and salt. Gradually add flour, adding a bit more milk if the batter's too thick. The batter should be much thinner than a typical american pancake batter. Set aside, and let stand for about 15 minutes.

Heat a 9 inch non-stick frying pan, and use a paper towel to lightly coat the skillet with vegetable oil. Then, using a ladle, pour about ¼ cup of batter into the skillet; enough to cover the bottom in one thin layer. Slightly tilt the pan to spread the batter evenly over a larger area if necessary. Cook until the top of the pancake begins to bubble and the underside is golden brown, about 45 seconds. Use a spatula to turn the pancake over, and cook for another 30 seconds.

Preheat oven to 375 degrees F. *To make the glaze/topping*, in separate mixing bowl, combine egg, sugar, and heavy cream. Set aside. Now, place approximately 2 to 3 tablespoons of cottage cheese filling on the bottom of each pancake, and roll carefully, closing both ends. Arrange pancakes in a greased 8 x 8 inch baking dish. Pour glaze over pancakes, and bake for 30 minutes, or until lightly browned.

Pumpkin Pancakes

"Another one of Silvia's specialties. You don't have to wait until Thanksgiving to enjoy these pumpkin pancakes. They're great year 'round!"

1½ cups milk
1 cup pumpkin puree
1 egg
2 tablespoons vegetable oil
2 tablespoons vinegar
1 cup unbleached flour
1 cup whole wheat flour
1/3 cup brown sugar
2 teaspoons baking powder
1 teaspoon baking soda
1 teaspoon allspice
1 teaspoon cinnamon
½ teaspoon ginger
½ teaspoon salt

In a medium mixing bowl, combine milk, pumpkin puree, egg, vegetable oil, and vinegar.

In a separate mixing bowl, combine white flour, wheat flour, brown sugar, baking powder, baking soda, allspice, cinnamon, ginger and salt. Blend into egg mixture, mixing just enough to combine. *Do not over-mix!*

Heat a non-stick griddle over medium-high heat, and use a paper towel to lightly coat the griddle with vegetable oil. Then, using a ladle, pour about ¼ cup of batter onto the griddle. Make 1 or 2 more pancakes, evenly spaced apart.

Cook until the top of the pancake begins to bubble and the underside is golden brown. Use a spatula to turn the pancake over, and cook until brown on both sides, about 3 minutes. Repeat with remaining batter, adding more vegetable oil to the griddle as needed. Serve hot, with butter and maple syrup.

Schmarren

"Another recipe from the swabian kitchen; schmarren is essentially a scrambled pancake best served with fresh fruit or compote."

1 tablespoon sugar
1 teaspoon cinnamon
½ cup chopped raisins
¼ cup dark rum or brandy; schnapps
4 eggs, separated
½ teaspoon lemon extract
1½ cups milk
2 tablespoons melted butter
2 tablespoons brown sugar
¼ teaspoon salt
2 cups unbleached flour
Vegetable oil, for pan frying

In a small bowl, use a whisk to combine the sugar and cinnamon. Set aside.

In a separate bowl, combine the raisins and dark rum, and set aside to soak.

In a medium mixing bowl, beat the egg whites until stiff peaks form, at least 5 to 7 minutes. Set aside.

Now, in a separate mixing bowl, combine the egg yolks, lemon extract, milk, butter, brown sugar, salt, and *drained* raisins. Gradually add the flour, *adding a bit more milk if the batter becomes too thick*. Use a whisk to gently fold-in the egg whites.

Heat a 9 inch non-stick frying pan, and use a paper towel to lightly coat the skillet with vegetable oil. Then, using a ladle, pour about ¼ cup of batter into the skillet; enough to cover the bottom in one thin layer. Slightly tilt the pan to spread the batter evenly over a larger area if necessary.

Cook until the top of the pancake begins to bubble and the underside is golden brown, about 45 seconds. All the while, use a wooden spoon and spatula (*as you would a fork and knife*) to break apart large pieces as they form. Turn the pancake over and cook for another 30 seconds, continuing to break apart large pieces as they form.

Sprinkle with sugar/cinnamon mixture and serve immediately, preferably with fresh fruit.

Zucchini Pancakes

1½ cups milk
1 cup grated zucchini
1 egg
1 teaspoon vanilla extract
2 tablespoons vegetable oil
2 tablespoons white vinegar
1 cup unbleached white flour
1 cup whole-wheat flour
1/3 cup brown sugar
2 teaspoons baking powder
1 teaspoon baking soda
½ teaspoon cinnamon
½ teaspoon salt
½ cup chopped walnuts

In a medium mixing bowl, combine milk, grated zucchini, egg, vanilla extract, vegetable oil, and white vinegar.

In a separate mixing bowl, combine the white flour, wheat flour, brown sugar, baking powder, baking soda, cinnamon, and salt. Gradually blend into the egg mixture and add the chopped walnuts, mixing just enough to combine. *Do not over-mix!*

Heat a non-stick griddle over medium-high heat, and use a paper towel to lightly coat the griddle with vegetable oil. Then, using a ladle, pour about ¼ cup of batter onto the griddle. Make 1 or 2 more pancakes, evenly spaced apart.

Cook until the top of the pancake begins to bubble and the underside is golden brown. Use a spatula to turn the pancake over, and cook until brown on both sides, about 3 minutes. Repeat with remaining batter, adding more vegetable oil to the griddle as needed. Serve hot, with butter and maple syrup.

Cakes

American Flag Cake

1 (18.25 ounce) package yellow cake mix
½ cup (4 ounces) fresh blueberries
1 quart fresh strawberries

Frosting Ingredients:
2 cups butter, *at room temperature*
3 (8 ounce) packages cream cheese, *at room temperature*
4 cups powdered sugar
1½ teaspoons vanilla extract

Slice the strawberries in half, lengthwise, and allow them to drain on a paper towel.

Preheat the oven (*refer to package directions for temperature*). Then, lightly grease and flour a 9 x 13 inch baking dish. Line it with parchment paper, and set aside.

To prepare the cake batter, follow the package directions, but be sure to *pour the batter into the prepared 9 x 13 inch baking dish*. Bake according to directions, or until a toothpick inserted near the center comes out clean. Let cool to room temperature, and invert the cake onto an appropriately sized serving tray.

To prepare the frosting; in a medium mixing bowl, beat the butter, cream cheese, powdered sugar, and vanilla extract until smooth and creamy.

Frost the top and sides of the cake. Then, place the fruit on top, in a pattern resembling that of the American Flag. *Though, you probably won't be able to fit seven rows of strawberries on the cake.*

Transfer the remaining frosting to a gallon freezer bag, and cut the corner (*about ½ inch*) off the bottom of the bag. Hold the bag tightly above the cake, and pipe the frosting in between the rows of strawberries. *Refrigerate for at least 2 hours before serving.*

*If you prefer, you can also pipe a decorative border around the cake.

Apple Cinnamon Cake

"This is my great-grandmother's apple cinnamon cake recipe. My great-grandparents apple tree always provided an abundant supply of fresh apples perfect for baking."

Cake Ingredients:
1 cup butter
1 cup sugar
½ cup brown sugar
2 eggs
2½ cups unbleached flour
1 teaspoon baking powder
1 teaspoon baking soda
1 teaspoon cinnamon
½ teaspoon salt
1 cup buttermilk
4 medium apples, peeled, cored, and sliced

Topping Ingredients:
½ cup sugar
½ cup walnuts, chopped
1 teaspoon cinnamon

Preheat oven to 350 degrees F.

To make the cake, in medium mixing bowl, beat butter and sugar until light and fluffy. Add eggs, and mix well. Gradually add flour, baking powder, baking soda, cinnamon, and salt. Then, add buttermilk, fold in the apples, and spread the batter into a greased 9 x 13 inch baking dish.

To make the topping, in a separate mixing bowl, combine sugar, chopped walnuts, and cinnamon. Sprinkle over batter, and bake for 50 minutes.

Banana Fanna Foe Fanna Cake

Cake Ingredients:
2½ cups sugar
1 cup butter, softened
4 eggs
1 cup sour cream
2 teaspoons baking soda
3 cups unbleached flour
1 tablespoon vanilla extract
2½ cups mashed, very ripe bananas (*about 6 bananas*)

Frosting Ingredients:
6 cup powdered sugar
½ cup cocoa powder
½ cup butter, softened
½ cup strong, brewed coffee (*cooled to room temperature*)

Preheat oven to 350 degrees F.

To make the cake, in a medium mixing bowl, beat sugar and butter until mixture resembles crumbs. Add the eggs and beat well. Then, mix-in the sour cream. In a separate bowl, use a whisk to combine the flour and baking soda. Blend into the egg mixture, add mashed bananas and vanilla extract, and mix well.

Pour the batter into 3 greased and floured (9 inch) round baking pans, and bake for 30 to 35 minutes, or until a tooth pick inserted in the center comes out clean. Remove from oven, and let cool to room temperature.

To make the frosting, in a medium mixing bowl, use a whisk to combine the powdered sugar and cocoa powder. Add butter, and blend until well incorporated. Now, gradually add the coffee, and beat until smooth and creamy.

Bee Sting Cake

"Bienenstich, German for 'Bee Sting' Cake, is traditionally made with almonds and honey. An old legend claims that two bakers once managed to chase away the tax collector by throwing a bee's nest at him. To celebrate, they baked a special cake, the Bienenstich."

Topping Ingredients:
¼ cup sugar
3 tablespoons milk
1 cup toasted, sliced almonds

Cake Ingredients:
1 cup unbleached flour
1 cup granulated white sugar, divided
6 large eggs, separated
1 teaspoon almond extract
1 tablespoon water
2 teaspoons lemon zest
¾ teaspoon cream of tartar

Honey Glaze Ingredients:
½ cup brown sugar
1 cup water
¼ cup honey

Filling Ingredients:
2 (3.75 ounce) packages instant vanilla pudding mix
2½ cups milk
1 cup heavy cream

To make the topping, in a small saucepan, combine milk and sugar. Cook over medium-low heat, almost to boiling. Stir constantly, until the sugar has fully dissolved. Add sliced almonds, remove from heat, and let cool.

To make the cake, let the eggs stand for approximately 30 minutes, in order to reach room temperature. Then, preheat oven to 350 degrees F. In a small mixing bowl, use a whisk to combine the flour and ¼ cup sugar. Set aside. In a separate mixing bowl, beat the egg yolks and ½ cup sugar on high speed for approximately five minutes, or until light and fluffy. Add almond extract, water, and lemon zest. Mix well. Beat the egg whites until stiff peaks form, at least 5 to 7 minutes. Then, gradually add cream of tartar and remaining ¼ cup sugar. Use a whisk to gently mix in the flour mixture and egg whites into egg yolk mixture, just enough to incorporate (a few quick strokes). *Over-mixing will deflate the batter.* Line the bottom of a 10 inch springform pan with parchment paper, and apply a light coating of nonstick cooking spray. Then, pour the batter into the pan and use a rubber spatula to evenly distribute the cake batter.

Spread the topping on top of the dough, and bake for 30 to 35 minutes, or until a toothpick inserted into the center is clean when removed. *Remove from oven and immediately invert.* Let stand for at least one hour before carefully *splitting the cake into two horizontal layers.*

To make the honey glaze, in a small saucepan, combine the brown sugar, water, and honey. Cook over medium-low heat, stirring constantly, until the sugar has fully dissolved. Set aside to cool. Then, generously brush both cake layers with the honey glaze.

To make the filling, in a medium mixing bowl, combine vanilla pudding mix and milk. Beat at a low speed for 2 minutes. In a separate bowl, whip the heavy cream until soft peaks form, at least 5 to 7 minutes. Then, fold the whipped cream into the pudding mixture, and gently use a whisk to combine.

To assemble the cake, spread the filling over the bottom layer and carefully place the remaining layer on top. *Refrigerate for at least 4 hours.*

Carrot Cake with Cream Cheese Frosting

"This is my mom's carrot cake recipe. One of my all-time favorites! In fact, I used to ask her to make it for my birthday... Topped with cream cheese frosting and chopped walnuts, this Carrot Cake is exceptionally moist. Be sure to save a piece for the Easter Bunny!"

Carrot Cake Ingredients:
4 eggs
2 cups sugar
1½ cups vegetable oil
2 cups unbleached flour
1 teaspoon baking powder
1 teaspoon baking soda
¼ teaspoon salt
2½ teaspoons cinnamon
¼ teaspoon nutmeg
2 cups finely grated carrots

Cream Cheese Frosting Ingredients:
¾ cup butter, softened
4½ ounces cream cheese, softened
1½ teaspoons vanilla extract
5 2/3 cups powdered sugar
1¾ cups chopped walnuts, *divided*
3 to 5 tablespoons milk
Carrot curls, for garnish

Preheat oven to 350 degrees F.

To make the carrot cake, in a medium mixing bowl, combine the eggs, sugar, and vegetable oil. Mix well.

In a separate mixing bowl, use a whisk to combine the flour, baking powder, baking soda, salt, cinnamon, and nutmeg. Blend the flour mixture into the egg mixture, and gradually add the grated carrots.

Pour the cake batter into 2 greased and floured (9 inch) round baking pans. Bake for 35 to 40 minutes, or until a toothpick inserted near the center comes out clean. Let cool for 10 to 15 minutes before removing from baking pans.

To make the cream cheese frosting, in a medium mixing bowl, beat the butter, cream cheese, and vanilla extract until light and fluffy.

Gradually add the powdered sugar, *1¼ cups chopped walnuts*, and milk (*a little at a time, until the desired consistency is achieved*).

Spread a thin layer of frosting on top of each cake layer, and place the layers on top of each other. Frost the sides of the cake with the remaining frosting, and garnish with carrot curls and remaining *½ cup chopped walnuts*. Refrigerate for at least 2 hours before serving.

Aunt Mary's Chocolate Cake

"This is my great-grandaunt, Mary Beer's recipe. It's another one of my great-grandmother's favorite recipes. She used to write little comments in the margins of her cookbook, and wrote 'this is an extra good recipe' above this prelatus torten recipe. I'm happy to say that I still have a pink and blue receiving blanket Aunt Mary knitted for me when I was born."

Cake Ingredients:
¾ cup brown sugar
6 egg yolks
2 ounces baking chocolate, finely grated
2 tablespoons unbleached flour
6 egg whites
2/3 cup walnuts, finely chopped and rolled

Preheat oven to 325 degrees F.

To make the cake, line two 9 inch round baking pans with waxed paper, grease the paper, and set aside.

In a medium mixing bowl, beat egg whites until stiff peaks form, at least 5 to 7 minutes.

In a separate mixing bowl, use a whisk to combine brown sugar, egg yolks, baking chocolate, flour, and egg whites. Then, mix in chopped walnuts, and evenly distribute batter into prepared cake pans.

Bake for 25 to 30 minutes, or until a toothpick inserted near the center comes out clean. *Let cool before carefully splitting each cake into two horizontal layers.*

Filling Ingredients:
2/3 cup walnuts, finely chopped and rolled
1 cup warm milk
2/3 cup butter, softened
2/3 cup powdered sugar

To make the filling, in a small bowl, combine chopped walnuts and warm milk. Let stand for approximately 10 minutes, until cool. Then, in a separate mixing bowl, cream the butter and powdered sugar. Gradually add the milk and walnuts, about 1 tablespoon at a time, and beat until well combined. *A slightly wet appearance is normal.* Place one cake layer on a serving plate, spread with filling, and repeat.

Frosting Ingredients:
1½ cups powdered sugar
½ cup butter
1½ - 2 tablespoons milk
2 tablespoons cocoa powder
¼ cup walnuts, chopped

In a medium mixing bowl, cream powdered sugar and butter. Add a small amount of milk (*1 to 2 tablespoons*). Add cocoa and beat until light and fluffy. If frosting is too sweet add a little more milk. Frost the top and sides of the cake, sprinkle with chopped walnuts, and *refrigerate overnight before serving!*

Chocolate Fudge Cake

Cake Ingredients:
½ cup butter, softened
1 cup sugar
1 egg
2 ounces baking chocolate, finely grated
1 teaspoon vanilla extract
2 cups unbleached flour
2 teaspoons baking powder
½ teaspoon salt
¾ cup milk

Frosting Ingredients:
¼ cup water
¾ cup sugar
1 ounce baking chocolate
2 egg yolks

Preheat oven to 325 degrees F.

In a large mixing bowl, beat butter and sugar until light and fluffy. Add egg, baking chocolate, and vanilla extract. Mix well.

In a separate mixing bowl, combine flour, baking powder, and salt. Gradually, blend into egg mixture, and add milk.

Bake in a greased 8 x 8 inch baking dish for 1 hour.

To make the frosting, boil water and sugar to form a thick syrup. Add baking chocolate, and pour mixture over beaten egg yolks, stirring constantly. Beat until thick enough to spread. Cover cake with frosting, and serve.

Chocolate Layer Cake with Butter Cream Frosting

Chocolate Cake Ingredients:
3½ cups unbleached flour
2 cups cocoa powder
1 tablespoon baking soda
½ teaspoon salt
1½ cups butter, *at room temperature*
1 1/3 cups granulated white sugar
1 1/3 cups brown sugar
4 eggs, *at room temperature*
1 tablespoon vanilla extract
¼ cup strong, brewed coffee, *at room temperature*
1 cup sour cream, *at room temperature*
2 cups buttermilk, *at room temperature*

Chocolate Butter Cream Frosting:
16 ounces bittersweet baking chocolate, *chopped*
12 ounces semisweet baking chocolate, *chopped*
5 egg whites, at room temperature
1½ cups granulated white sugar
¼ teaspoon cream of tartar
¾ teaspoon salt
3 cups butter, at room temperature
1 tablespoon vanilla extract
1 tablespoon strong, brewed coffee, *at room temperature*
3 tablespoons dark rum

Preheat oven to 350 degrees F.

To make the cake, lightly grease and flour 2 (9 inch) round baking pans. Line the bottom of each pan with parchment paper, and set aside. Now, in a medium mixing bowl, use a whisk to combine the flour, cocoa powder, baking soda, and salt.

In a separate mixing bowl, beat the butter, white sugar, and brown sugar until light and fluffy, about 5 minutes. Add the eggs and vanilla extract, and mix well. Then, gradually add the flour mixture alternately with the brewed coffee, sour cream, and buttermilk (*a little at a time*). Mix just enough to blend well. *Do not over-mix!* Evenly distribute the batter among the prepared cake pans, and bake for 85 to 90 minutes, or until a toothpick inserted near the center comes out clean. *Let stand for 1 hour before removing from pans, and splitting each cake into two horizontal layers.*

To make the butter cream frosting, in a medium saucepan, melt the chocolate over low heat, stirring constantly. Let cool to room temperature, about 20 minutes. In a medium mixing bowl, beat egg whites, sugar, cream of tartar, and salt until stiff peaks form; at least 5 to 7 minutes. Gradually add the butter, vanilla extract, coffee, rum, and melted chocolate. Beat until smooth.

To assemble the cake, place an individual cake layer on a serving plate, frost the top and sides with butter cream, and repeat. Garnish with grated chocolate, and *refrigerate overnight*.

Coconut Grove Cake

"This is one of Silvia's specialty cakes. It's named after one of my favorite songs. Ah, how the ocean breezes cool my mind! It just may be a piece of paradise."

Cake Ingredients:
2 cups sugar
½ cup butter, softened
½ cup vegetable oil
5 eggs, separated
2 cups unbleached flour
1 teaspoon baking soda
½ cup pecans, finely ground
1 cup buttermilk
1½ cups sweetened coconut flakes

Frosting Ingredients:
½ cup butter, softened
8 ounces cream cheese, softened
1½ pounds powdered sugar
1 teaspoon vanilla extract
2 tablespoons milk
1 cup pecans, chopped
1 cup sweetened coconut flakes

Preheat oven to 350 degrees F.

To make the cake, in a medium mixing bowl, beat sugar and butter until light and fluffy. Gradually add vegetable oil, and incorporate thoroughly. Add egg yolks, one at a time. Mix well.

In a separate mixing bowl, combine flour, baking soda, and ground pecans. Alternately blend the flour mixture and buttermilk into the egg mixture. Add coconut flakes, and mix thoroughly.

In a separate mixing bowl, beat egg whites until stiff peaks form, at least 5 to 7 minutes. Gently use a whisk to incorporate the egg whites into the batter.

Pour the batter into 2 greased and floured (9 inch) round baking pans. Bake for 35 to 40 minutes, or until a toothpick inserted near the center comes out clean. Remove from oven, and *let cool to room temperature before splitting each cake into two horizontal layer*s.

Optional: In a medium saucepan, heat ½ cup sugar and ½ cup water over medium heat. Stir continuously, until sugar dissolves. Increase heat and let boil for 3 to 5 minutes. Set aside to cool for approximately 15 minutes. Then, stir-in 1 teaspoon vanilla extract, and gently brush the syrup over each layer of cake, *except the top layer*.

To make the frosting, in a medium mixing bowl, beat the butter and cream cheese until smooth and creamy. Gradually add powdered sugar, vanilla extract, and milk. Mix well. Then, stir-in the chopped pecans.

Spread a thin layer of frosting on top of each cake layer, and place the layers on top of each other. Frost the sides of the cake with the remaining frosting, sprinkle coconut flakes on top and on sides of cake, and refrigerate for at least 4 hours before serving.

Old Fashioned Cream Cake

Cake Ingredients:
2 eggs
½ cup heavy cream
¾ cup sugar
1½ cups unbleached flour
1½ teaspoons baking powder
½ teaspoon salt

Frosting Ingredients:
1 cup sugar
6 tablespoons water
1 tablespoon plain gelatin
1/3 cup cold water
4 egg whites
1/8 teaspoon salt
1/8 teaspoon cream of tartar
1 cup powdered sugar
1 teaspoon vanilla extract

Preheat oven to 375 degrees F.

To make the cake, in a large mixing bowl, combine eggs, heavy cream, and sugar. Mix well. In a separate mixing bowl, combine flour, baking powder, and salt. Blend into egg mixture. Bake in greased (9 inch) round cake pan for 25 to 30 minutes, or until golden brown.

To make the frosting, boil sugar and 6 tablespoons water until sugar is dissolved. Soak gelatin in 1/3 cup water and dissolve in hot syrup. Let cool to room temperature. Then, beat egg whites, salt, and cream of tartar until stiff. Alternately add powdered sugar and gelatin. Mix-in vanilla extract, and chill until frosting stiffens slightly. Cover cake with frosting, and refrigerate for at least 4 hours before serving.

Date Coffee Cake

2 packages quick-rise yeast
½ cup warm water
½ cup milk, heated almost to boiling
½ cup sugar
1 teaspoon salt
½ cup butter
2 eggs
4½ to 5 cups unbleached flour
¼ cup melted butter
1½ cups dates, chopped
½ cup walnuts, ground
1 tablespoon powdered sugar, *optional*

Preheat oven to 375 degrees F.

Dissolve quick-rise yeast in ½ cup warm water.

In a medium mixing bowl, combine milk, sugar, salt, and butter. Let stand 5 minutes. Add yeast mixture and eggs. Mix well. Gradually add flour; just enough to make a soft dough.

On a floured work surface, knead the dough until smooth. Place in a greased bowl, turning once to bring greased side up. Cover, and allow mixture to double (about 1½ hours).

Roll out the dough to a ¼ inch thickness. Brush with melted butter, and top with dates and walnuts. Roll lengthwise, and place in a greased 9-inch bundt pan, joining the ends. Cover, and allow mixture to double (about 1 hour).

Bake for 30 to 35 minutes. Let cool to room temperature, and garnish with powdered sugar if desired.

Date Nut Torte

"This is one of my great-grandmother's favorite recipes. She loved dates, and had a tendency toward recipes that made use of dried fruit as a natural sweetener."

2 eggs
½ cup sugar
1 teaspoon vanilla extract
¼ cup unbleached flour
1 teaspoon baking powder
¼ teaspoon salt
1 cup dates, chopped
½ cup walnuts, chopped

Preheat oven to 350 degrees F.

In a medium mixing bowl, beat eggs, sugar, and vanilla extract together. In a separate bowl, combine flour, baking powder, and salt. Add dates and walnuts. Gradually blend into egg mixture.

Spread batter into a greased 8 x 8 inch baking dish and bake for 20 to 25 minutes, or until golden brown. Let cool.

Dobos Torte

Cake Ingredients:
1½ cups butter, softened
1 teaspoon vanilla extract
1 teaspoon almond extract
¼ cup powdered sugar
10 eggs, separated
1 cup brown sugar
¾ cup unbleached flour

Chocolate Butter Cream, Topping Ingredients:
½ cup shortening
½ cup butter, softened
2 cups powdered sugar
½ cup cocoa powder
½ teaspoon vanilla extract
¼ cup honey
½ cup heavy cream
¼ cup *Torani caramel sauce*

Preheat the oven to 400 degrees F.

To make the cake, in a medium mixing bowl, cream butter, vanilla extract, and almond extract. Add powdered sugar, and beat for 5 minutes, until smooth. Add egg yolks, and blend for 2 to 3 minutes, until light and fluffy.

In a separate mixing bowl, whip egg whites until soft peaks begin to form. Add brown sugar, and continue to whip until stiff, but not dry. Blend into egg yolk mixture, and gradually add flour to egg mixture.

Spread a thin (*about ¼ inch thick*) coating of batter into the bottom of a greased, floured 9 inch cake pan. Bake for 6 to 8 minutes. If you have the pans, bake 2 layers at a time. When the cakes are lightly browned, turn onto a cake board or cooling rack, and continue with the other layers, for a total of 6 layers.

To make the chocolate butter cream, in a medium mixing bowl, beat the shortening and butter together. Add the powdered sugar and the cocoa powder, and beat until light and fluffy, about 2 minutes. Gradually beat in the vanilla and honey, until thoroughly incorporated. Add the heavy cream, and refrigerate.

To assemble: reserve half of the chocolate butter cream. Using the remaining butter cream, spread a 1/8 inch layer on top of the first cake layer. Repeat; continuing to layer the remaining cake circles and butter cream. When all layers have been assembled, frost the sides and top of the cake.

Place the caramel sauce in a small zip-lock bag and cut one corner (*about 1/8 inch*) off the bottom of the bag. Hold the bag tightly above the cake, and drizzle caramel sauce over the top in a decorative manner.

Frankfurter Kranz

"Frankfurter Kranz, also known as Frankfurt Crown Cake, is a specialty of Frankfurt, Germany. It's typically shaped like a ring (or crown), filled with butter cream and fruit preserves, and is topped with chopped nuts. My cousins live in Echzell, near Frankfurt, and occasionally serve this at family get-togethers."

Cake Ingredients:
1 cup butter, softened
1 1/3 cups sugar
1 tablespoon vanilla sugar
6 eggs
2 tablespoons dark rum
3½ cups unbleached flour
½ cup cornstarch
1 tablespoon baking powder
½ teaspoon salt

Kirsch Syrup:
½ cup sugar
¾ cup water
2 tablespoons kirsch

Butter Cream Frosting:
2 cups milk
1/3 cup unbleached flour
2 cups butter, *softened**
2 teaspoons vanilla extract
1½ cups sugar

Almond Topping:
2 tablespoons butter
2/3 cup brown sugar
1 cup toasted, slivered almonds
12 ounce jar cherry preserves

*In order to prepare the ingredients for the butter cream frosting, it's important to let the butter stand at room temperature, overnight.

To make the cake, preheat oven to 350 degrees F. Then, in medium mixing bowl, beat butter, sugar, and vanilla sugar until light and fluffy. Add eggs and rum, and beat until well mixed. Then, gradually add flour, cornstarch, baking powder, and salt. Spread batter into a well-greased bundt pan. Bake for 35 to 45 minutes. Let stand for 15 minutes. Carefully, invert the bundt pan onto a platter and let cool to room temperature.

To make the syrup, in a small saucepan, combine water and sugar. Bring to a boil, stirring constantly. When sugar has fully dissolved, remove from heat, add the kirsch, and set aside to cool.

To make the butter cream, in a medium saucepan, use a whisk to combine milk and flour. Cook over medium heat, stirring continuously, until mixture thickens and begins to bubble, about 10 to 15 minutes. Cover with waxed paper (*placed directly on the surface of the frosting*) and let cool to room temperature, about 30 minutes. In a medium mixing bowl, beat butter and vanilla extract until light and fluffy. Gradually add sugar, and beat until well incorporated. Add the milk/flour mixture a little at a time, and beat until noticeably whiter in color, at least 5 to 7 minutes. Cover and refrigerate for *exactly* 15 minutes. *Use immediately to frost cake.*

To make the topping and assemble the cake, in a medium skillet, heat butter over medium-high heat. Add brown sugar and almonds, and sauté for 3 to 5 minutes, stirring continuously. Set aside to cool. After the cake cools, split it into three horizontal layers. Place the bottom layer on a platter, drizzle with syrup, spread preserves over top, and then spread butter cream over the preserves. Top the first layer with the second and repeat. Lay the third layer on top. Frost the exterior of the cake with the remaining butter cream. Sprinkle almond topping over top, and refrigerate for 2 to 3 hours before serving.

German Apple Cake

"This cake is actually the kind that used to be common in Austria and Hungary, and was one of my great-grandmother's favorites."

Filling Ingredients:
5 apples, peeled, cored, and thinly sliced
1/3 cup brown sugar
2 teaspoons cinnamon

Cake Ingredients:
3 cups unbleached flour
1½ cups sugar
½ teaspoon salt
4 eggs
1 cup vegetable oil
2 teaspoons vanilla extract
1/3 cup orange juice
1½ teaspoons baking soda
1½ teaspoons baking powder

Glaze Ingredients:
2 tablespoons melted butter
1½ cups powdered sugar
1½ teaspoons vanilla extract
1 to 2 tablespoons water

Preheat oven to 350 degrees F.

To make the filling, in a medium mixing bowl, combine apples with brown sugar and cinnamon. Set aside.

To make the cake, in separate mixing bowl, combine flour, sugar, salt, eggs, vegetable oil, vanilla extract, orange juice, baking soda and baking powder. Blend for 3 to 4 minutes, forming a thick dough.

In a greased and floured 10-inch bundt pan, alternate layers of batter and apples, for a total of 3 batter layers and 2 apple layers. Remember to start, and finish with a layer of batter.

Bake for 1 hour, or until a toothpick inserted into the center of the bread is clean when removed. Let cool for 10 minutes, then invert cake and remove pan. Let cool to room temperature.

To make the glaze, in a medium mixing bowl, use a whisk to combine the melted butter, powdered sugar, and vanilla extract. Add the water (*a tablespoon at a time*), and blend until mixture forms a thick syrup. Once cake has cooled to room temperature, drizzle on top of the cake.

Hawaiian Cake

"A quick and easy Hawaiian cake. This is one of my dad's favorites!"

1 (18.5 ounce) package white cake mix
2 (3.4 ounce) packages instant vanilla pudding mix
1¼ cup milk
1 (20 ounce) can crushed pineapple, drained
2 (8 ounce) containers frozen whipped topping
1 (3 ounce) package cream cheese, softened
¼ cup sugar
½ teaspoon vanilla extract
½ cup sweetened flaked coconut, toasted

In a medium mixing bowl, combine 1 package instant vanilla pudding mix and 1 package white cake mix. Bake cake in a 13 x 9 inch baking pan, according to package directions. Let cool.

In a medium mixing bowl, use a whisk to combine the milk and instant vanilla pudding mix. Let stand to thicken, about 5 minutes. Stir in crushed pineapple, and spread over cake.

In a separate mixing bowl, beat softened cream cheese, sugar, and vanilla extract until smooth. Mix in 1 (8 ounce) container whipped topping, and spread over pudding mixture. Cover loosely with plastic wrap, and refrigerate overnight.

Spread the remaining container of whipped topping on top of the cake, using a spatula to form small peaks. Sprinkle with toasted coconut flakes, and serve.

Hungarian Nut Torten

"One of my great-grandmother's tortes. It's made with ground walnuts and bread crumbs instead of flour."

Frosting Ingredients:
1 cup heavy whipping cream
½ cup powdered sugar
1 teaspoon vanilla extract

Torte Ingredients:
8 eggs, separated
¾ cup sugar
½ teaspoon vanilla extract
1 cup ground walnuts
1 teaspoon baking powder
½ teaspoon salt
2 tablespoons plain bread crumbs

To make the frosting, in a small mixing bowl, beat the heavy whipping cream until it begins to thicken. Then, add the powdered sugar and vanilla extract. Beat until stiff peaks form, at least 5 to 7 minutes. *Cover and refrigerate.*

Preheat oven to 325 degrees F.

To make the cake, in a medium mixing bowl, beat egg whites until stiff peaks form, at least 5 to 7 minutes. Set aside.

In separate mixing bowl, beat sugar, egg yolks, and vanilla extract until creamy. Gradually add ground walnuts, baking powder, salt, and bread crumbs; and mix well. Then, use a whisk to gently fold-in the egg whites.

Spread the batter on the bottom of a greased 9 inch round baking pan, and bake for 20 to 25 minutes, or until a toothpick inserted near the center comes out clean. Let cool to room temperature. Then, spread frosting evenly over top and sides of cake. *Refrigerate for at least 1 hour before serving.*

Pistachio Puddin' Cake

Cake Ingredients:
1 (18.25 ounce) package white cake mix
1 (3.4 ounce) package instant vanilla pudding mix
1 cup lemon-lime soda
1 cup vegetable oil
3 eggs
1 cup walnuts, chopped

Frosting Ingredients:
1½ cups milk
1 (3.4 ounce) package instant pistachio pudding mix
1 (8 ounce) tub whipped topping

Preheat oven to 350 degrees F.

To make the cake, in a medium mixing bowl, combine white cake mix, instant vanilla pudding mix, lemon-lime soda, vegetable oil, and eggs. Mix well. Gradually stir in walnuts, and pour batter into a greased 13 x 9 inch baking pan.

Bake for 45 to 50 minutes, or until a toothpick inserted near the center comes out clean. Let cool.

To make the frosting, in a separate mixing bowl, beat milk and instant pistachio pudding mix on a low speed for approximately 2 minutes. Mix in the whipped topping, and spread evenly over cake. Refrigerate for at least 30 minutes before serving.

Poppy Seed Coffee Ring Cake

"This is my great-grandmother's poppy seed coffee ring recipe. The cake is especially decorative given that it forms ripples."

½ cup butter
¾ cup sugar
2 eggs
1½ cups unbleached flour
2 teaspoons baking powder
1 teaspoon salt
2/3 cup milk
1 (12 ounce) can poppy seed filling

Preheat oven to 350 degrees F.

In a medium mixing bowl, beat butter and sugar until light and fluffy. Add eggs, and blend well. Gradually add flour, baking powder, salt, and milk.

Pour the batter into a well greased 9 inch bundt pan, alternating spoons of batter and poppy seed filling. Then, with the end of a wooden spoon, gently draw swirls through the batter to marbleize it.

Bake for 35 minutes, or until golden brown. Let cool for 5 minutes, turn out of mold. Once cake has cooled completely, serve with glaze.

Coffee Ring Cake Glaze:

¼ cup melted butter
2 cups powdered sugar
1 teaspoon vanilla extract
2 to 3 tablespoons brandy or dark rum

In a medium mixing bowl, use a whisk to combine the melted butter, powdered sugar, and vanilla extract. Add brandy or dark rum (*a tablespoon at a time*), and blend until mixture forms a thick syrup. Drizzle over cooled cake.

Pumpkin Cake

Cake Ingredients:
2 cup unbleached flour
2 teaspoons baking powder
1 teaspoon ginger
¾ teaspoon salt
½ teaspoon ground cloves
½ teaspoon cinnamon
½ teaspoon mace
1½ cup brown sugar
¾ cup pumpkin puree
½ cup butter, softened
2 eggs
¼ cup milk

Icing Ingredients:
1/3 cup butter, softened
1/8 teaspoon salt
3 cups powdered sugar, divided
3 tablespoons lemon juice

Preheat oven to 375 degrees F.

To make the cake, in a large mixing bowl, use a whisk to combine the flour, baking powder, ginger, salt, cloves, cinnamon, mace, and brown sugar. Add pumpkin puree and butter. Mix just enough to blend well. Then, beat-in eggs and milk.

Pour the batter into 2 greased and floured (8 inch) round baking pans, and bake for 30 to 35 minutes, or until a toothpick inserted near the center comes out clean. Remove from oven, and let cool to room temperature.

To make the lemon butter cream icing, in large mixing bowl, cream together butter, salt and 1 cup powdered sugar. Alternately mix-in lemon juice and remaining 2 cups of powdered sugar, until mixture is smooth and creamy. Spread a thin layer of the icing on top of each cake layer, and place the layers on top of each other. Cover the sides of the cake with the remaining icing.

Silvia's Red Velvet Cake

Red Velvet Cake:
1½ cups buttermilk
1½ teaspoons vinegar
¾ cup butter, softened
2 cups sugar
3 eggs, at room temperature
3 tablespoons cocoa powder
1½ teaspoons vanilla extract
6 tablespoons red food coloring
3 1/3 cups unbleached flour
1½ teaspoons baking soda
1½ teaspoons salt

Almond Syrup:
½ cup sugar
¾ cup water
1 teaspoon almond extract

Butter Cream Frosting:
2 cups milk
1/3 cup unbleached flour
2 cups butter, *softened**
2 teaspoons vanilla extract
1½ cups sugar
Finely grated chocolate, *for garnish*

*In order to prepare the ingredients for the butter cream frosting, it's important to let the butter stand at room temperature, overnight.

To make the cake, preheat oven to 350 degrees F. Then, lightly grease and flour three 9 inch round baking pans. Line the bottom of each pan with parchment paper, and set aside. In a small bowl, combine buttermilk and vinegar. Set aside. In a separate, medium mixing bowl, beat butter and sugar until light and fluffy. Add eggs, cocoa powder, vanilla extract, and red food coloring, and beat until well mixed. Then, gradually add flour, baking soda, and salt *alternately with buttermilk/vinegar mixture*. Mix just enough to blend well. *Do not over-mix!* Evenly distribute batter among prepared cake pans, and bake for 25 to 30 minutes, or until a toothpick inserted near the center comes out clean. Let cool for about 1 hour before removing from pans.

To make the syrup, in a small saucepan, combine water and sugar. Bring to a boil, stirring constantly. When sugar has fully dissolved, remove from heat, add almond extract, and set aside to cool.

To make the butter cream, in a medium saucepan, use a whisk to combine milk and flour. Cook over medium heat, stirring continuously, until mixture thickens and begins to bubble, about 10 to 15 minutes. Cover with waxed paper (*placed directly on the surface of the frosting*) and let cool to room temperature, about 30 minutes. In a medium mixing bowl, beat butter and vanilla extract until light and fluffy. Gradually add sugar, and beat until well incorporated. Add the milk/flour mixture a little at a time, and beat until noticeably whiter in color, at least 5 to 7 minutes. Cover and refrigerate for *exactly* 15 minutes. *Use immediately to frost cake.*

To assemble the cake, place 1 cake layer on a serving plate; drizzle with syrup, spread with approximately ¾ cup frosting, and repeat. Frost the top and sides of the cake with remaining frosting, garnish with finely grated chocolate, and refrigerate overnight.

"Yo, Ho, Ho and a Bottle of Rum" Cake

"The type of rum you use for this recipe is very important. It should be golden brown in color, and no less than 70 proof. I'd recommend using Captain Morgan's Gold Rum or Bacardi's Gold Rum"

Cake Ingredients:
1 (18.5 ounce) package yellow cake mix
½ cup dark rum
4 Eggs
½ cup water
½ cup vegetable oil
1 (3.5 ounce) package instant vanilla pudding mix
1 cup walnuts, chopped

Glaze Ingredients:
¼ cup butter
½ cup sugar
½ cup water
¼ cup dark rum

To make the cake, preheat oven to 325 degrees F. Grease and flour a 10" bundt pan. Sprinkle walnuts over bottom of pan.

Mix together the yellow cake mix, ½ cup dark rum, eggs, ½ cup water, vegetable oil, and instant vanilla pudding mix. Pour batter over chopped walnuts, in bundt pan.

Bake at 325 degrees F for 1 hour. When cake is cool, invert on a large plate. Using a fork, lightly prick the top of the cake.

To make the glaze, melt butter in small saucepan over medium flame. Stir in ½ cup water and ½ cup sugar. Boil 5 minutes, stirring constantly. Remove from heat. Add ¼ cup dark rum.

Drizzle and smooth glaze evenly over top and sides of cake. Allow cake to absorb glaze.

Special Occasion Cake

"Actually, my great-grandmother called this a 'three-occasion cake' but decided to I rename it 'special occasion cake' since I really have no idea which occasions, in particular, it's intended for. Birthday, Wedding, Other?"

Cake Ingredients:
4 egg whites
¾ cup butter
1½ cup sugar
1 teaspoon vanilla extract
½ teaspoon almond extract
2¾ cup unbleached flour
4 teaspoons baking powder
½ teaspoon salt
¾ cup milk

Preheat oven to 350 degrees F.

In a medium mixing bowl, beat egg whites until stiff peaks form, at least 5 to 7 minutes. Set aside. In separate mixing bowl, beat butter and sugar until light and fluffy. Add vanilla extract and almond extract. Then, gradually add flour, baking powder, salt, and milk. Use a whisk to gently fold-in the egg whites. Then, pour batter into a greased 13 x 9 inch baking pan, and bake 35 to 40 minutes, or until a toothpick inserted near the center comes out clean. Let cool.

Icing Ingredients:
1 1/8 cup sugar
3/8 cup water
1 teaspoon vanilla extract
3 egg whites, beaten
½ teaspoon rose water

To make the icing, in a small saucepan, boil water and sugar at 240 to 242 degrees F, to form a thick syrup. Keep the pan covered for the first three minutes. When sugar has fully dissolved and mixture spins an 8 inch thread, remove from heat and add vanilla extract. Let stand 5 minutes, and then pour mixture over beaten egg whites, stirring constantly. Beat until thick enough to spread.

Spread a thin layer of icing (*just enough to cover, don't use all the icing*) over the top and sides of the cake. Then, using a large chef's knife, make a criss-cross pattern on top of the cake, with lines about 2 inches apart. This will divide it into squares suitable for individual pieces.

Add the rose water to the remainder of the icing, and add a few drops of pink or yellow food coloring. Place a scant teaspoon of the colored icing in the center of each square, swirling with a fork, to resemble a rose.

Anna Beer's Spice Cake

"This spice cake recipe was passed down to my great-grandmother from her mother (my 2nd great-grandmother), Anna Beer, who was born in 1860. It's probably more than 125 years old, and must have been one of my great-grandmother's favorites considering that she wrote 'mother's best recipe' in the margin of her cookbook."

Spice Cake Ingredients:
½ cup butter
½ cup white sugar
1 cup brown sugar
2 eggs
1 cup buttermilk
½ cup sun dried raisins
½ cup walnuts, finely chopped
2 cups unbleached flour
1 teaspoon baking soda
1½ teaspoons cinnamon
½ teaspoon ground cloves
½ teaspoon nutmeg

Frosting Ingredients:
1/3 cup butter, softened
2 cups powdered sugar
1 teaspoon vanilla extract
2 to 3 tablespoons water

Preheat oven to 350 degrees F.

To prepare the spice cake, in a small bowl, combine raisins with ½ cup water. Set aside to soak.

In a medium mixing bowl, beat butter, white sugar, and brown sugar until light and fluffy. Add eggs, buttermilk, *drained* raisins, and chopped walnuts.

In a separate mixing bowl, combine flour, baking soda, cinnamon, ground cloves, and nutmeg. Gradually add flour mixture to egg mixture, and mix well.

Pour batter into a greased, floured, 9" x 13" rectangular cake pan. Then, bake for 30 to 35 minutes, or until a toothpick inserted into the center of the bread is clean when removed.

To prepare the frosting, in a medium mixing bowl, use a whisk to combine butter, powdered sugar, and vanilla extract. Gradually add water (*a tablespoon at a time*), and blend until smooth and creamy. Use to frost the top of the cake

Tiramisu Cake

"Tiramisu is Italian 'pick me up,' so be sure to use extra strong coffee or espresso for this cake. The recipe differs slightly from traditional tiramisu recipes; it's not made with savoiardi biscuits."

Cake Ingredients:
1 (18.25 ounce) package white cake mix
1 cup strong, brewed coffee (*cooled to room temperature*)
4 egg whites

Frosting Ingredients:
½ cup cream cheese, softened
½ cup sugar
½ cup chocolate syrup
2 teaspoons vanilla extract
2 (8 ounce) tubs whipped topping
6 tablespoons strong coffee, at room temperature
2 ounces chopped English toffee, *optional*

Preheat oven to 350 degrees F.

To make the cake, line two greased 9 inch round baking pans with waxed paper, grease the paper, and set aside.

In a large mixing bowl, combine cake mix, coffee, and egg whites. Pour batter into prepared cake pans.

Bake for 25 to 30 minutes, or until a toothpick inserted near the center comes out clean. *Let cool before splitting each cake into two horizontal layers.*

To make the frosting, in a medium mixing bowl, beat the cream cheese, sugar, chocolate syrup, and vanilla extract until smooth. Add the whipped topping, and stir until well combined.

Place one cake layer on a serving plate; drizzle with coffee, spread enough frosting (about ¾ cup) to cover, and repeat. Frost the top and sides with the remaining frosting, garnish with chopped toffee, and *refrigerate for at least 2 hours before serving.*

Vanilla Cheesecake

3 (8 ounce) packages cream cheese, *softened*
2 teaspoons vanilla extract
2 tablespoons unbleached flour
¼ cup vanilla sugar
½ cup granulated white sugar
4 eggs
2 tablespoons heavy cream
1 (9 inch) graham cracker pie shell
1 (8 ounce) tub whipped topping
1 teaspoon vanilla powder

Preheat oven to 350 degrees F.

In a medium mixing bowl, beat the cream cheese and vanilla extract until light and fluffy. Gradually add the flour, vanilla sugar, granulated white sugar, eggs, and heavy cream.

Then, use a rubber spatula to spread the cream cheese mixture into a 9 inch graham cracker pie shell, and bake for 50 to 60 minutes, or until set. The center shouldn't move when shaken.

Remove from oven, and *refrigerate overnight*. Garnish with whipped topping and vanilla powder before serving.

Walnut Cream Cake

Cake Ingredients:
1 (18.5 ounce) package yellow cake mix
1 teaspoon vanilla extract
2 tablespoons cocoa powder

Walnut Cream Ingredients:
½ cup ground walnuts
¾ cup warm milk
½ cup butter, softened
2 tablespoons sugar
2 teaspoons cornstarch
1 tablespoon rum

Topping Ingredients:
2 cups heavy whipping cream
½ cup cream cheese, softened
½ cup sugar
2 teaspoons vanilla extract
¼ cup chopped walnuts
½ cup chocolate syrup

Rum Sauce Ingredients:
1/3 cup milk
1 tablespoon rum
¼ cup sugar

Chocolate Cream Ingredients:
½ cup chopped raisins
¾ cup milk
1 egg
½ cup butter
1 tablespoon sugar
2 tablespoon cocoa powder
2 teaspoons cornstarch
1 cup whipped topping, *optional*

To prepare the cake, follow the package directions. Evenly distribute the batter into two separate bowls. Then, add vanilla extract to one bowl and cocoa powder to the other. Pour the batter into 2 greased 9 inch round baking pans. Bake according to directions, or until a toothpick inserted near the center comes out clean. *Let cool before splitting each cake into two horizontal layers.*

To prepare the rum sauce, in a small mixing bowl, combine the milk, rum, and sugar. Set aside.

To make the walnut cream, in a medium saucepan, combine the walnuts, milk, butter, and sugar. Bring to a boil, stirring frequently. Then, add the cornstarch, *stirring all the while*. Remove from heat, add the rum, and let cool to room temperature.

To prepare the chocolate cream, in a small bowl, combine the raisins with about ¼ cup amaretto, and set aside to soak. In a medium saucepan, use a whisk to combine the milk, egg, butter, sugar, and cocoa powder. Bring to *near-boil*, stirring frequently. Add the cornstarch, *stirring all the while*, until the mixture thickens. *Do not boil!* Let cool to room temperature before adding the whipped topping.

To prepare the topping and assemble the cake, in a medium mixing bowl, beat the heavy whipping cream, cream cheese, sugar, and vanilla extract until peaks form. Place a chocolate cake layer on a serving plate, drizzle with rum sauce, and spread with enough walnut cream to cover. Then, place a yellow cake layer on top, drizzle with rum sauce, and spread with enough chocolate cream to cover. *Repeat, alternating layers.* Frost the top and sides with whipped cream topping, and garnish with chopped walnuts. Now, place the chocolate syrup in a small zip-lock bag and cut one corner (about 1/8 inch) off the bottom of the bag. Hold the bag tightly above the cake, and drizzle chocolate syrup over top in a decorative manner. *Refrigerate for at least 2 hours before serving.*

Whiskey Cake

"This popular chocolate cake is laced with single malt whisky and is a traditional Scotch-Irish dessert. I bought one at the Glenlivet distillery near Ballindalloch once, as a gift for my cousin, Craig."

¾ cup butter
1 cup white sugar
1 cup brown sugar
1½ cups strong, brewed coffee (*cooled to room temperature*)
½ cup single malt scotch whisky
¾ cup cocoa powder
3 eggs
2 teaspoons vanilla extract
2 cups unbleached flour
1½ teaspoons baking soda
½ teaspoon cinnamon
¼ teaspoon nutmeg
1/8 teaspoon ground cloves
1 cup semisweet chocolate chips
¼ cup powdered sugar

Preheat oven to 325 degrees F.

In a medium saucepan, combine butter, white sugar, brown sugar, coffee, scotch whisky, and cocoa powder. Heat over medium-low heat, stirring occasionally. Once the sugar has dissolved, remove from heat and set aside. *When the mixture has cooled to room temperature*, use a whisk to incorporate the eggs and vanilla extract.

In a medium mixing bowl, combine flour, baking soda, cinnamon, nutmeg, and ground cloves. Gradually stir-in the egg mixture, and fold the chocolate chips into the batter.

Pour batter into a greased 9 inch bundt pan, and bake for 1 hour, or until a toothpick inserted into the cake is clean when removed. Let stand, and allow cake to cool 5 to 10 minutes. Remove from pan, and garnish with powdered sugar.

White Layer Cake

"This is my great-grandmother's basic layer cake recipe. You can use any kind of frosting and/or filling with this recipe."

Cake Ingredients:
½ cup butter
1 cup sugar
1 egg
2 egg yolks
½ cup milk
¼ teaspoon orange extract
¼ teaspoon lemon extract
2 cups unbleached flour
1 tablespoon baking powder

Frosting Ingredients:
1 cup sugar
1/3 cup water
2 egg whites

Preheat oven to 375 degrees F.

To make the cake, in a large mixing bowl, beat butter and sugar until light and fluffy. Add egg, egg yolks, milk, orange extract, and lemon extract. Blend well.

In a separate mixing bowl, combine flour and baking powder. Gradually blend into egg mixture.

Pour batter into 2 well greased 13 x 9 inch baking pans. Bake for 20 to 25 minutes, or until a toothpick inserted near the center comes out clean. Let cool.

To make the frosting, in a medium mixing bowl, beat egg whites until stiff peaks form, , at least 5 to 7 minutes. Set aside.

Boil sugar and water until a few drops form a soft ball when tested in cold water. Let stand for 5 minutes, and then beat-in egg whites.

Place one cake on a serving plate, spread with frosting, and repeat. Frost the top and sides of with remaining frosting.

Canning Recipes

Crisp Sweet Relish

"One of my mom's canning recipes... Like most canning recipes, this one freezes well too. Simply divide the relish into gallon freezer bags, and store them in the freezer."

8 cups cucumbers, chopped
4 cups onions, chopped
2 cups carrots, very thinly sliced
5 tablespoons salt
4 cups vinegar
7 cups sugar
2 teaspoons celery seed
1 teaspoon ground turmeric
1 teaspoon ground nutmeg
½ teaspoon freshly ground black pepper

In a large colander, combine cucumbers, onions, and carrots. Sprinkle with salt. Let stand for 6 hours. Drain thoroughly.

In a large pot, combine vinegar, sugar, celery seed, turmeric, nutmeg, and freshly ground black pepper. Add cucumbers, onions, and carrots, and bring to a boil over medium heat, stirring occasionally.

Reduce heat, and let simmer (*uncovered*) for 20 minutes, stirring occasionally.

Pack into hot jars, leaving approximately ½ inch headspace. Adjust caps, and process for 10 minutes in a boiling water bath.

Cucumber Relish

"My great-grandmother used red and green bell peppers to make this relish. It was one of her favorite recipes. In fact, she wrote 'best ever' in the margin of her cookbook."

2 quarts chopped cucumbers
1 quart chopped onions
5 large bell peppers, chopped
6 small vine-ripened tomatoes, diced
3 bunches celery, diced
½ cup salt
1 quart vinegar (*not too strong*)
1/3 cup unbleached flour
1 tablespoon dry mustard
4 cups sugar

In a large colander, combine the cucumbers, onions, bell peppers, tomatoes, and celery. Sprinkle with salt, mix well, and let stand for 1 hour. Drain thoroughly.

In a large pot, use a whisk to combine the vinegar, flour, dry mustard, and sugar. Add the cucumbers, onions, bell peppers, tomatoes, and celery. Bring to a boil, and cook over a medium-low flame for 12 minutes, stirring constantly.

Pack into hot jars, leaving approximately ½ inch headspace. Adjust caps, and process for 10 minutes in a boiling water bath.

Green Tomato Relish

1 quart cider vinegar
4 cups sugar
1 teaspoon allspice
1 teaspoon turmeric
1 teaspoon celery seed
1 teaspoon mustard seed
1 tablespoon salt
3 pounds green cabbage, cored and shredded
2 pounds green tomatoes, diced
3 green bell peppers, chopped
2 red bell peppers, chopped
4 large onions, chopped

In a large pot, use a whisk to combine the vinegar, sugar, allspice, turmeric, celery seed, mustard seed, and salt.

Add the cabbage, green tomatoes, bell peppers, and onions. Bring to a boil, and cook over a medium-low flame for 1 hour, or until thick and translucent.

Pack into hot jars, leaving approximately ½ inch headspace. Adjust caps, and process for 10 minutes in a boiling water bath.

Peach Relish

¾ cup cider vinegar
1½ cups sugar
1 teaspoon cinnamon
½ teaspoon ground cloves
2 teaspoons mustard seed
8 cups peaches (about 16 medium peaches), *peeled, pitted, and sliced*
1 cup sundried raisins
½ cup chopped walnuts

In a large pot, use a whisk to combine the vinegar, sugar, cinnamon, ground cloves, and mustard seed.

Add the peaches and raisins. Bring to a boil, and cook over a medium-low flame for 45 minutes, or until thick. Add the chopped walnuts, and let stand for 2 minutes.

Pack into half pint jars, leaving approximately ½ inch headspace. Adjust caps, and process for 10 minutes in a boiling water bath.

Pear Butter

"Rather than using a sieve or food mill, consider using a blender or food processor to puree the pear pulp."

20 medium, fully ripe pears, *peeled and chopped*
4 cups sugar
1 teaspoon grated lemon rind
1/3 cup orange juice
½ teaspoon nutmeg

In a large pot, cook pears over a medium-low flame until soft (*about 20 to 25 minutes*), adding just enough water to prevent sticking. Press through a sieve or food mill. Then, add sugar, grated lemon rind, orange juice, and nutmeg; and cook for an additional 15 minutes. As pulp thickens, stir more frequently to prevent sticking.

Pack into Ball jars, leaving approximately ½ inch headspace. Adjust caps, and process for 10 minutes in a boiling water bath.

Rhubarb Relish

"This is my mom's rhubarb relish recipe. Most likely, it came about as a means to preserve rhubarb during the winter months. It can be used as a sauce or used as a condiment."

2 cups rhubarb, finely chopped
2 medium onions, thinly sliced
2½ cups brown sugar
¾ cup cider vinegar
½ teaspoon cinnamon
½ teaspoon allspice
¼ teaspoon ground cloves
1 teaspoon salt
¼ teaspoon freshly ground black pepper

In a medium saucepan, combine rhubarb, onions, brown sugar, cider vinegar, cinnamon, allspice, ground cloves, salt, and pepper. Cook over medium heat for 30 minutes or until thickened, stirring occasionally.

Sliced Cucumber Pickles

12 large pickling cucumbers, *peeled and sliced ¼ inch thick*
12 medium onions, thinly sliced
½ cup salt
4 teaspoons cornstarch
4 teaspoons turmeric
2 tablespoons dijon mustard *(not dry mustard or mustard seed)*
5 cups cider vinegar
1½ cups white sugar
1 cup brown sugar

In a large colander, combine cucumbers and onions. Sprinkle with salt, mix well, and let stand overnight. Drain thoroughly.

In a small bowl, use a whisk to combine cornstarch, turmeric, and dijon mustard. Add just enough water to make a smooth paste.

In a large pot, bring cider vinegar, white sugar, and brown sugar to a boil. Gradually, stir in cornstarch mixture, and return to boil. Add cucumbers and onions; and once again, return to boil, stirring occasionally.

Pack into pint jars, leaving approximately ½ inch headspace. Adjust caps, and process for 10 minutes in a boiling water bath.

Cookies

Apple Oatmeal Cookies

"My great-grandmother used to make apple oatmeal cookies all the time. I'd forgotten how good they are until we re-discovered this recipe."

½ cup butter
2/3 cup brown sugar
2 eggs
½ cup unbleached flour
½ cup whole-wheat flour
1 teaspoon baking powder
1 teaspoon cinnamon
½ teaspoon nutmeg
½ teaspoon salt
1 cup rolled oats
2 small apples, peeled, cored, and chopped
1 cup walnuts, chopped

Preheat oven to 350 degrees F.

In medium mixing bowl, beat butter and brown sugar until light and fluffy. Add eggs, and beat until well incorporated. Then, gradually add flour, baking powder, cinnamon, nutmeg, and salt. Gradually mix-in oats, apples, and walnuts.

Drop by teaspoon onto greased baking sheets, about 2 inches apart. Bake for 15 minutes, or until golden brown.

Austrian Nut Butter Cookies

"This austrian nut butter cookie recipe is yet another of my great-grandmother's favorites. It makes use of ground walnuts blended with a little butter, though hazelnuts would work just as well."

1 cup unbleached flour
1/3 cup sugar
2/3 cup walnuts, ground
½ cup butter, softened
1/3 cup raspberry preserves

In medium mixing bowl, combine flour, sugar, and ground walnuts. Cut in butter using a pastry blender, to form an elastic dough. *Refrigerate for 2 hours.*

Preheat oven to 375 degrees F.

On a floured work surface, knead the dough until smooth. Then, roll out the dough to about a 1/8 inch thickness. Cut dough with a round cookie cutter, approximately 2 inches in diameter.

Bake on greased cookie sheets for 7 to 10 minutes, or until golden near the edges. Let cool.

Once the cookies have cooled completely, spread half of the cookies with raspberry preserves. Cover with the remaining cookies, forming '*sandwiches*.' Sprinkle with powdered sugar, and serve.

Banana Oatmeal Cookies

"My great-grandmother's recipe; these banana oatmeal cookies taste like banana bread, but are in the form of a cookie!"

1 cup brown sugar
¾ cup butter, softened
1 egg
1 cup mashed bananas
1 cup unbleached flour
½ cup whole-wheat flour
½ teaspoon baking soda
1/8 teaspoon salt
¼ teaspoon nutmeg
¼ teaspoon cinnamon
2 cups rolled oats
½ cup walnuts, chopped

Preheat oven to 400 degrees F.

In medium mixing bowl, beat brown sugar and butter until light and fluffy. Add egg and mashed bananas, and beat until well mixed. Then, gradually add white flour, wheat flour, baking soda, salt, nutmeg, cinnamon, rolled oats, and walnuts.

Drop mixture from teaspoon onto greased baking sheets, about 2 inches apart. Bake for 10 to 12 minutes.

Black Walnut Cookies

"This is my great-grandmother's black walnut cookie recipe. Black walnuts have a very rich, potent flavor. Either you love 'em or you hate 'em. When I was a kid, we had a black walnut tree in our back yard (yes, I've been hit in the head by a walnut or two – explains alot), but my great-grandfather was the only one who was any good at removing the husks and harvesting the nuts. It's a difficult, messy process..."

½ cup black walnuts, chopped
3 tablespoons milk
1/3 cup butter
1 cup brown sugar
1 egg
¼ cup peanut butter
½ teaspoon vanilla extract
1½ cups unbleached flour
¼ teaspoon salt
1/8 teaspoon baking soda

Preheat the oven to 400 degrees F.

In a small mixing bowl, combine chopped walnuts and milk. Set aside.

In a separate, medium mixing bowl, beat butter and brown sugar until light and fluffy. Add egg, peanut butter, and vanilla extract, and beat until well mixed. Then, gradually add flour, salt, and baking soda alternately with walnut-milk mixture.

Shape dough into 1 inch balls, and arrange approximately 2 inches apart on a greased baking sheet.

Bake 8 to 10 minutes.

Brazil Nut Sticks

"This is my great-grandmother's recipe. Cooking with brazil nuts used to be far more common than it is today, most likely due to the depletion of the rainforest. Still, if you can find them for a reasonable price, brazil nuts are extremely rich in potassium. On the other hand, they go bad quickly, and should probably be refrigerated. At any rate, I think you'll enjoy this recipe."

2 eggs
1 cup brown sugar
1 teaspoon vanilla extract
1½ cups unbleached flour
½ teaspoon baking powder
1 cup brazil nuts*, ground
¼ cup powdered sugar (*optional*)

Blend brazil nuts in food processor until finely ground. Set aside.

In medium mixing bowl, beat eggs, brown sugar, and vanilla extract until light and fluffy. Then, gradually add flour, baking powder, and brazil nuts. Place in a greased bowl, cover with plastic wrap, and refrigerate overnight.

The next day, preheat oven to 350 degrees F.

On a floured work surface, use your hands to pat the dough to about a ½ inch thickness, and cut into ½ inch thick ropes, lengthwise. Then, cut the ropes crosswise into 2 inch pieces. If necessary, add a little flour (*about ¼ cup at a time*) to prevent the dough from sticking.

Place on a greased baking sheet, and bake for 12 to 15 minutes. Let stand for 10 minutes. Then, if desired, garnish with powdered sugar.

*If unavailable, substitute with almonds or macadamia nuts.

Buckeyes

"Buckeyes are a regional favorite. They're made from semi-sweet chocolate and peanut butter, resemble the nut of a buckeye tree, and are rumored to have been created when Ohio became known as 'The Buckeye State,' honoring the state tree. Unless freshly ground peanut butter is readily available, I'd recommend using Smucker's Natural Creamy Peanut Butter for this recipe."

1 package semi-sweet chocolate chips
1½ cups creamy peanut butter
2½ cups powdered sugar
½ cup butter
1 teaspoon vanilla extract

In small saucepan, melt the semi-sweet chocolate chips over medium-low heat.

Meanwhile, in a medium mixing bowl, mix together the peanut butter, powdered sugar, butter, and vanilla extract, only until the mixture resembles coarse crumbs.

Shape into ½ inch balls, and dip into melted chocolate, leaving the top of the ball uncovered, to resemble a buckeye.

Place buckeyes on waxed-paper-lined baking sheet, cover, and *refrigerate overnight*.

Cherry Winks

"A family favorite, this classic cookie recipe actually became part of our holiday tradition when my great-grandmother experimented with a recipe that appeared on the side of a box of Kellogg's Corn Flakes. A lot of people freeze cookies for holiday celebrations, but these are best served fresh."

2¼ cups unbleached flour
2 teaspoons baking powder
½ teaspoon salt
¾ cup butter, softened
1 cup brown sugar
2 eggs
2 tablespoons milk
1 teaspoon vanilla extract
1 cup walnuts *or pecans*, chopped
1 cup dates, pitted and finely chopped
½ cup maraschino cherries, finely chopped
2½ cups corn flakes, crushed
15 maraschino cherries, quartered

Preheat oven to 375 degrees F.

In a medium mixing bowl, combine flour, baking powder, and salt. Set aside. In a separate, large mixing bowl, beat butter and brown sugar until light and fluffy. Add eggs, and beat well. Stir in milk and vanilla extract.

Add flour mixture to egg mixture, and mix well. Stir in walnuts, dates, and chopped maraschino cherries.

Using approximately one tablespoon for each cookie, roll the dough in crushed corn flakes, shape into 1½ inch balls, and arrange approximately 2 inches apart on a greased baking sheet. Top each cookie with a maraschino cherry quarter.

Bake for 10 to 12 minutes, or until golden brown. *Do not stack or store until room temperature!*

Chocolate Chip Cookies

"Chocolate Chip Cookies were my sister's specialty all through Junior High School and High School. She loved to eat the cookie dough, and would occasionally try to make one big cookie."

½ cup butter, softened
¼ cup granulated white sugar
¼ cup brown sugar
1 egg
½ teaspoon vanilla extract
1½ cups unbleached flour
½ teaspoon baking soda
¼ teaspoon salt
¾ cup semisweet chocolate chips
¾ cup walnuts, chopped

Preheat oven to 325 degrees F.

In medium mixing bowl, beat butter, white sugar, and brown sugar until light and fluffy. Add egg and vanilla extract, and beat until well mixed. Then, gradually add flour, baking soda, and salt. Gently fold in chocolate chips and walnuts.

Drop by large spoonfuls onto ungreased baking sheet, about 2 inches apart.

Bake for 12 to 15 minutes, or until edges are slightly browned.

Coconut Thumbprints

"My mom's coconut thumbprint cookies were always a holiday favorite. Rolled in coconut flakes and filled with preserves, these festive cookies will brighten up any Christmas celebration."

2/3 cup butter
1/3 cup sugar
2 egg yolks
1 teaspoon vanilla extract
½ teaspoon salt
1½ cups unbleached flour
2 egg whites, slightly beaten
¾ cup sweetened coconut flakes
1/3 cup blueberry preserves

Preheat oven to 350 degrees F.

In a medium mixing bowl, cream butter and sugar until light and fluffy. Add egg yolks, vanilla extract, and salt. Gradually add flour, and mix well.

Shape dough into 1 inch balls, and dip in egg whites. Roll dough in sweetened coconut flakes, and arrange approximately 1 inch apart, on a greased baking sheet. Then, with your thumb or the handle of a wooden spoon, make an indentation in each ball.

Bake for 15 to 17 minutes, or until golden brown. Remove from baking sheets and while still warm, use a pastry bag to fill the center of each cookie with blueberry preserves.

Filled Crescent Cookies

"One of my great-grandmother's favorite recipes. In fact, she wrote 'Best recipe. Uses very little sugar (except for filling). Not very sweet.' in the margin of her cookbook."

Walnut Filling:
1 cup finely ground walnuts
1 cup brown sugar
½ cup milk, heated almost to boiling
1/8 cup melted butter

Crescent Cookies:
1 package quick-rise yeast
2 tablespoons warm milk
1½ cups butter
3 tablespoons sugar
1 tablespoon grated lemon rind
4 cups unbleached flour
½ teaspoon salt
3 eggs, *separated*
¾ cup sour cream
¾ cup chopped walnuts
½ cup powdered sugar

To make the walnut filling, in a medium mixing bowl, combine ground walnuts and brown sugar. Add just enough milk (*about 1 tablespoon at a time*) until filling is thick but relatively easy to spread. Set aside.

To make the crescent cookies, preheat oven to 350 degrees F. Then, dissolve quick-rise yeast in 2 tablespoons warm milk.

In medium mixing bowl, beat butter and sugar until light and fluffy. Add grated lemon rind, flour, and salt. Mix well. Then, add yeast mixture, egg yolks, and just enough sour cream to make a stiff dough. In a separate mixing bowl, beat egg whites until stiff peaks form, at least 5 to 7 minutes. Set aside.

Now, on a floured work surface, knead the dough until smooth. Roll out the dough as thin as possible (the dough should be nearly transparent). If the edges are a little thicker, cut them off.

Cut into 4 inch squares, and place about a teaspoon of walnut filling (or stiff jam) in the center of each square. Roll from corner to corner, shaping each section of dough into a small crescent. Dip into stiffly beaten egg white, roll in chopped walnuts, and arrange approximately 2 inches apart, on a greased baking sheet.

Bake for 35 minutes, or until golden brown. Allow cookies to cool. Then, sprinkle with powdered sugar.

Vanilla Crescent Cookies

"My great grandmother used to make these crescent shaped cookies, flavored with vanilla and dusted with powdered sugar. Traditionally, they're made at Christmas and appear to have originated from Austria."

2 cups unbleached flour
½ teaspoon baking powder
½ cup sugar
1 teaspoon vanilla extract
1 teaspoon almond extract
3 egg yolks
¾ cup butter
½ cup blanched, ground almonds
¼ cup powdered sugar

Preheat oven to 350 degrees F.

In a medium mixing bowl, combine the flour, baking powder, sugar, vanilla extract, almond extract, egg yolks, butter, and almonds. Mix until smooth, using a kneading attachment for your mixer.

Cover the bowl loosely with greased plastic wrap, and *refrigerate for 30 minutes.*

On a floured work surface, roll the dough to about a ¾ inch thickness, and cut into ¾ inch thick ropes. Then, cut the ropes crosswise into 2 inch pieces, gently pinching the ends to round off the edges.

Shape sections of dough into small crescents and place on a greased baking sheet.

Bake 10 to 12 minutes, or until golden brown. Allow cookies to cool. Then, sprinkle powdered sugar over top of the cookies.

Frosted Date Balls

"Along with the perennial Hickory Farms gift basket, we used to buy assortments of nuts and dried fruit during the holiday season. I particularly enjoyed dates and figs, whereas my mom was partial to dried apricots and mangoes."

½ cup butter, softened
1/3 cup powdered sugar
1 tablespoon water
1 teaspoon vanilla extract
1¼ cups unbleached flour
¼ teaspoon salt
2/3 cup dates, pitted and finely chopped
½ cup walnuts, chopped

Preheat oven to 300 degrees F.

In a medium mixing bowl, cream the butter and powdered sugar until mixture is light and fluffy. Stir in water and vanilla extract, and beat until smooth. Add flour and salt, and mix well. Then, gradually add dates and walnuts.

Roll into 1 inch balls. Place 2 inches apart on an un-greased cookie sheet. Bake for 20 minutes, or until cookies are set but not brown. *While cookies are warm, roll in powdered sugar.*

Date Drop Cookies

"This is one of my great-grandmother's date cookie recipes. It wasn't straightforward though, to say the least. There was no list of ingredients. Rather, the ingredients appeared in the instructions on an as-needed basis and the first step read, 'bake at 375 degrees F for 12 to 15 minutes,' Anyway, I hope it's easier to follow now. Enjoy!"

2 (8 ounce) packages pitted, pressed baking dates
½ cup brown sugar
½ cup boiling water
1 cup butter
1 cup granulated white sugar
1 cup brown sugar
3 unbeaten eggs
1 teaspoon vanilla extract
4 cups unbleached flour
1 teaspoon baking soda
1 teaspoon salt
1 cup walnuts, chopped

Preheat oven to 375 degrees F.

In a medium saucepan, combine dates, brown sugar, and boiling water. Let simmer over low flame until thickened, 10 to 15 minutes. Stir frequently. Let cool.

In a large mixing bowl, beat butter, white sugar, and brown sugar. Add eggs, and vanilla extract. Mix well.

In a separate mixing bowl, combine flour, baking soda, and salt. Blend into egg mixture. Add chopped walnuts and date mixture. Mix well.

Drop dough by rounded teaspoonfuls onto greased baking sheets, approximately 2 inches apart.

Bake for 12 to 15 minutes, or until golden brown.

Date Oatmeal Cookies

"This is one of my great-grandmother's favorite recipes. Needless to say, it's been in the family for years…"

¾ cup brown sugar
½ cup butter, softened
2 eggs
½ teaspoon vanilla extract
1½ cups unbleached flour
¼ teaspoon salt
1 teaspoon cinnamon
¼ teaspoon ground cloves
½ teaspoon nutmeg
¾ cup rolled oats
2 tablespoons buttermilk
¼ cup walnuts, chopped
1/3 cup chopped dates

Preheat oven to 350 degrees F.

In medium mixing bowl, beat sugar and butter until light and fluffy. Add eggs and vanilla extract, and beat until well mixed. Then, gradually add flour, salt, cinnamon, ground cloves, nutmeg, and oats. Add buttermilk, walnuts, and chopped dates. Mix well.

Shape dough into 1 inch balls, arrange approximately 3 inches apart on a greased baking sheet, and flatten each cookie with a large wooden spoon.

Bake for 15 to 18 minutes, or until golden brown.

Date Raisin Nut Cookies

"This recipe combines dates, raisins, and walnuts to make a delicious, wholesome cookie. It's one of several of my great-grandmother's cookie recipes that make use of dried fruit and walnuts. Although these cookies are naturally sweet, you might consider adding ½ cup sugar if you have a genuine sweet tooth."

1 cup flour
1 teaspoon baking powder
¼ teaspoon salt
½ cup butter, softened
1 cup walnuts, chopped fine
½ cup sweetened coconut flakes
½ cup dates, chopped
½ cup raisins
1 egg
2 teaspoons brandy

In a medium mixing bowl, combine flour, baking powder, and salt. Cut in butter using a pastry blender, mixture should resemble fine crumbs. Add walnuts, coconut, dates, raisins, egg, and brandy. Mix just enough to blend well. *Do not over-mix!* Place in a greased bowl, cover with plastic wrap, and refrigerate for 1 hour.

Preheat oven to 350 degrees F.

Shape dough into 1 inch balls, and arrange approximately 2 inches apart on a greased baking sheet. Using a fork dipped in flour, flatten to form 1½ inch cookies. Bake for 12 to 15 minutes, or until golden brown.

Gingersnaps

"Some gingersnap recipes include anise. Not this one! My mom couldn't stand anise, or any sort of licorice flavor. Rumor has it that gingersnaps originated long ago, at medieval fairs."

¾ cup butter
1 cup brown sugar
¼ cup molasses
1 egg
2¼ cups unbleached flour
2 teaspoons baking soda
½ teaspoon salt
1 teaspoon ginger
1 teaspoon cinnamon
¼ teaspoon ground cloves
½ cup coarse granulated sugar

Preheat oven to 375 degrees F.

In a medium mixing bowl, beat the butter, brown sugar, molasses, and egg until light and fluffy.

In a separate mixing bowl, combine the flour, baking soda, salt, ginger, cinnamon, and ground cloves. Gradually blend into the egg mixture.

Shape dough into 1 inch balls*, roll in coarse granulated sugar, and arrange approximately 2 inches apart on a greased baking sheet. Bake for 10 to 12 minutes. Let cool on baking sheets for 2 to 3 minutes before removing.

If dough is too soft, refrigerate for approximately one hour.

Hershey's Kiss Cookies

"Essentially a peanut butter cookie topped with a Hershey's Kiss, a variation of this recipe was a Pillsbury bake off winner."

½ cup butter
¾ cup creamy peanut butter
1/3 cup sugar
1/3 cup brown sugar
1 egg
2 tablespoons milk
1 teaspoon vanilla extract
1½ cups unbleached flour
1 teaspoon baking soda
½ teaspoon salt
4 dozen Hershey's Kisses

Preheat oven to 375 degrees F, and remove Hershey's Kiss wrappers.

In a large mixing bowl, beat the butter and peanut butter until well blended. Add the sugar and brown sugar, and beat until light and fluffy. Then, add the egg, milk, and vanilla extract. Mix well. In a separate mixing bowl, combine the flour, baking soda, and salt. Gradually blend into the egg mixture.

Shape dough into 1 inch balls, and arrange approximately 2 inches apart on an ungreased baking sheet. Bake 8 to 10 minutes, or until lightly browned.

Remove from oven, and immediately press a Hershey's Kiss into the center of each cookie. Most likely, the cookie will crack around edges. This is to be expected.

Honey Drops

"This is my great-grandmother's honey drop cookie recipe. They're naturally sweet (not too sweet) and have a soft cakelike consistency."

1/3 cup butter
½ cup honey
2 eggs
1 teaspoon vanilla extract
½ cup sour cream
1 teaspoon baking powder
½ teaspoon baking soda
¼ teaspoon salt
1¾ cups unbleached flour
½ cup walnuts, chopped
½ cup dates, chopped
1 cup rice krispies

Preheat oven to 375 degrees F.

In medium mixing bowl, combine the butter, honey, eggs, vanilla extract, and sour cream. Gradually add the baking powder, baking soda, salt, and flour. Now, add the walnuts, chopped dates, and rice krispies. *Mix just enough to blend well.*

Drop from the tip of a large wooden spoon, onto greased baking sheets, about 2 inches apart. Bake for 10 to 12 minutes, or until golden brown.

Brazil Nut Icebox Cookies

"One of several of my great-grandmother's icebox cookie recipes. Icebox cookies are made from cookie dough that's been refrigerated. Refrigerating the dough makes it stiffer and well suited for slicing into thin rounds. Once the cookie dough is chilled, you can simply bake however many cookies you need, rather than having to roll out all the dough, use cookie cutters, &c. It's a great time saver."

½ cup butter
1¼ cups brown sugar
1 egg
1½ teaspoons vanilla extract
1 cup *ground brazil nuts**
2¼ cups unbleached flour
2 teaspoons baking powder
¼ teaspoon salt

Blend brazil nuts in food processor until finely ground. Set aside. In a large mixing bowl, beat butter and brown sugar. Add egg, vanilla extract, and brazil nuts. Mix well.

In a separate mixing bowl, combine the flour, baking powder, and salt. Gradually blend into the egg mixture.

Shape dough into rolls, approximately 1½ inches in diameter. Roll in waxed paper, and *refrigerate overnight***.

Preheat oven to 425 degrees F.

With a sharp knife, slice dough into 1/8 inch slices. Bake on ungreased cookie sheet for 8 to 10 minutes, or until golden brown.

*If unavailable, substitute with ground almonds or macadamia nuts. ** You can also place the dough in the freezer for about an hour.

Granny's Sour Cream Icebox Cookies

1/3 cup butter, softened
¾ cup sugar
1 egg
1 teaspoon vanilla extract
2 tablespoons sour cream
½ cup walnuts, chopped
1 cup unbleached flour
1 cup whole-wheat flour
1 teaspoon nutmeg
2 teaspoons baking powder
1/8 teaspoon baking soda
½ teaspoon salt

In a large mixing bowl, beat butter, and sugar until light and fluffy. Add egg, vanilla extract, sour cream, and chopped walnuts. Mix well.

In a separate mixing bowl, combine flour, nutmeg, baking powder, baking soda, and salt. Gradually blend into egg mixture.

Shape dough into rolls, approximately 1½ inches in diameter. Roll in waxed paper, and refrigerate overnight.

The next day, preheat oven to 375 degrees F.

With a sharp knife, slice dough into 1/8 inch slices. Bake on well greased cookie sheet for 10 to 15 minutes.

Walnut Icebox Cookies

"My great-grandmother's icebox cookies are convenient, and can be prepared well in advance. In fact, they can be refrigerated for several days, or even frozen for a few weeks prior to baking. They can be cut and baked directly from the freezer."

½ cup butter
1 cup granulated white sugar
¼ cup brown sugar
1 egg
1½ teaspoons vanilla extract
1 cup walnuts, chopped
2 cups unbleached flour
2 teaspoons baking powder
¼ teaspoon salt

In a large mixing bowl, beat butter, granulated white sugar, and brown sugar. Add egg, vanilla extract, and chopped walnuts. Mix well.

In a separate mixing bowl, combine flour, baking powder, and salt. Gradually blend into egg mixture.

Shape dough into rolls, approximately 1½ inches in diameter. Roll in waxed paper, and *refrigerate overnight*.

Preheat oven to 425 degrees F.

With a sharp knife, slice dough into 1/8 inch slices. Bake on ungreased cookie sheet for 5 to 8 minutes.

Israeli Nut Cookies

"My great-grandmother didn't specify what type of nuts to use in this recipe, but if you'd like to stay true to the name, try using almonds, macadamia nuts, or pecans."

2 cups *finely ground* nuts
2 egg whites
¾ cup brown sugar
1 tablespoon unbleached flour
1/8 teaspoon ground cloves
1/8 teaspoon ground cardamom
¼ teaspoon lemon juice

Preheat oven to 350 degrees F.

Blend nuts in food processor until finely ground. Set aside.

In a medium mixing bowl, beat the egg whites until stiff peaks form, approximately 5 to 7 minutes.

In a separate mixing bowl, use a whisk to combine the brown sugar, flour, ground cloves, ground cardamom, and lemon juice.

Gently fold the egg whites into the flour mixture, gradually add the ground nuts, and drop from the tip of a teaspoon, on a parchment paper-lined baking sheet, approximately 2 inches apart.

Bake for 12 to 15 minutes.

Kipfels

2 cups unbleached flour
½ teaspoon salt
1 cup butter
¾ cup sour cream
1 egg yolk, *slightly beaten*
¾ cup ground walnuts
¾ cup granulated white sugar
¼ cup powdered sugar

In a medium mixing bowl, combine the flour and salt. Now, cut-in the butter using a pastry blender. The mixture should resemble coarse meal.

In a separate mixing bowl, combine the sour cream and egg yolk. *Blend into dry mixture.*

On a lightly floured work surface, knead the dough until smooth. Cover with plastic wrap, and *refrigerate overnight*.

Preheat oven to 375 degrees F.

In a small mixing bowl, combine the ground walnuts and granulated white sugar. Set aside.

On a lightly floured work surface, roll out the dough, cut it into 2 inch strips, and cut each strip into triangles. *Sprinkle with walnut mixture.*

Now, roll each triangle (starting at the wide end) and place on a greased baking sheet, with the tip tucked under and the ends slightly curved, to form a crescent.

Bake for 20 to 25 minutes, or until golden brown. Let cool. Then, sprinkle powdered sugar over top.

Macaroons

4 egg whites
1/8 teaspoon salt
½ cup sugar
1 cup sweetened flaked coconut, *lightly toasted*

Preheat oven to 350 degrees F.

In a medium mixing bowl, beat egg whites and salt until stiff peaks form, at least 5 to 7 minutes. Add sugar, a little at a time. Then, use a rubber spatula to fold-in the coconut.

Drop by teaspoon on parchment paper-lined baking sheet, approximately 2 inches apart.

Bake for 15 to 20 minutes, or until golden brown (*the outside should be golden but the insides should still be moist*). Let cool completely before removing from baking sheet.

Maple Cookies

"I remember taking several family vacations to Niagara Falls when I was a child and of course, I always looked forward to the maple cookies and candy made in the shape of a maple leaf."

1 cup butter, softened
1 cup brown sugar
1 egg
1 cup pure maple syrup
1 teaspoon vanilla extract
3 cups unbleached flour
1 cup whole wheat flour
½ teaspoon salt
2 teaspoons baking soda

Maple Glaze

¼ cup pure maple syrup
1 teaspoon maple extract
¼ cup butter
1 cup confectioner's sugar

Preheat oven to 350 degrees F.

In a large mixing bowl, beat butter and brown sugar. Add egg, maple syrup, and vanilla extract. Mix well.

In a separate mixing bowl, combine flour, salt, and baking soda. Blend into egg mixture.

Drop mixture from tip of spoon, onto greased baking sheets, about 2 inches apart.

Bake 8 to 10 minutes.

Meanwhile, mix maple syrup, maple extract, butter, and confectioner's sugar in a medium saucepan. Stir continuously, over medium heat, until glaze reaches boiling point.

Brush top of the cookies with maple glaze while still hot. Let cool.

Mini Cheesecakes

Cheesecake Ingredients:
1/3 cup sliced almonds, ground
1 (8 ounce) package cream cheese, softened
1 egg
½ cup sugar
½ teaspoon vanilla extract
½ teaspoon almond extract

Topping Ingredients:
1/3 cup sour cream
2 tablespoons powdered sugar
¼ teaspoon vanilla extract
¼ cup sliced almonds

Preheat oven to 350 degrees F.

Grease 24 (1¾ inch) muffin cups. Sprinkle about a teaspoon of ground almonds into each cup. Then, gently shake the muffin cups, to coat the bottoms and sides.

In a medium mixing bowl, combine cream cheese, egg, sugar, vanilla extract, and almond extract. Beat until smooth. Then, spoon into muffin cups, approximately ¾ full.

Bake for 18 minutes, or until golden brown. Set aside, and let cool. Using a butter knife, loosen sides and carefully remove the mini cheesecakes.

To make the topping, in a separate mixing bowl, combine sour cream, powdered sugar, and vanilla extract. Once mini cheesecakes have cooled completely, top with sour cream mixture and slivered almonds. Cover, and refrigerate overnight.

Molasses Cookies

"I'm not sure exactly when molasses became obsolete or old fashioned, but my mom used to bake with it fairly often. She added it to baked beans, glazes, barbecue sauce, and of course cookies. These cookies are ideal for making ice cream sandwiches. All you have to do is place scoop of softened ice cream between two molasses cookies, and enjoy!"

2/3 cup butter
½ cup brown sugar
1 egg
½ cup molasses
½ cup buttermilk
1½ cups unbleached flour
1 cup whole-wheat flour
1 teaspoon baking soda
¼ teaspoon salt
½ teaspoon cinnamon
¼ teaspoon ginger
½ cup sun dried raisins, *chopped*

Preheat oven to 350 degrees F.

In a small bowl, combine raisins with about ½ cup water, and set aside to soak. Now, in a large mixing bowl, cream the butter and brown sugar. Add egg, molasses, and buttermilk, *drained* raisins, and mix well.

In a separate, medium mixing bowl, combine flour, baking soda, salt, cinnamon, and ginger. Add the flour mixture to the egg mixture.

Drop mixture from tip of spoon onto an un-greased baking sheet, about 2 inches apart, and bake for 1 2 to 15 minutes.

Oatmeal Cookies

"Aside from eating a bowl of oatmeal for breakfast, using oats to make cookies was by far the most common use in the McClellan household. Old fashioned, rolled oats are preferable when making these cookies."

½ cup milk
¾ cup vegetable oil
¾ cup maple syrup
½ cup brown sugar
1 teaspoon vanilla extract
½ teaspoon baking soda
½ teaspoon salt
½ teaspoon cinnamon
1 cup whole wheat flour
1½ cups unbleached flour
3 cups rolled oats
½ cup sun dried raisins
½ cup chopped walnuts

Preheat oven to 350 degrees F.

In a small bowl, combine raisins with about ½ cup water, and set aside to soak.

In a large mixing bowl, combine milk, vegetable oil, maple syrup, brown sugar, and vanilla extract.

Gradually mix-in baking soda, salt, cinnamon, flour, oats, *drained* raisins, and chopped walnuts. Mix well.

Drop mixture from tip of spoon onto un-greased baking sheets, about 2 inches apart.

Bake for 20 to 25 minutes, or until golden brown.

Peanut Butter Cookies

1 cup creamy peanut butter
½ cup butter, softened
½ cup maple syrup
2 mashed bananas
1½ cups unbleached white flour
1 cup whole-wheat flour
1½ teaspoons baking powder
¼ teaspoon salt
1½ cups chopped peanuts

Preheat oven to 375 degrees F.

In medium mixing bowl, beat peanut butter, butter, and maple syrup until light and fluffy. Add mashed bananas, and beat until well mixed. Then, gradually add white flour, wheat flour, baking powder, salt, and chopped peanuts.

Shape dough into 1 inch balls, and arrange approximately 2 inches apart on an ungreased baking sheet. Bake for 8 to 10 minutes, or until golden brown.

Peanut Butter Roundup Cookies

½ cup butter
½ cup brown sugar
1/3 cup white sugar
1 egg
½ cup chunky peanut butter
¾ cups unbleached flour
¼ cup whole-wheat flour
1 teaspoons baking soda
¼ teaspoon salt
½ cup rolled oats

Preheat oven to 350 degrees F.

In medium mixing bowl, beat butter, brown sugar, and white sugar together, until light and fluffy. Add egg and peanut butter, and beat until well mixed. Then, gradually add white flour, wheat flour, baking soda, salt, and oats.

Shape dough into 1 inch balls, and arrange approximately 2 inches apart on an ungreased baking sheet. Use a fork to flatten the cookies, and bake for 12 to 15 minutes, or until golden brown.

Peanut Cookies

½ cup brown sugar
½ cup white sugar
½ cup butter
½ cup chunky peanut butter
1 egg
2 tablespoons milk
1 teaspoon vanilla extract
1¾ cups unbleached flour
1 teaspoon baking soda
½ teaspoon salt

Preheat oven to 375 degrees F.

In medium mixing bowl, beat brown sugar, white sugar, butter, and peanut butter until light and fluffy. Add egg, milk, and vanilla extract, and beat until well mixed. Then, gradually add flour, baking soda, and salt.

Shape dough into 1 inch balls, and arrange approximately 2 inches apart on a greased baking sheet. Bake for 10 to 12 minutes, or until golden brown.

Peanuttiest Cookies

"Here's a (pea)nutty recipe. If you really want to get crazy, add ½ cup crushed peanuts!"

1 cup butter
1 cup creamy peanut butter
1 cup brown sugar
2 eggs
2 teaspoons vanilla extract
3 cups unbleached flour
½ teaspoon cinnamon
½ teaspoon salt

Preheat oven to 350 degrees F.

In medium mixing bowl, beat butter, peanut butter, and brown sugar until light and fluffy. Add eggs and vanilla extract, and beat until well mixed. Then, gradually add flour, cinnamon, and salt.

Shape dough into 1 inch balls (*about 1 tablespoon*), and arrange approximately 2 inches apart on a greased baking sheet. Bake for 10 to 12 minutes, or until golden brown.

Pine Nut Cookies

2 egg whites
1 (8 ounce) cans almond paste or marzipan
1/3 cup sugar
1/3 cup powdered sugar
1 1/3 cups pine nuts

Preheat oven to 350 degrees F.

In a medium mixing bowl, beat egg whites until stiff peaks form, *at least 5 to 7 minutes*.

In a separate mixing bowl, combine almond paste, sugar, and powdered sugar (*mixture should resemble coarse crumbs*). Then, use a whisk to gently fold-in egg whites.

Shape into ½ inch balls, roll in pine nuts, and arrange on a parchment paper-lined baking sheet, approximately 2 inches apart.

Bake for 18 to 20 minutes, or until golden brown. *Let cool completely before removing from baking sheet.*

Poppy Seed Cookies

Filling Ingredients:
½ cup poppy seeds
3 tablespoons milk
2 tablespoons honey
¼ cup brown sugar
1 tablespoon butter
¼ cup sun dried raisins, chopped
½ teaspoon vanilla extract
½ teaspoon lemon juice
1 egg, slightly beaten

Cookie Ingredients:
1 cup butter
½ cup granulated white sugar
2 eggs
2 teaspoons lemon zest
½ teaspoon cinnamon
1 teaspoon baking soda
2½ cups unbleached flour
¼ cup powdered sugar

To prepare the filling, in a small saucepan, combine the poppy seeds, milk, honey, brown sugar, butter, and chopped raisins. Bring to boil over medium heat. Then reduce heat and let simmer for approximately 30 minutes, stirring frequently, until most of the liquid is absorbed. Remove from heat, add vanilla extract and lemon juice, and let stand for 10 minutes. In a separate bowl, beat the eggs, and slowly whisk into poppy seed mixture. *Refrigerate for 1 hour, or until filling is thick enough to spread.*

To prepare the cookies, in a medium mixing bowl, beat the butter and sugar until light and fluffy. Add the egg, lemon zest, cinnamon, baking soda, and flour. Then, on a large sheet of wax paper, roll out the dough to form two 12" x 10" rectangles. Cover with another sheet of waxed paper and *refrigerate for 30 minutes*, or until firm.

Preheat oven to 350 degrees F.

Remove the waxed paper from one side of the dough and spread the poppy seed filling over top, leaving about ¼ inch between the filling and the edge of the dough. Now, fold the edges of the dough over the filling and *tightly* roll the dough, starting from the longer edge and peeling off the waxed paper as you go.

Cut the rolls into ½ inch slices, and place each slice on greased baking sheets. Bake for 10 to 12 minutes, or until edges are golden brown. Let stand for 5 minutes and sprinkle with powdered sugar before serving.

Poppy Seed Kolachky Cookies

"This is an old Slavic recipe; typically served at holiday gatherings. Actually, you can use any type of filling you want, including cream cheese, walnuts, and of course, poppy seed."

1 package quick-rise yeast
¼ cup warm milk
3 cups unbleached flour
1 tablespoon sugar
1 teaspoon salt
1/8 teaspoon nutmeg
½ cup butter
3 egg yolks
1 cup heavy whipping cream
1 (12 ounce) can poppy seed pastry filling

Dissolve the quick-rise yeast in ¼ cup warm milk, and set aside. Now, in a medium mixing bowl, use a whisk to combine the flour, sugar, salt, and nutmeg. Cut in the butter, until the mixture resembles coarse meal. Then, add the egg yolks, heavy whipping cream, and dissolved yeast, and mix well. Place in a greased bowl, cover with plastic wrap, and *refrigerate for about 1 hour*.

Divide the dough into 4 equal pieces. In separate batches, roll out the dough on a lightly floured work surface (*to about a ¼ inch thickness*). Cut into rounds with a floured drinking glass or cookie cutter. Then, place the cookies on a greased baking sheet and *let rise for 1 hour*.

Preheat the oven to 350 degrees F. Then, with your thumb (or the handle of a wooden spoon), make an indentation in each cookie. Fill with poppy seed pastry filling, and bake for 15 minutes, or until lightly browned.

Puppy Cookies

Vanilla Cookie Dough Ingredients:
¼ cup butter
½ cup sugar
1 egg
¼ cup sour cream
½ teaspoon vanilla extract
¼ teaspoon baking soda
½ teaspoon baking powder
¼ teaspoon salt
1½ cups + *2 tablespoons* unbleached flour

Chocolate Cookie Dough Ingredients:
¼ cup butter
½ cup sugar
1 egg
¼ cup sour cream
2 tablespoons unsweetened cocoa powder
¼ teaspoon baking soda
½ teaspoon baking powder
¼ teaspoon salt
1½ cups unbleached flour

Icing Ingredients:
¾ cup powdered sugar
1 teaspoon meringue powder
1/8 teaspoon vanilla extract
1 tablespoon warm water

Additional Ingredients:
1 (14 ounce) bag plain M&Ms

Preheat oven to 425 degrees F.

To prepare the vanilla cookies, in medium mixing bowl, beat the butter and sugar until light and fluffy. Add the egg, sour cream, and vanilla extract; and beat until well mixed. Then, gradually add the baking soda, baking powder, salt, and flour.

To prepare the chocolate cookies, in separate mixing bowl, beat the butter and sugar until light and fluffy. Add the egg, sour cream, and cocoa powder; and beat until well mixed. Then, gradually add the baking soda, baking powder, salt, and flour.

Now, on a floured work surface, knead the vanilla cookie dough until smooth. Roll out the dough to a ½ inch thickness, and cut-out the cookies using a 3 inch heart-shaped cookie cutter. *Repeat using chocolate cookie dough.*

Place the vanilla heart cookies about 3 inches apart on a greased baking sheet. Then, slice the chocolate hearts in half lengthwise, place on either side of the vanilla heart cookies (overlapping, to give the appearance of ears), and bake until just golden, about 8 to 10 minutes. Let cool completely.

To prepare the icing, in a medium mixing bowl, use a whisk to combine the powdered sugar and meringue powder. Add the vanilla extract and water (a little at a time), and beat until stiff peaks form, about 5 to 7 minutes. If necessary, add more powdered sugar or water. The icing must be used immediately because it hardens when exposed to air. Place the icing in a pastry bag and pipe three dots of frosting on each cookie, where the eyes and nose will go. *Then, for each cookie, attach two brown M&Ms for the eyes, and one red M&Ms for the nose.*

Rock Cookies

"My great-grandmother used to make these, but I didn't have a copy of her recipe. So, I was thankful when my neighbor, Elaine Marzano, shared this recipe, which appeared on the back of a Spry vegetable shortening container. Probably one of Aunt Jenny's recipes…"

¾ cups brown sugar
½ cup butter, softened
2 eggs
½ teaspoon baking soda
¼ teaspoon salt
½ teaspoon cinnamon
1/8 teaspoon ground cloves
1½ cups unbleached flour
1 cup sun dried raisins
1 cup semisweet chocolate chips
½ cup chopped walnuts

Preheat oven to 350 degrees F.

In a small bowl, combine raisins with approximately 1 cup water, and set aside to soak.

In a medium mixing bowl, beat the brown sugar and butter until light and fluffy. Add the eggs, and beat until well mixed. Then, add the baking powder, salt, cinnamon, ground cloves, flour, *drained* raisins, chocolate chips, and walnuts. Mix well.

Drop by large spoonfuls onto greased baking sheet, and bake for 12 minutes, or until edges are slightly browned.

Rum Balls

Shortbread Ingredients:
1 cup butter, softened
1 cup sugar
1 egg
2 cups unbleached flour
1 cup cornstarch
¼ teaspoon salt

To make the shortbread, preheat oven to 300 degrees F. In a large mixing bowl, beat butter, sugar, and egg. Add flour, cornstarch, and salt. Mix well, and shape dough into 1 inch balls. Bake cookies on un-greased baking sheet, about 2 inches apart, for 20 to 25 minutes. *Set aside, and let stand overnight.*

Rum Ball Ingredients:
2 cups fine shortbread crumbs
1 cups powdered sugar, plus ½ cup
½ cup walnuts, finely chopped
¼ cup dark rum, plus 1 tablespoon
¼ cup honey
2 tablespoons butter, melted

To make the rum balls, the next day, crush the shortbread to make fine crumbs. In a medium mixing bowl, combine the shortbread crumbs, 1 cup powdered sugar, chopped walnuts, rum, honey, and butter. Mix well.

Place in a greased bowl, cover with plastic wrap, and refrigerate for 1 hour. Then, roll into ½ inch balls and roll in ½ cup powdered sugar. Arrange rum balls on a baking sheet, cover with plastic wrap, and *let stand overnight.*

Shortbread Cookies

"Originating from Scotland, shortbread is primarily made from shortening or butter, which during lean years was once reserved only for Christmas."

1 cup butter *or shortening*
1 cup sugar
1 egg
2 cups unbleached flour
1 cup cornstarch
¼ teaspoon salt

Preheat oven to 300 degrees F.

In a medium mixing bowl, beat the butter and sugar until light and fluffy. Add the egg and beat until well mixed. Then, gradually add the flour, cornstarch, and salt. Mix well, and shape dough into 1 inch balls.

Bake on an ungreased cookie sheet, about 2 inches apart, for 20 to 25 minutes; or until lightly browned.

Sour Cream Cookies

"My great-grandmother made these during the holidays, but they're good anytime. In fact, they're perfect served with hot coffee or tea."

½ cup butter
1 cup sugar
1 egg
½ cup sour cream
3¼ cups unbleached flour
½ teaspoon baking soda
1 teaspoon baking powder
½ teaspoon salt
¼ teaspoon nutmeg

Preheat oven to 425 degrees F.

In medium mixing bowl, beat butter and sugar until light and fluffy. Add egg, and sour cream, and beat until well mixed. Then, gradually add flour, baking soda, baking powder, salt, and nutmeg.

On a floured work surface, knead the dough until smooth. Then, roll out the dough to a 1/8 inch thickness. Cut-out cookies using a 2½ inch cookie cutter, and bake on a greased cookie sheet for 8 to 10 minutes, or until golden near the edges.

Granny's Sour Cream Sugar Cookies

"My great-grandmother developed this recipe. It's more or less a variation on a kipfel cookie. Kipfels are typically horn shaped. In fact, the word's derived from the German "kipf," meaning "horn." Though, these sour cream sugar cookies have a somewhat unusual shape for a kipfel. Like many immigrants, my great-grandmother often substituted ingredients, modified traditional recipes, and came up with some truly great variations."

3½ cups unbleached flour
1 teaspoon salt
1 cup butter
1 package quick-rise yeast
¼ cup warm water
¾ cup sour cream
1 teaspoon vanilla extract
1 egg, well-beaten
2 egg yolks, well-beaten
¼ cup melted butter
1 cup sugar

In a medium mixing bowl, combine flour and salt. Cut in butter using a pastry blender.

Dissolve quick-rise yeast in ¼ cup warm water. Add quick-rise yeast, sour cream, vanilla extract, well-beaten egg and egg yolks to flour mixture. Knead the dough with your hands, to mix well. Place in a greased bowl, cover with plastic wrap, and refrigerate for at least 2 hours.

Preheat oven to 375 degrees F.

Roll out the dough on a lightly floured surface, to about a ¼ inch thickness. Brush lightly with melted butter, and sprinkle sugar on top. Fold the dough, brush with melted butter, and sprinkle with sugar once more. Repeat until you have at least four layers. Liberally sprinkle sugar on top layer.

Then, cut the dough into a crescent circles using the top of a small floured drinking glass or a cookie cutter. Place on greased cookie sheet, and bake at 375 degrees F for 10 to 15 minutes, or until golden brown. Be sure to check on the progress of the cookies every few minutes.

Thumbprints

"My mom always made thumbprint cookies for Christmas. Although this recipe uses strawberry preserves, you can use any kind you like."

2/3 cup butter
1/3 cup sugar
2 egg yolks
1 teaspoon vanilla extract
½ teaspoon salt
1½ cups unbleached flour
2 egg whites, slightly beaten
¾ cup walnuts, finely chopped
1/3 cup strawberry preserves

Preheat oven to 350 degrees F.

In a medium mixing bowl, cream butter and sugar until light and fluffy. Add egg yolks, vanilla extract, and salt. Gradually add flour, and mix well.

Shape dough into 1 inch balls, and dip in egg whites. Roll dough in chopped walnuts, and arrange approximately 1 inch apart, on a greased baking sheet. Then, with your thumb or the handle of a wooden spoon, make an indentation in each ball.

Bake for 15 to 17 minutes, or until golden brown. Remove from baking sheets and while still warm, use a pastry bag to fill the center of each cookie with strawberry preserves.

Wine Cookies

"Like most wine cookie recipes, this recipe is basically a sugar cookie with a bit of wine added. Although similar to some Italian wine cookie recipes, this recipe is dependent on the type of wine used. You must use a fortified wine such as sherry or port! Otherwise the cookies will have very little flavor."

½ cup butter
1 cup brown sugar
1 egg
1 teaspoon vanilla extract
¼ cup sherry or port wine
1½ cups unbleached flour
1 cup whole wheat flour
½ teaspoon salt
½ teaspoon baking soda
¼ cup powdered sugar (*optional*)

Preheat oven to 375 degrees F.

In a large mixing bowl, beat butter and brown sugar. Add egg, vanilla extract, and sherry or port wine. Mix well.

In a separate mixing bowl, combine flour, salt, and baking soda. Gradually blend into egg mixture.

Shape dough into 1 inch balls, and arrange on a greased baking sheet. Bake for 15 to 18 minutes.

Let stand for 10 minutes. Then, if desired, garnish with powdered sugar.

Zucchini Cookies

"One of my mom's many uses for zucchini. I really enjoyed these when I was a kid. She pretty much stopped making them at some point though. Not sure why. Maybe she lost the recipe? At any rate, I'm glad I found it!"

½ cup butter
¾ cup brown sugar
1 egg
½ teaspoon vanilla extract
1 teaspoon cinnamon
½ teaspoon baking soda
1 cup grated zucchini
1½ cups whole wheat flour
½ cup sweetened, flaked coconut
½ cup raisins
1¾ cups whole oats

Preheat oven to 375 degrees F.

In a small bowl, combine raisins with ¼ cup warm water, and set aside to soak.

In a medium mixing bowl, combine butter and brown sugar, and mix on medium speed. Add egg, vanilla extract, cinnamon, baking soda, and grated zucchini. Then, add flour, coconut, *drained* raisins, and oats.

Drop dough, by rounded teaspoonfuls, about 2 inches apart, onto greased cookie sheet. Bake for 5 to 7 minutes, or until golden brown.

Christmas

Fruitcake

Cake Ingredients:
1 cup sundried raisins, chopped
1 cup dates, chopped
2 tablespoons candied citron peel, chopped
½ cup butter, softened
½ cup brown sugar
2 eggs
¼ cup honey
1 tablespoon sherry or port wine
1¼ cups unbleached flour
1 teaspoon baking powder
¼ teaspoon salt
¼ teaspoon cinnamon
¼ teaspoon nutmeg
1/8 teaspoon ground cloves
¼ cup milk
¼ cup chopped walnuts
¼ cup chopped pecans or brazil nuts
¼ cup chopped almonds

Glaze Ingredients:
¼ cup butter
½ cup water
½ cup brown sugar
¼ cup dark rum

To make the cake, preheat the oven to 350 degrees F. In a small bowl, combine the chopped raisins and 1 cup water. Set aside to soak.

In a large mixing bowl, beat butter and brown sugar until light and fluffy. Add eggs, honey, and sherry. Mix well. Now, in a separate mixing bowl, use a whisk to combine the flour, baking powder, salt, cinnamon, nutmeg, and ground cloves. Blend into the egg mixture; *adding the milk a little at a time*. Gradually add the *drained* raisins, chopped dates, candied citron peel, chopped walnuts, pecans, and slivered almonds.

Pour batter into a greased 9 inch bundt pan, and bake for 45 to 50 minutes, or until a toothpick inserted into the center of the cake is clean when removed. Let cool for 20 minutes before removing from pan. *When the cake has cooled completely, use a fork to lightly prick the top of the cake.*

To make the glaze, melt the butter in a small saucepan, over a medium flame. Stir-in the water and brown sugar. Boil for approximately 5 minutes. Then, remove from heat, and add the rum. *Let cool to room temperature*. Drizzle the glaze evenly over the top and sides of the cake. Allow the cake to fully absorb the glaze before serving.

Gingerbread Men

"This recipe is inspired by the Raleigh Tavern Bakery in Colonial Williamsburg, one of my family's favorite vacation spots when I was a child. The bakery sold mouth-watering gingerbread cookies, fresh from the oven!"

Gingerbread Ingredients:
½ cup brown sugar
1 teaspoon ginger
½ teaspoon nutmeg
½ teaspoon cinnamon
¼ teaspoon salt
1 teaspoon baking soda
½ cup butter, melted
¼ cup heavy cream
½ cup molasses
½ teaspoon vanilla extract
Zest of ½ lemon
2¼ cups unbleached flour

Icing Ingredients:
1½ cups powdered sugar
2¼ teaspoons meringue powder
1/8 teaspoon vanilla extract
2 tablespoons warm water

To make the gingerbread, in a large mixing bowl, combine brown sugar, ginger, nutmeg, cinnamon, salt, and baking soda. Mix well. Then, add the melted butter, heavy cream, molasses, vanilla extract, and lemon zest. Mix well. Add flour 1 cup at a time. Place in a greased bowl, cover with plastic wrap, and refrigerate overnight.

The next day, preheat oven to 375 degrees F.

On a floured work surface, knead the dough until smooth. Then, using a rolling pin, roll out the dough to a ¼ inch thickness. Cut-out cookies using a gingerbread-man shaped cutter, and bake on a greased cookie sheet for 10 to 12 minutes, or until golden brown. When thoroughly cool, decorate with icing.

To make the icing, in a medium mixing bowl, use a whisk to combine the powdered sugar and meringue powder. Add the vanilla extract and water (*a little at a time*), and beat until stiff peaks form, about 5 to 7 minutes. If necessary, add more powdered sugar or water. *The icing must be used immediately because it hardens when exposed to air.* Place the icing in a pastry bag fitted with a decorative tip, and decorate the gingerbread men as desired.

Lebkuchen

"Lebkuchen, also known as honey cake, is a traditional German Christmas favorite and is very much like gingerbread. However, the dough is typically placed on a communion wafer, to celebrate the Catholic Eucharist."

Lebkuchen Ingredients:
1 egg
¾ cup brown sugar
½ cup honey
½ cup molasses
3 cups unbleached flour
1¼ teaspoons nutmeg
1¼ teaspoons cinnamon
½ teaspoon baking soda
¼ teaspoon ground cloves
½ teaspoon allspice
½ cup dates, pitted and finely chopped
½ cup sliced almonds

Lemon Glaze Ingredients:
1 egg white, slightly beaten
1 tablespoon lemon juice
½ teaspoon grated lemon peel
¼ teaspoon salt
1½ cups powdered sugar

To make the Lebkuchen, beat egg, brown sugar, honey, and molasses in a medium mixing bowl. In a separate mixing bowl, combine flour, nutmeg, cinnamon, baking soda, ground cloves, and allspice. Gradually blend into egg mixture. Add dates, place in a greased bowl, cover with plastic wrap, and refrigerate overnight.

The next day, preheat oven to 350 degrees F.

On a floured work surface, knead the dough until smooth. Then, using a rolling pin, roll out the dough to a ¼ inch thickness. Cut-out cookies using a round or heart shaped cutter, and bake on a greased cookie sheet for 12 to 15 minutes, or until golden brown.

Let cool slightly. While cookies are still warm, brush with lemon glaze, and decorate with sliced almonds.

To make the lemon glaze, beat egg white, lemon juice, grated lemon peel, salt, and powdered sugar in a small mixing bowl.

Linzer Cookies

"Named after the city of Linz, Austria, these cookies are an Austro-Hungarian holiday tradition."

¾ cup butter
½ cup sugar
1 egg
1 teaspoon grated lemon rind
½ teaspoon vanilla
1½ cups ground walnuts
½ teaspoon baking powder
½ teaspoon cinnamon
2¼ cups unbleached flour
¾ cup raspberry preserves
¼ cup powdered sugar

In a medium mixing bowl, beat butter and sugar until light and fluffy. Add egg, grated lemon rind, vanilla extract, and ground walnuts. Beat until well mixed. Then, add baking powder, cinnamon, and flour, a little at a time. *Place in a greased bowl, cover with plastic wrap, and refrigerate for at least 2 hours.*

Preheat oven to 350 degrees F.

On a floured work surface, knead the dough until smooth. Then, roll out the dough to a 1/8 inch thickness. Cut rounds using a cookie cutter, 2 inches in diameter. Then, cut out the center of *exactly half the rounds* using a 1 inch tree-shaped cutter.

Bake on greased cookie sheets for 10 to 12 minutes, or until golden near the edges. Remove from oven, and while still warm, use a pastry bag to spread a thin layer of raspberry preserves over the solid rounds. Cover with cut-out rounds, pressing down lightly to form 'sandwiches.' Then, sprinkle with powdered sugar, and let the cookies stand for 10 or 15 minutes before serving.

Marzipan Stollen

"Stollen is a traditional German fruitcake that's prepared during the Christmas holiday season. The best stollen I ever had was a Christstollen from a bakery in Nürnberg, near my friend, Jens Arweiler's apartment."

1½ cups chopped sundried raisins
½ cup rum, brandy, or amaretto
1 package quick-rise yeast
1 teaspoon brown sugar
½ cup lukewarm milk
2 teaspoons vanilla extract
2 cups unbleached flour
1/3 cup sugar
¼ teaspoon cardamom
¼ teaspoon allspice
1/8 teaspoon salt
½ cup butter
1 egg
1/3 cup chopped candied lemon peel or citron
1/3 cup chopped walnuts
1 (8 ounce) can almond paste or marzipan
½ cup melted butter, divided
¼ cup powdered sugar

In a small bowl, combine the chopped raisins and rum. Set aside to soak.

Dissolve the yeast and brown sugar in lukewarm milk. Let stand for about approximately 5 minutes. Then, add vanilla extract.

In medium mixing bowl, combine the flour, sugar, cardamom, allspice, and salt. Add the butter, egg, and yeast mixture, and mix just enough to blend well. Knead the dough until smooth. Then, place dough in a greased bowl, cover loosely with plastic wrap, and *set aside to rise in a warm place for 1 hour.*

On a lightly floured work surface, work in the *drained* raisins, candied lemon peel, and walnuts. Then, roll out the dough onto on a large floured tablecloth, brush with melted butter, and pull the dough very gently to form a 12" x 8" rectangle.

Knead the almond paste, and roll it out to a 12 x 6 inch rectangle. Place on top of the dough, leaving about 1 inch along the edges.

Fold the edges of the dough over the filling, and use the table cloth to roll the dough from the longer edge, starting with the almond paste filling. Roll tightly, to maintain shape and tuck-in the edges as you go.

Roll onto a greased baking sheet, with the seam on the bottom, and brush with melted butter. Once again, *set aside to rise in a warm place, for about 1 hour.*

Preheat oven to 325 degrees F. Then, bake stollen for 40 to 45 minutes, or until golden brown. *If necessary, cover with foil for the last 10 to 15 minutes, to prevent the crust from burning.* Remove from oven, brush with melted butter, and dust with powdered sugar.

Mince Pie

"Mince Pie is traditionally prepared for Christmas or New Year's Day. Although Mince Pie was originally made with a type of spiced meat known as mincemeat, modern pies are made with dried fruit and nuts."

Pie Crust:
2 cups unbleached flour
1 teaspoon salt
¾ cup shortening
¼ cup cold water

Pie Filling:
¼ cup butter
6 apples, peeled, cored, and sliced
¼ cup sun dried raisins
¼ cup chopped dates
¼ cup dried figs
¼ cup dried currants
¼ cup chopped walnuts
½ cup brown sugar
¼ cup molasses
1/3 cup dark rum
¼ cup orange juice
1 tablespoon grated orange peel
1 teaspoon grated lemon peel
1 teaspoon cinnamon
¼ teaspoon nutmeg
¼ teaspoon allspice
¼ teaspoon ground cloves

To make the pie crust, in a medium mixing bowl, combine flour and salt. Cut-in shortening using a pastry blender, until mixture resembles coarse meal. Gradually add cold water, stirring all the while, until a dough forms.

On a lightly floured work surface, knead dough until smooth. Add just enough flour to keep the dough from sticking. Then, divide the dough into two equal parts, and roll into 2 (12 inch) circles, about 1/8 inch thick. Cover loosely with plastic wrap, and *refrigerate for 1 to 3 hours.*

To make the pie filling, in a large pot or dutch oven, combine butter, apples, raisins, dates, figs, currants, walnuts, brown sugar, molasses, rum, orange juice, grated orange peel, grated lemon peel, cinnamon, nutmeg, allspice, and ground cloves. Cook over low heat until apples are tender (*about 1½ hours*), stirring occasionally. Let cool to room temperature, and set aside.

Preheat oven to 400 degrees F. Use a metal spatula to carefully place one of the 12 inch circles onto a 9 inch pie pan, gently pressing the dough into the corners and using your fingertips to create a rim around sides of the pan. Now, spoon-in the mince pie filling.

Gently place the second 12 inch circle on top. Pinch the dough together, and trim any excess (leaving about a ¾-inch overhang). Then, fold the dough under, and flute the edges using your thumb and forefinger. Lightly brush the pie crust with milk, and bake for 40 minutes, or until golden brown. Let cool to room temperature before serving with vanilla ice cream.

Pfeffernüsse

"Pfeffernüsse, meaning 'pepper nuts' in German, are small round cookies made with a pinch of black pepper. My grandmother loves pfeffernüsse cookies, which are generally available at local grocers during the holiday season. Still, there's nothing like freshly baked pfeffernüsse."

¾ cup molasses
½ cup butter
2 eggs
4¼ cups unbleached flour
½ cup brown sugar
1¼ teaspoons baking soda
1½ teaspoons cinnamon
¼ teaspoon ground cloves
½ teaspoon nutmeg
¼ teaspoon black pepper
½ cup powdered sugar

In a medium saucepan, combine molasses and butter. Melt the butter, over medium heat, stirring all the while. Remove from heat, and let cool to room temperature.

In a medium mixing bowl, combine flour, brown sugar, baking soda, cinnamon, ground cloves, nutmeg, and black pepper. Add eggs and flour mixture to molasses mixture. Mix well, place in a greased bowl, cover with plastic wrap, and refrigerate overnight.

The next day, preheat oven to 375 degrees F.

Shape dough into 1 inch balls, and arrange approximately 2 inches apart on a greased baking sheet. Bake for 12 to 15 minutes.

Remove from oven, and let cool slightly. Roll in powdered sugar, while still warm.

Springerle Cookies

"Springerle cookies are traditional swabian cookies made with a special type of rolling pin that leaves a detailed impression on the dough. The dough should stand overnight, in order for the cookies to retain the detail of the pattern. Although springerle cookies are usually flavored with anise, this recipe is made with vanilla extract. Almond extract works well too."

¾ cup sugar
½ cup butter, softened
1 egg
1 tablespoon vanilla extract
Zest of one lemon
2 cups unbleached flour
¼ teaspoon baking powder
¼ teaspoon salt

In medium mixing bowl, beat sugar and butter until light and fluffy. Add egg, vanilla extract, and lemon zest, and beat until well mixed. Then, gradually add flour, baking powder, and salt. *Place in a greased bowl, cover with plastic wrap, and refrigerate for at least 1 hour.*

Knead the dough until smooth. Then, on a floured work surface, roll out the dough to a ½ inch thickness with smooth rolling pin.

Be sure to use a floured springerle rolling pin and add enough flour to keep the dough from sticking. Slowly roll over the dough with the springerle rolling pin (*don't be afraid to apply pressure*).

Cut cookies according to design, place on a greased baking sheet about 1½ inches apart, and repeat with remaining dough. *Loosely cover with plastic wrap, and let stand overnight, in order to set the design.*

Preheat oven to 375 degrees F.

Bake for approximately 1 minute at 375 degrees F. Then, reduce oven temperature to 300 degrees F and bake for an additional 10 to 12 minutes, or until tops are pale and bottoms are lightly browned.

If desired, use a brush to highlight the springerle design with egg wash (1 egg white and 2 teaspoons water) and a few drops of food coloring, and/or edible gold leaf prior to baking.

Spritz Cookies

"Spritz cookies are traditional Christmas cookies that can be formed into a variety of shapes using a cookie press. My mom almost always made tree shaped cookies, but occasionally made a wreath or two. They're probably my favorite Christmas cookie. In fact, when my sister and I were kids we used to love to decorate them with red or green granulated sugar, jimmies, nonpareils, and my personal favorite, silver dragées that we'd place at the top of the tree, like a shining star! Evidently, the secret to a perfect spritz cookie lies in the consistency of the dough, which can be attained simply by using softened butter."

1½ cups butter, softened
1 cup sugar
1 egg
1 teaspoon vanilla extract
½ teaspoon almond extract
4 cups unbleached flour
1 teaspoon baking powder
A few drops of green food coloring

*Optional: egg wash (made by beating 1 egg white lightly, with 2 teaspoons water)
Green and red decorating sugar*

Preheat the oven to 400 degrees F.

In a medium mixing bowl, cream the butter with the sugar until the mixture is light and fluffy. Add egg, vanilla, and almond extract, and add a few drops of green food coloring. Beat until smooth.

In a separate mixing bowl, combine the flour and baking powder. Then, gradually add the flour mixture to the egg mixture. Beat just enough to blend well. *Do not over-mix!*

Pack the dough into a cookie press, fitted with a tree-shaped disk, and press the cookies (*about an inch apart*) onto an un-greased baking sheet.

Optional: brush cookies lightly with the egg wash, and sprinkle with decorating sugar.

Bake at for 8 to 12 minutes.

Classic Christmas Sugar Cookies

"Christmas just wouldn't be the same without my mom's sugar cookies. She used to decorate them with red or green granulated sugar, baked in various shapes. Some were shaped like Santa, some like a snowman, an angel, or even a bell. Simple, but delightful."

¾ cup sugar
½ cup butter, softened
1 egg
1 teaspoon vanilla extract
2 cups unbleached flour
¼ teaspoon baking powder
¼ teaspoon salt
Egg wash (*made by beating 1 egg white lightly, with 2 teaspoons water*)
Red and green decorating sugar

In a medium mixing bowl, beat sugar and butter until light and fluffy. Add egg and vanilla extract, and beat until well mixed. Then, gradually add flour, baking powder, and salt. *Place in a greased bowl, cover with plastic wrap, and refrigerate overnight.*

The next day, preheat oven to 325 degrees F.

On a floured work surface, knead the dough until smooth. Then, roll out the dough to a 1/8 inch thickness. Cut-out cookies using a santa, angel, star, bell, snowman, or tree shaped cutter.

Brush cookies lightly with the egg wash, and sprinkle with decorating sugar. Then, bake on greased cookie sheets for 10 to 12 minutes, or until golden near the edges.

Easter

Babka

"Babka is a traditional eastern european sweetbread that's made by doubling and twisting the dough. It typically contains cinnamon, raisins, and walnuts, and is topped with glaze."

Filling Ingredients:
¾ cup brown sugar
3 tablespoons cinnamon
1½ tablespoons finely grated orange peel
¾ cup chopped raisins
¾ cup chopped walnuts
1/3 cup melted butter

Glaze Ingredients:
2 tablespoons melted butter
1 cup powdered sugar
1 tablespoon finely grated orange peel
2 tablespoons milk

Dough Ingredients:
1 package quick-rise yeast
¼ cup warm water
¾ cup warm milk
1 teaspoon salt
½ cup sugar
¾ cup melted butter
2 large eggs
4 cups unbleached flour

To prepare the filling, in a medium mixing bowl, use a whisk to combine the brown sugar and cinnamon. Add the grated orange peel, chopped raisins, chopped walnuts, and melted butter; and set aside.

To prepare the dough, dissolve the quick-rise yeast in warm water (with a pinch of sugar). Let stand for ten minutes. Then, add the milk, salt, sugar, melted butter, and eggs. Gradually add the flour, and beat to make a soft dough. Knead until smooth, place in greased bowl, and cover. *Allow mixture to double (about 1 hour).*

On a lightly floured work surface, roll the dough into a rectangle, approximately 10" by 18". Spread the filling onto the dough, leaving about ½ inch between the filling and the edge of the dough. Now, tightly roll up the dough from the long end, and twist it a few times, as if you were wringing out a towel. Place on a greased baking sheet, and coil it around like a pinwheel, tucking the loose end of the dough under, so it won't unravel. *Cover, and let rise for 30 minutes.*

Brush the top of the dough with melted butter, preheat the oven to 325 degrees F, and bake for 45 to 60 minutes, or until golden brown.

To prepare the glaze, in a medium mixing bowl, use a whisk to combine the melted butter, powdered sugar, and grated orange peel. Add the milk (a little at a time) and blend until the mixture forms a thick syrup. Whisk to smooth out any lumps, and drizzle over top of the babka while still warm.

Baked Ham

"My mom always served baked ham for Christmas and Easter. When I was a kid, I didn't like it very much, and was a bit perplexed by the cloves. The tradition of serving baked ham at holiday get-togethers has grown on me, however, and now I readily look forward to it."

1 (7 - 11 pound) boneless half-ham
1 tablespoon whole cloves
1/3 cup butter
1 cup honey
3 tablespoons molasses
1 teaspoon dry mustard
½ teaspoon cinnamon
¼ teaspoon nutmeg
½ teaspoon freshly ground black pepper
Juice of 1 lemon

Preheat oven to 325 degrees F.

With a sharp knife, score parallel lines in a diagonal pattern, approximately 1 inch apart and ¼ inch deep. Insert whole cloves at the crossings.

Place ham in roasting pan, scored side up, and bake for 1½ to 2½ hours. *Allow approximately 10 to 15 minutes per pound, but be sure that an instant read thermometer reaches an internal temperature of 140 degrees F.*

While the ham is baking, combine butter, honey, molasses, dry mustard, cinnamon, nutmeg, black pepper, and lemon juice in a medium sauce pan.

Bring to a boil over medium heat. Then reduce heat to medium low, and cook for 1 minute more, stirring all the while.

Baste ham on all sides, with glaze and pan drippings, every 15 minutes. When ham is done, remove from oven and let rest for 10 to 15 minutes before carving. Serve remaining glaze with ham.

Easter Bread

"Symbolic of the regeneration of life, this traditional yeast-based Easter Bread is garnished with poppy seeds, and is made with milk, honey, raisins, butter, and eggs."

1 cup sundried raisins
1 package quick-rise yeast
1 teaspoon sugar
1 cup warm milk
2 eggs
3 egg yolks
3 tablespoons vegetable oil
1/3 cup honey
1 teaspoon salt
4 cups unbleached flour
2 tablespoons butter, softened
½ tablespoon poppy seeds

In a small bowl, combine raisins with about ½ cup water, and set aside to soak. Then, in a separate bowl, dissolve quick-rise yeast and sugar in warm milk. Let stand 15 minutes.

In a large mixing bowl, use a whisk to combine 1 egg, 3 egg yolks, vegetable oil, honey, and salt with 1 cup flour. Mix well, and cut in butter using a pastry blender.

Add yeast mixture, remaining 3 cups flour, and *drained* raisins. On a lightly floured work surface, knead dough for approximately 10 minutes, until smooth. Add enough flour (*about 1 cup*) to keep the dough from sticking.

Place dough in a greased bowl, cover loosely with greased plastic wrap, and let rise until doubled in size, about 1 hour.

Divide the dough into 3 equal pieces. Roll the dough into 1 inch thick ropes of equal length. Arrange ropes side by side, and loosely braid the ropes, pinching the ends together.

Place on greased baking sheet, and *let rise until doubled in size, about 1 hour.*

Preheat oven to 375 degrees F.

Beat remaining egg. Brush loaf with egg, and sprinkle with poppy seeds. Bake for 20 to 25 minutes, or until golden brown.

German Wreath Cake

"Kranzkuchen, German for 'wreath cake,' is a traditional Easter bread my great-grandmother used to make. It's braided and made into the shape of a wreath, which is symbolic of the crown of thorns."

1 package quick-rise yeast
2/3 cup warm milk
2¾ cups unbleached flour, divided
¼ cup sugar
1 teaspoon salt
2 tablespoons butter, softened
2 eggs
4 uncooked eggs, dyed
1 egg and 2 tablespoons water for egg wash
2 tablespoons melted butter

Dissolve quick-rise yeast in warm milk. Let stand 15 minutes. In a large mixing bowl, combine yeast mixture with 1 cup flour, sugar, and salt. Mix well. Cut in butter using a pastry blender. Add 2 eggs and ¾ cup flour, and beat well. Gradually add the remaining 1 cup of flour (½ cup at a time), until dough pulls away from sides of bowl. A slightly sticky dough is normal.

On a lightly floured work surface, knead dough for approximately 10 minutes, or until dough is smooth and elastic. If necessary, add a little flour to keep the dough from sticking. *Place the dough in a greased bowl, cover loosely with plastic wrap, and let rise in a warm place until double in size, about 1 hour.*

Punch down dough to remove air bubbles if necessary. Then, divide dough into 2 equal size rounds. Roll the dough into 1 inch thick ropes of equal length. Loosely braid the ropes, leaving space for the four dyed eggs. Pinch the ends together, and distribute the eggs evenly within the braids.

Place wreath on greased baking sheet. Then, using 1 egg and 2 tablespoons water, make an egg wash solution. *Brush the wreath cake with egg wash, sprinkle with sugar, and let rise for 1 hour.*

Preheat oven to 350 degrees F. Brush with melted butter, and bake for 30 to 35 minutes, or until golden brown.

Hot Cross Buns

"This is my great-grandmother's hot cross buns recipe. These traditional sweet buns are made with raisins and are glazed crosswise, while still warm. Traditionally hot cross buns are baked and served on Good Friday and represent the crucifixion of Jesus."

Dough Ingredients:
3 tablespoons lukewarm warm water
1 package quick-rise yeast
1 cup milk, scalded
1/3 cup sugar
½ teaspoon salt
1/3 cup butter
4 cups flour, divided
2 eggs
1 teaspoon grated lemon rind
½ teaspoon cinnamon
¾ cup sun dried raisins
¼ cup melted butter

Frosting Ingredients:
1 cup powdered sugar
1 tablespoon melted butter
½ teaspoon vanilla extract
1 tablespoon hot water

To prepare the dough, in a small mixing bowl, dissolve quick-rise yeast in warm water. Let stand for 5 minutes. In a separate bowl, combine raisins with approximately 1 cup water, and set aside to soak.

In a medium saucepan, heat milk until almost boiling. Add salt, sugar, and butter, and cook over medium-low heat until sugar has completely dissolved and butter has melted. Remove from heat, and let cool to room temperature.

Transfer to a medium mixing bowl, add 1½ cups flour, and beat until smooth. Then, add yeast, eggs, grated lemon rind, cinnamon, and remaining 2½ cups of flour. Knead the dough until smooth, adding just enough flour to keep the dough from sticking. Cover loosely with a clean kitchen towel or dish cloth, and *let rise in a warm place for 1 hour.*

Then, drain the raisins and add them to the dough, little by little; kneading as you work them into the dough. Now, on a floured work surface, roll out the dough to about a 1 inch thickness. Cut biscuit rounds using a cookie cutter, approximately 2 inches in diameter. Arrange the rounds (*so that they touch*) in a greased 9 x 13 inch baking dish, brush with melted butter, and let rise for 1 hour.

Preheat oven to 375 degrees F. When the buns have doubled in bulk, bake for 20 minutes, or until golden brown.

Meanwhile, to prepare the frosting, in a medium mixing bowl, use a whisk to combine the powdered sugar, melted butter, vanilla extract, and hot water (*a tablespoon at a time*), and beat until smooth. *While the buns are still warm,* decorate each bun with the frosting, making the sign of the cross.

New Year's Day

Pork Roast

"One of my favorite holiday meals is my mom's pork roast. If I'm not mistaken, it's a traditional German meal, prepared on New Year's Day to ensure good luck and wealth in the up coming year. In fact, my mom was a little superstitious about this, and never ate beef on New Year's Day. The reason being, that a cow routs backwards for its food which suggests a regression for the upcoming year; that things will only get worse as time passes. In contrast, a pig routs forward, representing growth and improvement; a step forward."

1 (2- 3 pound) center cut, boneless pork loin roast
2 tablespoons vegetable oil
2 medium onions, sliced
3 cloves garlic, minced
1 tablespoon brown sugar
Salt and freshly ground black pepper, to taste

Preheat oven to 325 degrees F.

In a large dutch oven, heat vegetable oil over medium high flame. Add pork loin, and sear on all sides, for about 5 minutes. Then, add onion, garlic, and brown sugar. Cover, and place in oven for 30 minutes. Turn the roast over, and cook for an additional 45 minutes. Stir onions periodically, and *prepare sauerkraut in the meantime*:

2 (14.5 ounce) cans of sauerkraut, drained and rinsed
1 tablespoon vegetable oil
1 medium onion, sliced
¼ pound bacon, chopped
1 tablespoon brown sugar
1 (12 ounce) bottle of beer

In a large saucepan, heat vegetable oil over medium high flame. Add onion and bacon, and cook until tender, about 3 to 5 minutes. Add brown sugar, beer, and sauerkraut, and let simmer for 40 to 45 minutes. Remove from heat, cover, and set aside.

When the pork roast is finished, a meat thermometer inserted into the thickest part of the roast should read 160 degrees F. Transfer the roast to a carving board or platter, and let rest for 10 to 15 minutes before carving and serving.

For the gravy, whisk 2 tablespoons of flour and 2 cups of water together in a small mixing bowl. Add to dutch oven, and continue to cook over low heat, stirring frequently, until sauce thickens. Carefully scrape the remnants from the bottom and sides of the dutch oven. Season with salt and pepper, and simmer for approximately 5 minutes. Then, strain to remove any small particles.

Sauerkraut Balls

"My mom enjoyed making sauerkraut balls during the holidays, especially New Year's Eve. She didn't always make them from scratch though, since they were readily available at most local supermarkets."

Sauerkraut Ingredients:
¼ pound bacon, chopped
1 medium onion, cut in half and very thinly sliced
½ teaspoon paprika
1 teaspoon caraway seeds
1 (16 ounce) can of sauerkraut, *drained and rinsed*
½ (12 ounce) bottle of beer

Breading Ingredients:
1 egg
2 cups milk
2 cups unbleached flour
1¼ cups bread crumbs
Vegetable oil, for pan frying

To prepare the sauerkraut, in a medium saucepan, sauté the bacon until crisp. Add the onion, paprika, and caraway seeds, and cook over medium heat until tender, about 3 to 5 minutes. Add the sauerkraut and beer, and cook until softened; about 45 minutes more.*

Transfer the sauerkraut mixture to a medium colander, and *let stand for about 1 hour*. Drain thoroughly, and pat dry using a paper towel. Then, loosely shape into 1 inch balls and arrange approximately 2 inches apart on a greased baking sheet. *Place in freezer, and chill for at least 2 hours.*

To prepare the breading, in a medium mixing bowl, whisk the egg, milk, and flour together. Place the bread crumbs in a separate bowl.

Heat approximately 1½ inches of vegetable oil in a heavy skillet, to 375 degrees F.

Now, dip each frozen sauerkraut ball into the egg mixture, roll in bread crumbs, and fry until golden brown; approximately 1 to 2 minutes on each side. Drain on paper towels, and serve with dijon mustard, horseradish, and/or sour cream.

* An even better approach would be to use a slow cooker. To do so, place combined ingredients in a 3½ quart slow cooker, cover, and cook on 'high' for approximately 4 hours.

Saint Patrick's Day

Blarney Stones

"Blarney Stones are an ideal Saint Patrick's Day treat. Rumor has it that, much like the Blarney Stone found at Blarney Castle, these delicious pastries bestow the gift of eloquence and flattery."

Cake Ingredients:
4 eggs
1¾ cups sugar
1 teaspoon vanilla extract
1¾ cups unbleached flour
1 tablespoon baking powder
½ teaspoon salt
1 cup milk
¼ cup melted butter

Frosting Ingredients:
2 pounds powdered sugar
1 cup milk
2 teaspoons vanilla extract
1/8 teaspoon salt
5 cups chopped nuts

Preheat oven to 350 degrees F.

To make the cakes, in a large mixing bowl, combine the eggs, sugar, and vanilla extract. Gradually add the flour, baking powder, salt, milk, and melted butter. Mix just enough to blend well. *Do not over-mix!*

Pour into a greased 9 x 13 inch baking dish and bake for 30 to 35 minutes, or until a toothpick inserted near the center is clean when removed. Let cool to room temperature. *Then, cut into 4 inch squares, cover with plastic wrap, and freeze overnight.*

To make the frosting, in a large mixing bowl, beat the powdered sugar, milk, vanilla extract, and salt until light and fluffy. Submerge the frozen cakes in the frosting, and place on wire racks. Let stand for 5 minutes (allow excess frosting to drip if necessary). Then, roll in chopped nuts, and place on a baking sheet, to set, before serving.

Corned Beef & Cabbage

"Corned Beef and Cabbage is more of an Irish American tradition than an Irish tradition per se. If I'm not mistaken, the Irish traditionally serve pork or lamb. At any rate, I'm partial to my mom's Saint Patrick's Day meal, which is great with Irish Stout and soda bread."

4 to 5 pounds corned beef brisket
6 quarts water *(just enough to cover the brisket)*
2 teaspoons coarsely ground black peppercorns
4 whole allspice berries
2 whole cloves
2 bay leaves
2 teaspoons salt
4 medium carrots, chopped
2 medium onions, thinly sliced
4 medium red potatoes, chopped
2 stalks celery, finely chopped
1 medium cabbage, chopped

Place the corned beef in a large dutch oven. Then add water, peppercorns, allspice berries, cloves, bay leaves, and salt.

Cover, and bring to a boil over high heat. Then reduce the heat to medium low, and simmer for 2 to 2½ hours.

Add carrots, onions, potatoes, and celery. Then, return to a simmer and cook uncovered for 15 to 20 minutes.

Finally, add the cabbage and cook for an additional 15 to 20 minutes, or until potatoes and cabbage are tender. Remove bay leaf and serve.

Irish Cream Cheesecake

12 ounces cream cheese
1 teaspoon vanilla extract
1/3 cup sugar
½ cup sour cream
3 tablespoons irish cream
2 eggs
1 (9 inch) graham cracker pie shell
1 (8 ounce) tub whipped topping

Preheat oven to 350 degrees F.

In a medium mixing bowl, beat the cream cheese and vanilla extract until light and fluffy. Gradually add the sugar, sour cream, irish cream, and eggs. Mix just enough to blend well.

Then, use a rubber spatula to spread the cream cheese mixture into a 9 inch graham cracker pie shell, and bake for 50 to 60 minutes; until set. The center shouldn't move when shaken.

Remove from oven, and *refrigerate overnight*. Garnish with whipped topping and ground nutmeg before serving.

Shamrock Cookies

"These shamrock cookies are symbolic of the three-leafed clover that Saint Patrick once used to represent the Holy Trinity. Naturally, they're perfect for Saint Patrick's Day!"

½ cup butter
1 cup sugar
1 egg
½ teaspoon vanilla extract
½ cup sour cream
¼ teaspoon green food color*
½ teaspoon baking soda
1 teaspoon baking powder
½ teaspoon salt
3¼ cups unbleached flour
1 cup white chocolate candy wafers
2 tablespoons vegetable oil

In medium mixing bowl, beat the butter and sugar until light and fluffy. Add the egg, vanilla extract, and sour cream; and beat until well mixed. Then, add the baking soda, baking powder, and salt. Gradually add the flour, *place in a greased bowl, cover with plastic wrap, and refrigerate overnight.*

The next day, preheat oven to 425 degrees F.

On a floured work surface, knead the dough until smooth. Then, roll out the dough to a 1/8 inch thickness, and cut-out the cookies using a 2 inch *shamrock-shaped* cookie cutter.

Bake on greased cookie sheets for 3 minutes. Then, rotate the baking sheets, and bake for an additional 3 minutes.

Now, in a small saucepan, melt the candy wafers and vegetable oil in a double boiler** or hot-water bath, stirring continuously. It's important that the candy be allowed to melt over a gentle, indirect heat.

Using a wooden spoon, drizzle the melted wafers in a zigzag pattern over the shamrock cookies. Let stand until firm.

* *You can also use a small amount of green icing color, such as "Wilton's Kelly Green Icing Color."*

**If you don't own a double boiler, any metal bowl that fits over the top of a saucepan can be used.*

Thanksgiving

Traditional Bread Stuffing for Thanksgiving Dinner

"My mom used to make a traditional bread stuffing for Thanksgiving, and yes, she actually stuffed the turkey. Actually it was the best stuffing I've ever had. There were rarely leftovers. When I was a kid, I wasn't entirely sure what to think of giblets, but they definitely add a lot of flavor. Nowadays we have cornbread stuffing with our turkey (baked separately) because everyone seems to freak out over giblets, and somehow the notion that stuffing a turkey can be "dangerous" has prevailed. If you'd like to have a politically correct Thanksgiving dinner, you might consider making cornbread stuffing instead..."

Turkey giblets (*neck, heart, and gizzard*)
1 tablespoon vegetable oil
½ cup butter
2 medium onions, finely chopped
3 medium celery stalks (*with leaves*), finely chopped
1 pound stale white bread, cut into ½ inch cubes
2 teaspoons parsley
1 teaspoon poultry seasoning
½ teaspoon thyme
1 teaspoon salt
½ teaspoon freshly ground black pepper
2 cups chicken broth, as needed

Chop the turkey neck into 2 to 3 inch pieces, and trim the liver. In a large saucepan, heat vegetable oil over medium high flame, and cook the neck, heart, and gizzard for 10 to 12 minutes, until browned. Add salt and water (*about an inch above the giblets*). Cover, and bring to a boil. Then, reduce heat to medium low, partially cover, and simmer, until giblets are tender, about 1½ hours. Add the turkey liver and simmer for an additional 15 to 20 minutes, until cooked throughout. Strain, and let the giblets cool before pulling the meat off the neck. Chop the neck meat, heart, gizzard, and liver. Then, set aside.

In a large heavy skillet, melt the butter over medium heat. Add the onions and celery, and cook for approximately 6 to 8 minutes, or until the onions are tender. In a large mixing bowl, combine giblets, onion and celery mixture, bread cubes, parsley, poultry seasoning, thyme, salt, and freshly ground black pepper. Gradually mix-in 1½ - 2 cups of chicken broth, *until the stuffing is moist but not soggy*. Use as stuffing; or place in a greased casserole dish, mix-in another ½ cup chicken broth, cover, and bake at 350 degrees F for 30 to 40 minutes.

Herbed Corn

"Thanksgiving just wouldn't be the same without this family favorite. Much better than con on the cob…"

½ teaspoon dill weed
1 teaspoon parsley
½ teaspoon oregano
½ teaspoon basil
¼ teaspoon thyme
½ teaspoon garlic powder
1 teaspoon salt
¼ teaspoon black pepper
4 (12 ounce) packages frozen corn
2 cups water
1/3 cup butter, cubed

In a small mixing bowl, use a whisk to combine the dill, parsley, oregano, basil, thyme, garlic powder, salt, and black pepper. Set aside.

In a large pot, combine the corn and water. Bring to boil. Then, reduce heat, cover, and let simmer for 4 to 6 minutes, or until tender. Drain thoroughly, add the butter, and stir in the herb mixture. Serve immediately.

Cornbread Stuffing

Cornbread Ingredients:
3 cups cornmeal
2 cups unbleached flour
2 tablespoons baking powder
2 teaspoons salt
2 cups milk
2 eggs
1/3 cup butter, melted

Stuffing Ingredients:
2 loaves cornbread, cubed
¼ cup butter
2 medium onions, chopped
1 celery stalk, chopped
8 ounces fresh mushrooms, sliced
1 teaspoon parsley
1 teaspoon basil
1 teaspoon paprika
1 egg
½ cup heavy cream
3 cups chicken broth
Salt and freshly ground black pepper, to taste

To prepare the cornbread, preheat oven to 425 degrees F

In a medium mixing bowl, whisk together cornmeal, flour, baking powder, and salt.

In small mixing bowl, whisk together milk, eggs, and butter. Add egg mixture to cornmeal, stirring only until combined. Do not over-mix!

Pour batter into a greased 9 x 13 inch baking dish, and bake for 20 to 25 minutes, or until golden brown. A toothpick inserted into the center of the bread should be clean when removed. Let stand for 5 minutes. Then, invert cornbread onto a cutting board and set aside to let cool completely.

If you'd like to use the corn bread for stuffing (without waiting for it to stale), simply cut the loaf into cubes, place the cubes on a baking sheet and bake for 30 minutes, at 300 degrees F. After you turn the oven off, leave the baking sheet in the oven for another 30 minutes.

To prepare the stuffing, preheat oven to 375 degrees F.

In a large heavy skillet, heat butter over medium high heat. Sauté onions, celery, and mushrooms until tender, about 5 minutes. Add parsley, basil, and paprika. Remove from heat, and set aside.

In a large mixing bowl, combine cornbread and onion mixture. Add egg, heavy cream, and *just enough chicken broth to moisten the stuffing, without making it soggy* (about ½ cup). Mix well, and season with salt and pepper.

Place cornbread stuffing in a greased 9 x 13 inch baking dish, and bake for 35 to 40 minutes, or until golden brown.

Cranberry Sauce

1 (12 ounce) package fresh cranberries
¼ cup cream sherry
½ cup brown sugar
1 teaspoon cinnamon
Juice of 1 orange
Zest of 1 orange
1 tablespoon cornstarch
1 tablespoon water

In a medium saucepan, combine cranberries, cream sherry, brown sugar, cinnamon, orange juice, and orange zest.

Bring to a boil over high heat. Then, reduce heat to medium low and simmer, stirring frequently, 10 to 15 minutes, or until cranberries are tender.

In a small mixing bowl, whisk cornstarch and water together, and add to the cranberry sauce. Continue to cook over low heat, stirring frequently, until sauce thickens.

Garlic Mashed Potatoes

2 whole bulbs garlic
2 tablespoons extra-virgin olive oil
5 pounds yukon gold potatoes
½ cup milk
½ cup butter
½ teaspoon salt
¼ teaspoon freshly ground black pepper

Preheat oven to 400 degrees F

Peel the outermost layer of the garlic bulb's skin and cut about ½ inch off the top, exposing each clove of garlic. Drizzle with olive oil, and wrap in aluminum foil. Place on an ungreased baking sheet, and bake for 35 to 40 minutes, or until tender. Let stand for approximately 15 minutes. Then, gently squeeze the roasted garlic cloves out of the skins.

In a large pot, combine potatoes, 1 teaspoon salt, and just enough cold water to cover the potatoes. Bring to a boil over high heat. Then reduce the heat to medium low, and simmer until fork tender, about 45 minutes. Peel the potatoes. Mash the potatoes with a potato masher while they're still warm, gradually adding the milk, butter, salt, and pepper.

Add the garlic to the mashed potatoes and once again, mash the potatoes with a potato masher.

Pumpkin Pie

"This is my great-grandmother's pumpkin pie recipe. Made of pumpkin, heavy cream, eggs, brown sugar, and spices. It's ideal for any Thanksgiving or Christmas festivity."

Pie Filling:
2/3 cup brown sugar
½ teaspoon cinnamon
½ teaspoon nutmeg
¼ teaspoon ginger
1/8 teaspoon ground cloves
½ teaspoon salt
1 cup heavy cream
1 cup pumpkin puree
2 eggs
1 teaspoon vanilla extract
1 tablespoon melted butter

Pie Crust:
1 cup unbleached flour
½ teaspoon salt
1/3 cup shortening
2 tablespoons cold water

To make the pie filling, in a medium mixing bowl, use a whisk to combine the brown sugar, cinnamon, nutmeg, ginger, ground cloves, and salt. In a separate mixing bowl, combine the heavy cream, pumpkin puree, eggs, vanilla extract, and melted butter. Now, use the whisk to gradually blend the brown sugar mixture into the egg mixture. *The batter should be thin enough to pour.*

To make the pie crust, in a medium mixing bowl, combine the flour and salt. Cut-in the shortening using a pastry blender. The mixture should resemble coarse meal. Gradually add the cold water, stirring all the while, until a dough forms.

On a lightly floured work surface, knead the dough until smooth. Add just enough flour to keep the dough from sticking. Then, roll into a 12 inch circle, about 1/8 inch thick.

Preheat oven to 375 degrees F.

Use a metal spatula to carefully place the 12 inch circle onto a greased 9 inch pie pan, gently pressing the dough into the corners and using your fingertips to create a rim around sides of the pan. Now, use a rubber spatula to spread the pie filling into the pie shell.

Bake for 30 minutes at 375 degrees F. Then, reduce oven temperature to 325 degrees F, and *bake for an additional 20 minutes*, or until golden brown. *Refrigerate overnight*, and serve with whipped cream.

Roast Turkey

1 (12 - 14 pound) whole turkey
½ cup butter (*refer to rosemary and sage butter recipe*)
1 large onion, quartered
1 medium carrot
1 medium celery stalk, *with leaves*
3 cloves garlic
1 sprig fresh rosemary
1 sprig fresh sage
1 lemon
2 cups chicken stock
8 slices bacon
¼ cup unbleached flour
1 cup chicken broth
Salt and freshly ground black pepper, to taste

The night prior, place thawed turkey in brine solution (*refer to turkey brine recipe*), and fill the remainder of the bucket with ice. Cover, and let stand overnight, in a cool dry place.

About an hour before you're ready to roast the turkey, remove top rack from oven and preheat to 350 degrees F. Rinse the turkey with cold water and pat it dry with a paper towel. Then, season liberally with salt and pepper, and gently work butter under the skin, mainly near the breast and legs. Fill the cavity with onion, carrot, celery, garlic, rosemary, sage, and ½ a lemon. Tie the drumsticks and wingtips together using kitchen twine. Set the turkey on a rack, in a large roasting pan, and place in oven.

Meanwhile, use the chicken stock to baste the turkey, about every 30 minutes. The turkey should take about 3½ to 4 hours to cook (15 to 20 minutes per pound), but be sure to begin checking after 3 hours. If the legs or breast brown too quickly, cover with foil.

Halfway through cooking, about 2 hours, wrap bacon slices around the breast and legs, stretching slightly to cover. Continue to roast for another hour or so, basting every 30 minutes. The turkey's done when an instant-read meat thermometer placed deep in the thigh reaches 170 degrees F. Also, the juices should be clear when pricked with a knife, not reddish pink. When done, transfer the turkey to a carving board or platter and let rest for 15 to 20 minutes before serving.

For the gravy, use a wooden spoon to skim off any excess fat. Pour the drippings from the turkey roasting pan into a medium saucepan, and set to medium-high heat. Be sure to reserve the brown bits that remain on the bottom of the pan and whisk the flour into the drippings, stirring continuously as it thickens to prevent lumps. Add the chicken broth, and bring to a simmer. Season with salt and pepper, and add juice of ½ a lemon. Simmer for approximately 5 minutes. Then, strain to remove any small particles before serving.

Rosemary and Sage Butter

1 cup butter, softened
1 sprig fresh rosemary, finely chopped
½ bunch fresh sage, finely chopped
Salt and freshly ground black pepper, to taste

In a medium mixing bowl, whip butter until smooth. Add rosemary, sage, salt, and freshly ground black pepper.

Sweet Potatoes with Maple Syrup & Marshmallows

6 medium sweet potatoes, mashed
½ teaspoon salt
2 tablespoons brown sugar
¼ cup pure maple syrup
1 teaspoon cinnamon
¼ teaspoon nutmeg
¼ cup milk
¼ cup butter
1 (10.5 ounce) package miniature marshmallows

Preheat oven to 400 degrees F.

Bake the sweet potatoes for about 1 hour or until tender and easily pierced with a fork. Peel the sweet potatoes while still hot. Then, mash with a potato masher until smooth.

In a medium mixing bowl, combine the sweet potatoes, salt, brown sugar, maple syrup, cinnamon, nutmeg, milk, and butter.

Spread sweet potato mixture into a greased 9 x 13 inch baking dish. Top with approximately 6 to 8 ounces marshmallows, and bake until marshmallows begin to melt or are golden brown.

Turkey Brine

2 gallons cold water
1 (7 pound) bag of ice
½ cup brown sugar
1 cup salt
1 onion, peeled and quartered
6 cloves garlic, chopped
1 apple, peeled and quartered
1 tablespoon crushed peppercorns
4 sprigs rosemary, coarsely chopped
6 sage leaves, chopped
1 lemon, quartered

The night prior, in a 5 gallon plastic bucket; combine the water, brown sugar, salt, onion, garlic, apple, peppercorns, rosemary, and sage. Stir briskly, to dissolve brown sugar and salt. Then, *remove the giblets and the neck*, place the thawed turkey (*breast side down*) in the brine, and fill the remainder of the bucket with ice. Cover, and let stand overnight, in a cool, dry place.

About an hour before roasting, add the lemon, squeezing it to release the juice. When you're ready to roast the turkey, remove the turkey and discard the brine.

Main Course Dishes

Beef Chow Mein

"My mom liked to use beef to make chow mein. However, chicken, shrimp, or pork are certainly acceptable substitutes. She also used canned vegetables, though you can use stir fry vegetables such as red bell peppers, broccoli, carrots, and sugar snap peas."

2 tablespoons tamari soy sauce
¼ cup beef stock
1 tablespoon sherry or port wine
1 tablespoon cornstarch
2 teaspoons brown sugar
2 pounds boneless top sirloin, *thinly sliced and cut into bite-size pieces*
4 cups water
2 cups long-grain white rice
2 tablespoons vegetable oil, divided
1 medium onion, cut in half and thinly sliced
3 cloves garlic, minced
½ teaspoon ginger
Salt and freshly ground black pepper, to taste
1 (14 ounce) can bean sprouts, *drained*
1 (14 ounce) can straw mushrooms, *drained*
1 (8 ounce) can water chestnuts, *drained*
1 (8 ounce) can bamboo shoots, *drained*
2 cups chow mein noodles

In a medium mixing bowl, use a whisk to combine the soy sauce, beef stock, sherry, cornstarch, and brown sugar. Add the beef sirloin and marinate for 1 hour.

In a medium saucepan, bring 4 cups water and 1 teaspoon salt to a boil. Add 2 cups long-grain white rice and cook, stirring repeatedly, until water returns to a boil. Reduce to low heat and simmer for 8 to 10 minutes. Cover pan, and cook rice until water is absorbed, about 15 minutes more. Remove pan from heat, and let stand.

Meanwhile, place a wok over high heat until hot. Coat sides with *1 tablespoon* vegetable oil. Drain the beef (reserving the marinade) and brown on all sides for approximately 5 minutes; stirring continuously. Remove from wok, and set aside.

Add the remaining *1 tablespoon* vegetable oil, and sauté the onion, garlic, ginger, salt, and freshly ground pepper for 2 to 3 minutes. Add the bean sprouts, mushrooms, water chestnuts, bamboo shoots, and beef. Cook for an additional 3 minutes, or until sirloin has cooked throughout.

Add the soy sauce marinade to the wok, reduce to medium-low heat, and let simmer for 3 to 5 minutes; until sauce has thickened slightly. Serve on a bed of white rice, and top with chow mein noodles.

Beef Stroganoff & Egg Noodles

1 (6 ounce) package egg noodles
1 pound lean ground beef
1 tablespoon extra-virgin olive oil
1 medium onion, cut in half and thinly sliced
3 cloves garlic, minced
1 teaspoon oregano
½ teaspoon freshly ground black pepper
2 teaspoons worcestershire sauce
2 (10¾ ounces) cans cream of mushroom soup
8 ounces mushrooms, sliced

Bring a large pot of water to boil. Cook egg noodles according to package directions. Drain noodles in colander, but *do not rinse*. Return noodles to pot and set aside.

In a medium saucepan, brown the ground beef. Drain the excess fat, and add olive oil, onion, garlic, oregano, and freshly ground black pepper. Cook over medium heat, 3 to 5 minutes, until tender. Add the worcestershire sauce, cream of mushroom soup, and sliced mushrooms. Mix well, and heat throughout.

To serve, place egg noodles in a serving bowl. Top with ground beef mixture.

Black Bean Chili

"My mom typically used dried black beans to make her chili. A couple of cans of black beans work just as well though. If you decide to use dried beans, however, just be sure to soak them overnight."

2 tablespoons vegetable oil
1 medium onion, chopped
6 cloves garlic, minced
2 teaspoons basil
1 teaspoon cilantro, *optional*
4 teaspoons cumin
1 teaspoon freshly ground black pepper
2 tablespoons chipotle pepper sauce
1¾ cups chicken broth
2 (16 ounce) cans black beans
1 (16 ounce) can diced tomatoes
1 tablespoon cider vinegar
½ cup grated jack or white cheddar cheese.

Drain and rinse the black beans in strainer. Set aside. In a medium saucepan, heat the vegetable oil over a medium flame. Add the onion, garlic, basil, cilantro, cumin, freshly ground black pepper, and chipotle pepper sauce. Cook for 15 minutes. Then, add the chicken broth and black beans. Cover, and cook for an additional 30 minutes. Now, add the diced tomatoes and cider vinegar. Cover, and let simmer for 30 minutes more. Ladle into bowls, top with grated cheese, and serve immediately.

Boxty

"Boxty is a traditional potato pancake that's common in the Ulster province of Ireland. Although my dad's side of the family is originally from Kirkcudbright, a town in the south of Scotland, the McClellans settled in Ulster before coming to America."

Sautéed Vegetables:
2 tablespoons extra-virgin olive oil
1 medium onion, chopped
2 cloves garlic, minced
1 carrot, very thinly sliced
2 small zucchini, cut into thin strips
2 small yellow summer squash, cut into thin strips
4 ounces frozen chopped spinach, thawed and drained
8 ounces mushrooms, sliced
1 small bunch fresh parsley, chopped
Salt and freshly ground black pepper, to taste

Boxty:
1½ cups unbleached flour
1½ teaspoons salt
½ teaspoon freshly ground black pepper
1 tablespoon baking powder
3 medium raw potatoes, grated
3 medium potatoes, cooked, peeled and mashed
3 eggs
1/3 cup buttermilk
Vegetable oil, for pan frying

Béchamel Sauce:
5 tablespoons butter
¼ cup unbleached flour
4 cups milk
2 teaspoons salt
½ teaspoon nutmeg

To prepare the sautéed vegetables, in a medium skillet, heat the olive oil over medium high heat. Add onion, garlic, carrot, zucchini, and summer squash, and increase to high heat. Sauté, stirring frequently, until tender, 5 to 7 minutes. Add the spinach, mushrooms, parsley, salt, and pepper. Cook for another 3 to 5 minutes. Set aside.

To make the boxty, in a medium mixing bowl, use a whisk to combine the flour, salt, freshly ground black pepper, and baking powder. Add raw potatoes, mashed potatoes, eggs, and just enough buttermilk to make a thick batter. *Add more milk if needed.* Then, heat approximately ¼ inch vegetable oil in a heavy skillet, over a medium flame. Drop batter (*by the cupful*) into the skillet. Gently press down with spatula to flatten into pancakes, and fry until golden brown, about 4 minutes on each side. Drain on paper towels before serving with butter and sour cream.

To make the béchamel sauce, in a medium saucepan, heat butter over medium-low flame until melted. Add flour and stir until smooth. Increase to medium heat, and cook for approximately 5 to 7 minutes, stirring all the while. Meanwhile, heat the milk in a separate pan almost to boiling. Add milk to butter mixture (*about 1 cup at a time*), whisking continuously until smooth. Bring to a boil, and cook for 10 minutes, stirring constantly. Remove from heat. Add salt and nutmeg, and set aside. To serve, fill half the boxty with sautéed vegetables, fold in half, invert, and top with béchamel sauce.

Brunswick Stew

"Evidently, this recipe originated in Brunswick County, Virginia. My mom had it for the first time at Colonial Williamsburg, a well known historic district in Williamsburg, Virginia. Her variation is relatively straightforward, but tasty."

1 large, whole chicken, cut into pieces
1 (14.5 ounce) can stewed tomatoes, quartered and drained
1 (16 ounce) package frozen corn, thawed
3 medium red potatoes, cut into ½ inch cubes
1 large onion, cut in half and thinly sliced
1 whole bay leaf
1½ teaspoons chicken soup base
½ teaspoon freshly ground black pepper
1 teaspoon brown sugar
2 cups dried baby lima beans

Place the beans in a medium pot, and add enough water to cover by approximately 2 inches. Soak overnight. Then, drain, rinse thoroughly, and set aside.

To prepare the stew, place the chicken in a large pot, and add enough water to cover, about 3 quarts. Bring to a boil over high heat. Then reduce the heat to medium low, and simmer, partially covered, until the chicken falls off the bones and the broth is well flavored, about 2 to 3 hours.

With a slotted spoon, transfer the chicken to a medium-sized bowl to let cool. Skim the fat from broth, add the stewed tomatoes, corn, red potatoes, onion, bay leaf, chicken soup base, freshly ground black pepper, and brown sugar.

Bring to a simmer over medium heat. Then reduce heat to medium low and cook, stirring often, until the potatoes are tender; 20 to 30 minutes.

Meanwhile, pull the chicken off the bones, shredding it into bite size pieces. Add the baby lima beans and chicken, and let simmer over medium low heat for another 10 to 15 minutes. Remove bay leaf, and serve immediately.

Fried Cabbage & Bacon

½ pound bacon
1 medium onion, cut in half and thinly sliced
2 cloves garlic, minced
½ medium green cabbage, cored and shredded
1 teaspoon parsley
Salt, and freshly ground black pepper, to taste

In a heavy skillet, sauté bacon until crisp; 3 to 5 minutes. Remove bacon, and set aside to drain on a paper towel. Reserve approximately 2 tablespoons of bacon fat, and discard the rest.

Add the onion and garlic, and sauté in bacon fat for 2 to 3 minutes. Add cabbage, parsley, salt, and freshly ground black pepper. Cover, *reduce heat to low*, and cook until tender, about 35 to 40 minutes; stirring occasionally.

Crumble bacon over top, and serve immediately.

Cabbage & Noodles

"This dish is of Austro-Hungarian origin, and is a long standing family favorite. It's ideal when served with a quality smoked sausage."

1 small head of cabbage, shredded
1 (12 ounce) package wide egg noodles
¼ cup butter
1 medium onion, cut in half and thinly sliced
2 cloves garlic, minced
1 teaspoon caraway seeds
1 teaspoon basil
1 teaspoon parsley
1 teaspoons brown sugar
Salt and pepper, to taste

Bring a large pot of water to boil. Cook egg noodles according to package directions. Drain noodles in colander, but *do not rinse*. Return noodles to pot, add about a tablespoon of vegetable oil to prevent the noodles from sticking together. Stir briefly, and set aside.

In a large heavy skillet, melt the butter over medium-low heat. Sauté the onion, garlic, caraway seeds, basil, parsley, brown sugar, salt, and pepper; about 3 to 5 minutes.

Then, add the shredded cabbage, and cook approximately 5 to 7 minutes longer, stirring occasionally. Cover, *reduce heat to low*, and cook until tender, about 30 to 35 minutes; stirring occasionally.

Adjust heat to medium and add cooked egg noodles. Mix well, and cook until noodles are heated throughout, about 3 to 5 minutes.

Fried Catfish

¾ cup cornmeal
2 tablespoons unbleached flour
1 teaspoon salt
¼ teaspoon freshly ground black pepper
¼ teaspoon cayenne pepper
½ teaspoon garlic powder
1 pound boneless, skinless catfish fillets
Vegetable oil, for pan frying

In a small mixing bowl, use a whisk to combine the cornmeal, flour, salt, freshly ground black pepper, cayenne pepper, and garlic powder.

Rinse the fish fillets, and pat them dry with paper towel. Then, thoroughly cover each fillet with cornmeal mixture.

Heat approximately ½ inch of vegetable oil, in a heavy skillet, to 375 degrees F. Fry until golden brown, about 1½ to 2 minutes on each side. Drain on paper towels.

Honeyed Chicken Breast

1 medium onion, coarsely chopped
1 medium celery stalk (*including celery leaves*), quartered
1 carrot, peeled and quartered
½ bunch fresh parsley, coarsely chopped
1 teaspoon salt
½ teaspoon freshly ground black pepper
1 teaspoon rosemary
1 bay leaf
1 1/3 cups chicken broth
1 cup water
4 chicken breasts, halved
2 tablespoons butter
¼ cup sliced almonds
1/3 cup honey

In a large pot, combine the onion, celery, carrot, parsley, salt, freshly ground black pepper, rosemary, bay leaf, chicken broth, and water. Bring to a boil, add the chicken breasts, and cover. Reduce heat to medium-low, and let simmer fro 30 minutes, or until chicken is tender. Let cool to room temperature and *refrigerate overnight*.

The next day, in a medium skillet, heat the butter over medium-high heat. Add the almonds, and sauté for 3 to 5 minutes, stirring continuously. Set aside to cool.

Now, place the pot over low heat for 10 minutes. Remove the chicken breasts, and place in a large roasting pan. Discard onion, celery, carrot, and parsley. Add 1 cup of broth to the roasting pan, and brush the chicken with honey.

Broil for 2 minutes. Then, brush with honey again, and broil for an additional 1 to 2 minutes. Brush with honey once more, and broil until golden brown.

Remove from heat, arrange on serving platter, sprinkle with sliced almonds, and garnish with watercress sprigs, dandelion greens, or tender spinach leaves. Serve immediately.

Chicken Curry

1 small, whole chicken, cut into pieces
¼ cup vegetable oil
1 large onion, cut in half and thinly sliced
3 cloves garlic, minced
¼ teaspoon ginger
¼ teaspoon cayenne pepper
1½ teaspoons chicken soup base
1 medium tomato, chopped
½ cup water
1 teaspoon white vinegar
1 teaspoon garam masala

Rinse the chicken with cold water, and pat it dry with a paper towel. Then, cut the chicken into pieces, and remove the skin.

In a large pot, heat the vegetable oil over medium-high heat. Sauté the onion for 3 to 5 minutes, or until tender. Add the garlic, ginger, cayenne pepper, chicken soup base, and chopped tomato; and cook for an additional 3 minutes.

Add the chicken and water, and bring to a boil over medium heat. Then, cover, reduce heat to medium low, and let simmer (*stirring frequently*) about 1½ hours.

Add the vinegar, and cook for an additional 5 minutes. Sprinkle with garam masala, and serve immediately.

Chicken Fried Rice

4 cups chicken broth
2 cups long-grain white rice
3 tablespoons vegetable oil
1 pound chicken breast, *cut ½ inch pieces*
3 eggs, *lightly beaten*
3 cloves garlic, minced
½ teaspoon ginger
2 medium carrots, peeled and shredded
1 small red bell pepper, chopped
2 medium onions, finely chopped
½ cup frozen peas, *thawed*
1/3 cup tamari soy sauce

In a medium saucepan, bring the chicken broth to a boil. Add the rice, and reduce heat to medium-low. Then, cover the pan and cook for 15 to 18 minutes, or until tender. Remove from heat, and let stand.

Place wok over high heat until hot. Coat sides of wok with vegetable oil. Brown the chicken for approximately 5 minutes, stirring continuously.

Add lightly beaten eggs. Cook until the eggs begin to set. Then, scrape the eggs off the bottom of the wok, breaking them apart. Add the garlic, ginger, shredded carrots, red bell pepper, and onions; and cook until tender, about 2 minutes.

Add the rice, and cook for an additional 2 or 3 minutes. Then, add the peas and tamari soy sauce, and cook 1 minute more.

Chicken Soft Tacos

"My mom used to make tacos with fried corn tortillas filled with seasoned ground beef, cheese, lettuce, tomato, and sour cream. I never really liked hard-shell tacos though, and so she began to make chicken soft tacos made with whole-wheat tortillas."

Salsa Ingredients:
6 medium tomatoes, chopped
1 teaspoon salt
1 small red onion, finely chopped
½ bunch cilantro, finely chopped
1 teaspoon lemon juice
¼ teaspoon freshly ground black pepper
1 jalapeno pepper, seeded and finely chopped
2 cloves garlic, minced

Soft Taco Ingredients:
3 tablespoons extra-virgin olive oil
4 boneless, skinless chicken breasts, *cut in ½ inch pieces*
Salt and freshly ground black pepper, to taste
1 medium onion, cut in half and very thinly sliced
2 cloves garlic, minced
½ bunch parsley, chopped
½ teaspoon ancho chile powder
¼ teaspoon cayenne pepper
1 cup chicken stock
4 (9 inch) whole-wheat tortillas

Preheat oven to 350 degrees F.

To prepare the salsa, in a strainer, combine the chopped tomatoes and salt. *Let stand for approximately 30 minutes.* Drain any excess liquid. Now, in a large bowl, combine the red onions, cilantro, lemon juice, freshly ground black pepper, jalapeno pepper, and garlic. Salt and pepper to taste.

To prepare the soft tacos, in a large dutch oven, heat the olive oil over medium-high heat. Season the chicken with salt and freshly ground black pepper. Then, sear the chicken on all sides, for about 5 minutes, stirring continuously. Set aside.

Sauté the onion for 2 to 3 minutes, or until tender. Then, add the garlic, parsley, ancho chile powder, and cayenne pepper, and cook for an additional 2 to 3 minutes. Add the chicken breast and chicken stock, and bring to a boil. Cover, and bake for 10 to 15 minutes, or until the chicken is cooked through.

Warm the tortillas by placing them directly over the flame of a gas stove burner for about 10 to 15 seconds on each side. Then, using a slotted spoon, divide the chicken among the tortillas, top with salsa, and serve immediately.

Chicken Tandoori

¾ cup low-fat plain yogurt
2 teaspoons ground coriander seeds
2 teaspoons garam masala
1 teaspoon ground cumin
¼ teaspoon cayenne pepper
¼ teaspoon garlic powder
1 teaspoon salt
½ teaspoon freshly ground black pepper
6 boneless, skinless chicken breasts
2 tablespoons vegetable oil

In a small mixing bowl, use a whisk to combine the yogurt, ground coriander seeds, garam masala, ground cumin, cayenne pepper, garlic powder, salt, and freshly ground black pepper.

Now, make several diagonal cuts (*about ¼ inch deep*) in each chicken breast and rub spice mixture into cuts, and all over chicken. Let the chicken marinate for 30 minutes.

Preheat broiler and line the broiler pan with foil.

Arrange chicken breasts on rack of broiler pan. Brush with vegetable oil, and broil for 10 minutes. Turn the chicken over, brush with vegetable oil, and broil until lightly browned and just cooked through, about 8 to 10 minutes more.

Chicken with Sun dried Tomatoes and Basil

¼ cup extra-virgin olive oil
3 boneless, skinless chicken breasts, *cut in half (crosswise)*
Salt and freshly ground black pepper, to taste
½ cup unbleached flour
1 cup dry white wine
½ cup sundried tomatoes, chopped
½ teaspoon chicken soup base
½ teaspoon basil
½ cup water
½ cup heavy cream

In a large heavy skillet, heat the olive oil over medium-high heat. Season the chicken breasts with salt and freshly ground black pepper, coat with flour, and cook for 2 to 3 minutes per side, or until golden brown. Remove from skillet and set aside.

Add the white wine to the skillet and (*over medium heat*) deglaze the pan, using a spatula or wooden spoon to scrape the browned bits. Add the sundried tomatoes, and cook for approximately 2 to 3 minutes, allowing the wine to reduce until almost dry.

Now, add the chicken soup base, basil, water, heavy cream, and chicken breast; and cook for an additional 2 to 3 minutes.

Baked Chicken & Rice

3 tablespoons extra-virgin olive oil
2 medium onions, sliced
2 medium celery stalks (*with leaves*), finely chopped
2 medium carrots, thinly sliced
3 cloves garlic, minced
½ tablespoon parsley
½ teaspoon basil
½ teaspoon marjoram
1½ teaspoons cumin
½ teaspoon poultry seasoning
Salt and freshly ground black pepper, to taste
3 cups long-grain white rice
6 cups chicken broth
1 small, whole chicken, cut into pieces

Preheat oven to 400 degrees F.

In a large heavy skillet, heat olive oil over medium-high heat. Sauté onions, celery, carrots, garlic, parsley, basil, marjoram, cumin, poultry seasoning, salt, and pepper about 5 minutes. Add rice, and cook for about 1 minute more (stirring regularly), until translucent.

Transfer rice mixture to a greased 11 x 15 inch baking dish, and add chicken broth.

Rinse the chicken with cold water, pat it dry with a paper towel, and then cut it into pieces. *Do not remove the skin!* Season with salt and pepper, and place in baking dish.

Cover dish with foil, and bake for 1 hour, or until the chicken is cooked throughout and juices run clear. Remove foil, and bake for an additional 5 to 10 minutes, to allow the skin to brown.

Remove from oven, let stand approximately 10 minutes before serving.

Della's "Almost BBQ" Chicken

"Although Della's technically my first cousin, once removed, she's more like an aunt to me. Anyway, her 'Almost BBQ' Chicken is yet another recipe that my granduncle, John Kleindienst, shared with my mother via e-mail."

½ cup ketchup
¼ cup soy sauce
½ cup honey
¼ teaspoon garlic powder
3 pounds boneless, skinless, chicken breasts
Salt and freshly ground black pepper, to taste

Preheat oven to 450 degrees F.

To prepare the sauce, in a medium mixing bowl, use a whisk to combine the ketchup, soy sauce, honey, and garlic powder. Set aside.

Season the chicken breast with salt and freshly ground black pepper. Then, place in a greased *9 x 13 inch baking dish*, cover, and bake for 25 minutes. Drain the excess fat, and cut the chicken into bite-sized pieces.

Now, place the chicken in a greased *9 x 9 inch baking dish*, pour the sauce over top, and bake for an additional 10 to 15 minutes, or until the sauce is incorporated.

Fried Chicken

"Although sour cream isn't a typical marinade, it does a terrific job tenderizing meat. In fact, my great-grandmother made the best fried chicken I've ever had."

Sour Cream Marinade:

¾ cup sour cream
¼ teaspoon paprika
½ cup milk
1 clove garlic, minced
Salt and freshly ground black pepper, to taste

In a large mixing bowl, combine sour cream, paprika, milk, and garlic. Liberally season each piece of chicken with salt and freshly ground black pepper. Then, place chicken in mixing bowl, cover with plastic wrap, and refrigerate overnight.

Breading:

1 medium, whole chicken, cut into pieces
2 cups unbleached flour
3 eggs, beaten (*add a little milk if necessary*)
3 cups plain bread crumbs
Vegetable oil for frying

Place flour, eggs, and bread crumbs in 3 separate bowls. Then, coat each piece of chicken with flour, dip in egg wash, and thoroughly cover with bread crumbs.

Pour vegetable oil into a large skillet, no more than halfway up the sides.

Heat oil over medium flame for about 5 minutes, and cook 3 or 4 pieces of chicken at a time for 6 to 8 minutes on each side*, or until golden brown. Set aside, and let oil drain on a paper towel.

*Legs, thighs, and large pieces with bones may require additional time.

Jerk Chicken with Rice & Peas

"This well-liked Jamaican dish is made with chicken, rice, and coconut milk. Jamaicans typically refer to beans as 'peas,' kidney beans being the most commonly used."

2 tablespoons vegetable olive oil
2 medium onions, sliced
3 cloves garlic, minced
1 red bell pepper, chopped
2 teaspoons hot sauce
1 teaspoon parsley
½ teaspoon thyme
½ teaspoon poultry seasoning
Salt and freshly ground pepper
2½ cups long-grain white rice
1 (15 ounce) can red kidney beans, *drained and rinsed*
1 (13.5 ounce) can coconut milk
5 cups chicken broth
1 small, whole chicken
¼ cup walkerswood jerk seasoning

Rinse chicken with cold water, pat it dry with a paper towel, and cut the chicken into pieces. *Do not remove the skin!* Season with salt and pepper, and rub jerk seasoning all over the chicken. *Cover, and refrigerate overnight.*

Preheat oven to 400 degrees F.

In a large heavy skillet, heat vegetable oil over medium high heat. Sauté onions, garlic, red bell pepper, hot sauce, parsley, thyme, poultry seasoning, salt, and pepper until onions are tender, about 5 to 7 minutes. Add rice and kidney beans, and cook for about 1 minute more (stirring frequently), until rice is translucent.

Transfer rice mixture to a greased 9 x 13 inch baking dish, and add coconut milk and chicken broth.

Place the chicken in the baking dish, cover dish with foil, and bake for about 1 hour, or until the chicken is cooked throughout and juices run clear. Remove foil, and bake for an additional 5 to 10 minutes, to allow the skin to brown.

Remove from oven, let stand approximately 10 minutes before serving with Jamaican rum punch!

Roast Chicken & Vegetables

1 medium, whole chicken, cut into pieces
1 bunch fresh broccoli, cut into bite-sized florets
2 medium carrots, peeled and cut into thin 2 inch long strips
8 ounces mushrooms, quartered
½ teaspoon basil
1 teaspoon parsley
½ teaspoon thyme
½ teaspoon marjoram
Salt and freshly ground black pepper, to taste
1/3 cup extra-virgin olive oil

Preheat oven to 400 degrees F.

Rinse chicken with cold water, pat it dry with a paper towel, and then cut into pieces. Do not remove the skin! Season with salt and pepper, and place in a greased 9 x 13 inch baking dish.

In large mixing bowl, combine broccoli florets, carrots, mushrooms, basil, parsley, thyme, marjoram, salt, pepper, and olive oil. Mix well.

Distribute the vegetables around the perimeter of the baking dish, cover dish with foil, and bake for 1 hour, or until the chicken is cooked throughout and juices run clear. Remove foil, and bake for an additional 5 to 10 minutes, to allow the skin to brown.

Remove from oven, let stand approximately 15 minutes before serving.

Kathy's Classic Chili

"Occasionally, my mom would dish up her chili cincinnati-style, served over spaghetti and topped with shredded jack or white cheddar cheese. It's a great way to make use of leftover chili!"

1 pound ground beef
2 medium onions, chopped
2 cloves garlic, minced
1 red bell pepper, chopped
1 carrot, very thinly sliced
2 teaspoons hot sauce*
1 (16 ounce) can tomato sauce
1 (14.5 ounce) can diced tomatoes, *do not drain*
4 plum tomatoes, diced
½ cup ketchup
2 tablespoons brown sugar, *add more if desired*
1 tablespoon chili powder
2 teaspoons paprika
¼ teaspoon chipotle powder
2 (15 ounce) cans light red kidney beans, drained and rinsed
2 (15 ounce) cans dark red kidney beans, drained and rinsed
Salt and pepper, to taste

In a large saucepan, brown the ground beef over medium heat. Then, drain the excess fat, and add onions, garlic, red bell pepper, carrots, hot sauce, salt, and pepper, stirring occasionally. Cook until tender, about 5 to 7 minutes.

Add tomato sauce, diced tomatoes, plum tomatoes, ketchup, brown sugar, chili powder, paprika, and chipotle powder. Reduce the heat to medium low, and simmer for approximately 45 minutes. Add the kidney beans, and cook for an additional 15 minutes.

My mom used to grow red cayenne chili peppers. Usually, she'd let them dry, and add ¼ or ½ a chili pepper to her chili instead of using hot sauce. This recipe requires one whole red cayenne chili pepper, however.

Cockles and Mussels

"Inspired by the folk song 'Molly Malone.' Most people don't realize that cockles are basically small clams, and can be used interchangeably in cooking."

½ cup butter
2 medium onions, thinly sliced
4 cloves garlic, minced
1 (14.5 ounce) can diced tomatoes, drained
½ tablespoon parsley
2 teaspoons cilantro
½ teaspoon cayenne pepper
1 teaspoon salt
½ teaspoon freshly ground black pepper
2 cups white wine
2 pounds clams, scrubbed
2 pounds mussels, scrubbed and de-bearded
Juice of 1 lemon

In a large pot, heat butter over medium heat. Add the onions, garlic, diced tomatoes, parsley, cilantro, cayenne pepper, salt, and freshly ground black pepper. Cook for 3 to 5 minutes. Then, add the white wine, and bring to a boil over high heat.

Add clams and mussels, and reduce heat to medium low. Cover the pot, and let simmer for approximately 10 to 15 minutes, making sure all the shells have opened, discarding any shells that remain closed. Add the lemon juice, mix well, and serve.

Crab Cakes

"My family used to vacation at the Outer Banks of North Carolina, and this was undoubtedly one of my favorite regional dishes."

1 small onion, finely chopped
2 cloves garlic, minced
1 medium celery stalk (with leaves), finely chopped
2 tablespoons mayonnaise
1 teaspoon dijon mustard
1 egg
1 teaspoon old bay seasoning
Salt and freshly ground black pepper, to taste
2 (8 ounce) cans phillips crabmeat
¼ cup plain breadcrumbs
Vegetable oil, *for pan frying*

Drain crabmeat and lightly flake with a fork.

In a medium mixing bowl, combine the onion, garlic, celery, mayonnaise, dijon mustard, egg, old bay seasoning, salt, and freshly ground black pepper. Then, gently mix-in the crabmeat and bread crumbs.

Place bread crumbs in a small mixing bowl and heat vegetable oil in large skillet over medium flame. Now, use an ice cream scoop to portion each crab cake (*about 1/3 cup*). Thoroughly cover each cake with bread crumbs, and drop into hot vegetable oil. Using a metal spatula, press down lightly on the crab cakes, and cook for approximately 4 to 5 minutes on each side, or until golden brown. Let oil drain on paper towel, and serve with fresh coleslaw and hush puppies.

Hurricane

"One of the most popular drinks among tourists was the "Hurricane." It was my mom's favorite drink, and complements a meal such as this rather well. The recipe is as follows:"

1 ounce vodka
¼ ounce grenadine
1 ounce gin
1 ounce light rum
½ ounce dark rum
1 ounce amaretto
1 ounce triple sec
2 ounces orange juice
2 ounces grapefruit juice
2 ounces pineapple juice

Pour vodka, grenadine, gin, light rum, dark rum, amaretto, and triple sec into a 10 to 12 ounce glass that's approximately ¾ filled with ice. Add equal parts orange juice, grapefruit juice, and pineapple juice, and enjoy!

Singapore-Style Curry Noodles

"Absolutely, positively, my favorite 'Chinese' takeout."

Sauce Ingredients:
2 tablespoons vegetable oil
3 cloves garlic, minced
1 tablespoon brown sugar
¼ teaspoon ginger
2 tablespoons curry powder
1 teaspoon hot sauce, *optional*
¼ cup tamari soy sauce
1 cup chicken broth

Curry Noodles Ingredients:
1 (12 ounce) package rice vermicelli
2 tablespoons vegetable oil
1 pound pork tenderloin, cut into thin strips
1 medium onion, cut in half and thinly sliced
8 shiitake mushroom caps, sliced
2 medium celery stalks, very thinly sliced
1 red bell pepper, cut into thin 2 inch long strips
1 (8 ounce) can bean sprouts, rinsed and drained
8 green onions, chopped
3 cloves garlic, minced
¼ teaspoon ginger
1 pound frozen ready-to-eat shrimp, thawed
3 tablespoons oyster sauce

To prepare the sauce, in a medium saucepan, heat the vegetable oil over a medium flame. Add the garlic, brown sugar, ginger, curry powder, hot sauce, tamari soy sauce, and chicken broth. Mix well. Cover, and cook for 5 minutes. Then, remove from heat and set aside.

To prepare the noodles, bring a large pot of water to boil. Cook the vermicelli noodles according to package directions. Then, drain the noodles, rinse with cool water, and set aside. Place a wok over high heat, until hot. Coat the sides of the wok with vegetable oil, and brown the pork for approximately 5 minutes, stirring continuously. Add the onion, mushrooms, celery, red bell pepper, bean sprouts, green onions, garlic, and ginger; and cook until tender, about 3 minutes. Add the shrimp, and cook for an additional 2 minutes. Then, add the vermicelli noodles and oyster sauce, and cook 1 minute more. Toss noodles with sauce, transfer to a serving bowl, and serve immediately.

Dublin Coddle

"Made with sausage, bacon, onions, and potatoes, this traditional Irish dish is typically cooked in a slow oven and makes for a hearty meal, one that'll stick to your bones."

1 pound bratwurst sausage links
½ pound bacon scraps or end pieces, chopped
2 medium onions, thinly sliced
2 medium celery stalks (*with leaves*), finely chopped
3 medium carrots, thinly sliced
4 cloves garlic, minced
½ teaspoon marjoram
½ teaspoon sage
½ teaspoon rosemary
½ teaspoon thyme
Salt and freshly ground black pepper, to taste
3 pounds yukon gold or red potatoes, *sliced about ½ inch thick*
1½ cups dry white wine
½ bunch fresh parsley, chopped

Preheat oven to 325 degrees F.

In a heavy skillet, brown the sausage links on all sides, for about 5 minutes, using tongs to turn the links frequently. Remove from skillet, and set aside.

Sauté bacon scraps until crisp. Remove bacon, and drain on paper towel. Reserve approximately 2 tablespoons bacon fat, and discard the rest.

Add onions, celery, and carrots, and sauté in bacon fat for 2 to 3 minutes. Add garlic, marjoram, sage, rosemary, thyme, salt, and freshly ground black pepper. Cook for an additional 2 to 3 minutes.

Arrange the sliced potatoes in a greased 11 x 15 inch baking dish, slightly overlapping them if necessary. Add white wine, and top with sautéed vegetables, bacon scraps, and sausage links. Cover with foil, and bake for 60 minutes. Then, carefully remove foil, and bake for an additional 30 minutes.

Remove from oven, and let stand for 15 minutes before garnishing with fresh parsley, and serving with a crusty whole-grain bread and a good stout or porter.

Kathy's Egg Noodles with Potatoes, Creamy Cucumber Salad, and Croutons

Egg Noodles:
1 (12 ounce) package egg noodles
2 tablespoons extra-virgin olive oil

Cucumber Salad:
2 medium cucumbers
1 small onion, peeled and sliced
1 teaspoon salt
¼ teaspoon black pepper
1 tablespoon fresh dill, chopped
¾ cup sour cream

Potatoes:
8 small, red/new potatoes
1 teaspoon salt

Croutons:
4 slices whole-wheat bread, cut into ½ inch cubes
1 clove garlic, minced
3 tablespoons butter

To prepare the egg noodles, bring a large pot of water to boil. Cook egg noodles according to package directions. Drain noodles in colander, but *do not rinse*. Return noodles to pot, add olive oil and potatoes. Stir briefly, and set aside.

To prepare the potatoes, place the potatoes in a large sauce pan. Add salt, and enough cold water to cover the potatoes by an inch. Bring to a boil, lower the heat, and simmer until potatoes are tender. About 5 to 10 minutes. Cut the potatoes into quarters, and set aside.

To prepare the cucumber salad, peel and slice the cucumbers, and place them in a medium-sized mixing bowl. Add onion, and salt. Let stand for approximately 15 minutes, and drain any excess liquid. Add the black pepper, dill, and sour cream. Mix well, cover with plastic wrap, and refrigerate. *If you don't have any fresh dill, you can simply substitute a teaspoon of dried dill instead.*

To prepare the croutons, in a medium-sized frying pan, heat butter over medium heat. Add bread cubes and garlic, stirring periodically, about 5 to 10 minutes or until golden brown. If the bread should soak up all the butter, simply add more. Remove croutons from frying pan and set aside, in a small mixing bowl.

To serve, place egg noodles in a serving bowl. Top with cucumber salad, and then with croutons.

Eggplant & Beef Stew

2 medium eggplants, peeled and cut into ½ inch pieces
1 tablespoon vegetable oil
1 pound beef stew meat
2 tablespoons extra-virgin olive oil
1 medium onion, cut in half and thinly sliced
3 cloves garlic, minced
1 red bell pepper, cut into thin 2 inch long strips
1 teaspoon hot sauce, *optional*
1 tablespoon tomato paste
½ teaspoon parsley
Salt and freshly ground black pepper, to taste
2½ cups beef stock

Place the eggplant in a medium colander, sprinkle with salt, and let stand for about 1 hour. Drain thoroughly, and pat dry using a paper towel.

Lightly coat the inside of a large pot with vegetable oil. Heat over medium-high flame, and brown the beef on all sides, for about 5 minutes, stirring continuously. Remove from heat, and set aside.

In a heavy skillet, heat the olive oil over a medium-high flame. Add the eggplant, and cook for approximately 10 minutes. Then, add the onion, garlic, red bell pepper, hot sauce, tomato paste, parsley, salt, and freshly ground black pepper. Cook for an additional 3 to 5 minutes, or until tender.

Transfer eggplant mixture to pot, add beef stock, and bring to a boil. Cover, and cook over low flame for 1½ hours.

Eggplant Farfalle

2 tablespoons extra-virgin olive oil
1 medium onion, diced
1 red bell pepper, chopped
6 cloves garlic, minced
1 large eggplant, *peeled and sliced into ½ inch pieces*
2 tablespoons capers, drained and rinsed
¾ teaspoon tarragon
¾ teaspoon thyme
Salt and pepper, to taste
3 medium tomatoes, chopped
1 (14.5 ounce) can crushed tomatoes
½ cup dry red wine
2 teaspoons brown sugar
1 (16 ounce) package farfalle (bowtie pasta)

Bring a large pot of salted water to boil.

In a medium sauce pan, heat olive oil over medium high heat, add onion, red bell pepper, garlic, eggplant, capers, tarragon, thyme, salt and pepper. Cook for 10 to 12 minutes, or until most of the liquid has evaporated.

Add chopped tomatoes, crushed tomatoes, red wine, and brown sugar. Reduce heat to medium low and let simmer for 30 to 40 minutes, stirring occasionally.

Cook the farfalle according to package directions. Drain, but *do not rinse*. Return pasta to pot, add about a tablespoon of extra-virgin olive oil, stir briefly, and set aside.

To serve, place farfalle in a serving bowl. Top with eggplant mixture.

Eggplant Lasagna

1 large eggplant, peeled and thinly sliced
2 tablespoons extra-virgin olive oil
1 medium onion, chopped
3 cloves garlic, minced
8 ounces mushrooms, sliced
½ teaspoon basil
½ teaspoon oregano
½ teaspoon freshly ground black pepper
1 (12 ounce) package lasagna noodles
2 (16 ounce) cans crushed tomatoes
1 cup ricotta cheese
4 cups mozzarella cheese, shredded
1/2 cup freshly grated parmesan cheese

Preheat oven to 450 degrees F.

Line a shallow baking pan with aluminum foil. Arrange the eggplant in a single layer, and brush olive oil on both sides. Sprinkle with salt and freshly ground pepper. Bake until lightly browned and soft when pressed, about 15 to 20 minutes. Remove eggplant from oven, cover loosely with aluminum foil, and set aside.

In a large heavy skillet, heat 2 tablespoons extra-virgin olive oil over medium-high heat. Sauté the onion, garlic, mushrooms, basil, oregano, and freshly ground black pepper for 3 to 5 minutes, or until tender.

Cook the lasagna according to package directions. *You can also use no-boil lasagna noodles for this recipe. However, you'll probably have to add water to compensate for the moisture that the noodles will absorb.*

Preheat oven to 350 degrees F. Then, in a 15" x 11" greased baking dish, spread ¼ of the crushed tomatoes.

Reserve 2 cups of mozzarella cheese for topping.

Alternate layers of lasagna noodles, crushed tomatoes, and eggplant with mozzarella cheese, onion, garlic, mushrooms, ricotta cheese, and parmesan cheese. The last layer of lasagna noodles is topped with crushed tomatoes and reserved mozzarella cheese. Cover with parchment paper, then foil.

Bake for 30 to 40 minutes. Remove from oven, and carefully take off the foil and parchment paper. Let lasagna stand at least 5 minutes before serving.

Eggplant Moussaka

"Not long before Silvia and I were married, my mom became interested in learning how to make moussaka. It's popular in Bulgaria (where Silvia was born), and my mom wasn't all that familiar with it. Anyhow, she settled on the following recipe."

Moussaka:
2 medium eggplants, peeled and sliced about ¼ inch thick
Salt and freshly ground black pepper, to taste
Vegetable oil, for pan fyring
1 pound ground beef
2 medium onions, chopped
3 cloves garlic, minced
1 teaspoon parsley
1 tablespoon oregano or *chubritza*
1 (8 ounce) can crushed tomatoes, drained
2 tablespoons tomato paste
1 cup crumbled feta cheese
1 cup freshly grated parmesan cheese

Bechamel Sauce:
¼ cup butter
¼ cup unbleached flour
3 cups milk, *heated almost to boiling*
1 teaspoon salt
½ teaspoon nutmeg

To prepare the moussaka, season the eggplant with salt and freshly ground black pepper. Then, heat approximately ½ inch of vegetable oil in a heavy skillet. When the oil is hot, fry the eggplant until golden brown, about 2 to 3 minutes on each side. Let drain on paper towels, and discard remaining vegetable oil.

Now, brown the ground beef over medium heat. Drain the excess fat, and add the onions, garlic, parsley, and oregano. Cook until onion is tender, about 3 to 5 minutes. Add crushed tomatoes and tomato paste, and cook until most of the liquid has been absorbed; about 5 minutes.

Preheat the oven to 350 degrees F.

Line the bottom of a greased 9 x 13 inch baking dish with approximately 1/3 of the eggplant slices. Spread 1/3 of the sauce over top, sprinkle with 1/3 of the feta and parmesan cheese, and repeat to form layers. Bake for 1 hour, or until golden brown. Remove from oven, and let stand.

To prepare the bechamel sauce, in a medium saucepan, melt the butter over medium heat. Add the flour and whisk, continuously, until smooth. Cook for 5 to 7 minutes, or until lightly browned. Add hot milk to the butter mixture (*about 1 cup at a time*), whisking continuously, until very smooth. Then, bring to a boil, and cook for 10 minutes, stirring constantly. Remove from heat, season with salt and nutmeg, and set aside.

Place moussaka in serving bowls, topped with a generous portion of bechamel sauce. Serve immediately.

*Chubritza, or Summer Savory, plays an important role in Bulgarian cuisine.

Eggplant Parmesan

2 medium eggplants, peeled and sliced *about ¼ inch thick*
1 cup unbleached flour
2 eggs, beaten (add a little milk if necessary)
2 cups plain bread crumbs
½ cup vegetable oil
1 tablespoon olive oil
1 medium onion, cut in half and thinly sliced
3 cloves garlic, minced
½ teaspoon parsley
½ teaspoon basil
½ teaspoon oregano
Salt and freshly ground black pepper, to taste
2 (15 ounce) cans crushed tomatoes
1 tablespoon tomato paste
1 cup shredded mozzarella cheese
½ cup grated parmesan cheese

Place flour, eggs, and bread crumbs in 3 separate bowls. Coat each slice of eggplant with flour, dip in egg wash, and thoroughly cover with bread crumbs.

Heat vegetable oil in large skillet, over medium flame. Cook eggplant for approximately 2 to 3 minutes on each side, or until golden brown. Let oil drain on a paper towel.

Preheat oven to 350 degrees F.

In a separate heavy skillet, heat olive oil over medium-high heat. Sauté onion, garlic, parsley, basil, oregano, salt, and freshly ground black pepper; about 3 minutes. Add crushed tomatoes and tomato paste, and let simmer for approximately 5 minutes.

Pour approximately ½ the sauce into a greased 9 x 13 inch baking dish, and arrange the eggplant over top. Pour the remaining sauce on top, and add the mozzarella and parmesan cheeses. Cover with parchment paper and foil, and bake until heated throughout, about 20 minutes.

Carefully remove foil and parchment paper, and bake for an additional 15 minutes to allow the cheese to brown. Remove from oven, and let stand 5 minutes before serving.

Chinese Eggplant with Steamed Rice

4 cups water
2 cups long-grain white rice
2 tablespoons tamari soy sauce
3 tablespoons hoisin sauce
2 teaspoons plum sauce
1/2 cup dry white wine
1 cup chicken broth
2 tablespoons vegetable oil
2 medium chinese eggplants
1 clove garlic, minced
1 teaspoon ginger
2 teaspoons sesame seeds

In a medium saucepan, bring 4 cups water and 1 teaspoon salt to a boil. Add 2 cups long-grain white rice and return to a boil. Reduce heat to low, and simmer for 8 to 10 minutes. Cover, and cook until water is absorbed, about 15 minutes more. Remove pan from heat, and let stand.

In a small mixing bowl, combine soy sauce, hoisin sauce, plum sauce, dry white wine, and chicken broth. Mix well.

Peel eggplant. Cut lengthwise in quarters, then crosswise.

Place wok over high heat until hot. Coat sides of wok with vegetable oil. Add garlic, ginger, and eggplant. Cook until eggplant begins to brown, about 5 minutes.

Add sauce mixture and reduce heat to medium/low. Simmer for 10 to 15 minutes. Once sauce has been reduced to a thick glaze, garnish with sesame seeds and serve over long-grain white rice.

Enchilada Casserole

2 (15 ounce) can red kidney beans, drained and rinsed
1 ounce tequila
1 medium onion, chopped
1 *heaping* tablespoon chili powder
3 cloves garlic, minced
1½ teaspoons cumin
½ cup chicken broth
9 (6 inch) flour tortillas
1 (16 ounce) package frozen whole kernel corn, *thawed*
1 (4 ounce) can green chilies, chopped
2 (14 ounce) cans diced tomatoes, drained
3 cups white cheddar cheese, shredded
½ cup sour cream
¼ cup green onions, diced

Preheat oven to 350 degrees F.

Place kidney beans, tequila, onion, chili powder, garlic, cumin, and chicken broth in a food processor, and grind into a puree.

Cut the tortillas in half. Line a greased 11 x 7 baking dish with six tortilla halves, and spread half of the bean mixture on tortillas. Top with six more tortilla halves. Then, sprinkle corn, green chilies, and approximately half of the cheese on top.

Finally, top with the remaining six tortilla halves. Spread the remainder of the bean mixture and diced tomatoes on tortillas. Sprinkle with remaining cheese, cover tightly with foil, and bake for 40 to 50 minutes. *Serve topped with sour cream and green onions.*

Fettuccine Alfredo

1 (16 ounce) package fettuccine
1/3 cup butter
1 medium onion, minced
3 cloves garlic, minced
¼ cup dry white wine
1 cup heavy cream
1 cup finely grated parmesan cheese
Salt and freshly ground black pepper, to taste
1 small bunch fresh parsley, for garnish

Bring a large pot of water to boil. Cook the fettuccine according to package directions. Then, drain the noodles in colander, and rinse with cool water to stop the cooking process and help prevent sticking. Return to pot, and cover.

In a medium skillet, melt the butter over medium-high flame. Add the onion and garlic, and sauté until tender, about 3 to 5 minutes. Add the white wine and heavy cream, and bring to a boil. Cook until slightly reduced, about 5 minutes. Remove from the heat, and set aside.

Add the heavy cream mixture and grated parmesan cheese to the fettuccine, and season with salt and freshly ground black pepper. Top with fresh parsley, and serve.

Fish & Chips

"In Cleveland, fried walleye and lake perch (rather than cod or haddock) used to be a cheap, but popular food among the working class Irish. That's not the case anymore, however, since walleye and lake perch can be a bit pricey these days."

3 large russet potatoes, *peeled and cut lengthwise into ½ inch wide strips*
2 tablespoons olive oil
Vegetable oil, for pan frying
1 cup unbleached flour
1½ teaspoons baking powder
½ (12 ounce) bottle of beer, *preferably a good brown ale like Newcastle*
1 egg
4 to 6 cod or haddock fillets
½ cup unbleached flour, for dredging
1 (12 ounce) bottle malt vinegar
Salt and freshly ground black pepper, to taste

Preheat to 400 degrees F.

Place potato strips on baking sheet. Drizzle with olive oil, season with salt and freshly ground black pepper, and bake for 25 to 30 minutes. Turn chips over, and bake until golden brown, about 25 to 30 minutes longer. Allow chips to drain on paper towel.

Heat approximately 1½ inches of vegetable oil, in a heavy skillet, to 375 degrees F.

In a large mixing bowl, combine 1 cup flour, baking powder, salt, and freshly ground black pepper. Combine beer and egg, and blend into flour mixture. Whisk to form a smooth batter.

Rinse fish fillets, and pat dry with paper towel. Then, dredge fish in ½ cup flour, dip in batter, and allow excess to drip off.

Fry until golden brown, about 3 minutes on each side. Drain on paper towels before seasoning lightly with salt.

Serve with malt vinegar, tartar sauce, and a good dark brown ale (*or my personal favorite, a shandy, which can be made by adding ½ glass stout or porter to ½ glass of ginger ale*).

Granny's Battered Fish Fry

"My father and my great-grandfather used to enjoy fishing for walleye, smallmouth bass, and yellow perch in Lake Erie. They even brought home a freshwater sturgeon once. Anyway, my great-grandmother would typically use this batter recipe to fry the catch of the day."

Vegetable oil, for pan frying
½ cup unbleached flour
½ cup whole wheat flour
1 tablespoon brown sugar
1 teaspoon baking soda
½ teaspoon salt
½ teaspoon black pepper
½ - 1½ cups water
12 medium perch or walleye fillets
½ cup unbleached flour, for dredging

Heat approximately 1½ inches of vegetable oil in a heavy skillet to 495 degrees F.

In a large mixing bowl, combine flour, brown sugar, baking soda, salt, and pepper. Add ½ cup water at a time. Whisk, to make a smooth, thick, pancake-like batter.

Rinse fish fillets, and pat dry with paper towel. Then, dredge fish in ½ cup flour, dip in batter, and allow excess to drip off.

Fry until golden brown, about 3 minutes on each side. Drain on paper towels before serving with malt vinegar and tartar sauce.

Fish Pie

6 large yukon gold potatoes (*about 2 pounds*)
½ cup milk
½ cup + 2 tablespoons butter
½ teaspoon salt
¼ teaspoon freshly ground black pepper
2 tablespoons vegetable oil
2 slices bacon, finely chopped
1 medium onion, finely chopped
3 cloves garlic, minced
1 medium celery stalk (*with leaves*), finely chopped
1 small carrot, very thinly sliced
1 teaspoon parsley
½ teaspoon oregano
½ teaspoon basil
½ teaspoon ancho chile powder
1 cup heavy cream
1 cup grated jack or white cheddar cheese
1 (10 ounce) package frozen chopped spinach, *thawed and drained*
1 pound haddock or fresh cod fillets, cut into bite size pieces
Juice of 1 lemon
2 teaspoons paprika

Preheat the oven to 450 degrees F.

In a large pot, combine potatoes, 1 teaspoon salt, and just enough cold water to cover the potatoes. Bring to a boil over high heat. Then reduce the heat to medium low, and simmer until fork tender, about 45 minutes. Peel the potatoes. Mash the potatoes with a potato masher while they're still warm, gradually adding the milk, ½ cup butter, salt, and pepper. Set aside.

In a large heavy skillet, heat vegetable oil over medium-high heat. Add bacon, onion, garlic, celery, carrot, parsley, oregano, basil, and ancho chile powder. Sauté until tender, 7 to 9 minutes. Add heavy cream, and heat almost to boiling.

Season fish fillets with salt and pepper. Then, place the chopped spinach and fish in a 9 x 13 inch baking dish, and sprinkle with fresh lemon juice and cheese. Top with vegetable mixture, and spread mashed potatoes on top. Finally, sprinkle with paprika, top with 2 tablespoons butter, and bake for 25 to 30 minutes, or until golden brown.

Fish Tacos

"One of my wife, Silvia's specialties. If I'm not mistaken, these originated in Baja Mexico but have since become popular all over the world."

Cabbage Salad:
½ small green cabbage, cored and shredded
1 medium onion, cut in half and thinly sliced
4 medium carrots, peeled and shredded
Oil and vinegar, to taste
Salt and freshly ground black pepper, to taste

Guacamole:
2 large avocados, peeled and pitted
2 cloves garlic, minced
¼ cup sour cream
Zest of 1 lemon
Juice of 1 lemon

Beer Batter:
1 cup unbleached flour
1 teaspoon salt
1 teaspoon brown sugar
1 teaspoon baking powder
½ (12 ounce) bottle of beer
1 teaspoon hot sauce

Additional Ingredients:
Vegetable oil, for pan frying
1 pound fresh cod fillets, cut into bite size pieces
2 teaspoons smoked paprika
Salt and freshly ground black pepper, to taste
½ cup unbleached flour, *for dredging*
1 package (9 inch) whole-wheat wraps

To make the cabbage salad, in a large mixing bowl, combine cabbage, onion, and carrots. Toss with oil, vinegar, salt, and freshly ground black pepper. Set aside.

To make the guacamole, combine the avocados, garlic, sour cream, lemon zest, and lemon juice in a food processor and grind into a paste.

To make the beer batter, in a large mixing bowl, combine flour, salt, brown sugar, and baking powder. Use a whisk to gradually add the beer and hot sauce, forming a smooth batter.

Now, in a heavy skillet, heat vegetable oil over medium flame. Season the fish fillets with smoked paprika, salt, and pepper. Then, using a fork or tongs, dredge in ½ cup flour, dip in batter, and allow excess to drip off. Fry for 2 to 3 minutes on each side, or until golden brown. Then, let drain on paper towels.

Warm the whole-wheat wraps by placing them directly over the flame of a gas stove burner for about 10 to 15 seconds on each side. Prepare the fish taco immediately, by placing cabbage salad in the center of the wrap, adding 2 to 3 pieces of fish, and topping with guacamole. Fold the wrap in half, and serve immediately.

Goulash

"Goulash is a traditional Hungarian stew made of beef, onions, red peppers, and paprika. If I'm not mistaken, the dish was named after the herdsman that tended to the magyar oxen; the 'gulyas.'"

2 tablespoons vegetable oil
1½ pounds boneless veal stew meat, *cut into one-inch cubes*
2 medium onions, cut in half and thinly sliced
4 cloves garlic, minced
2 red bell peppers, cut into thin 2 inch long strips
2 medium carrots, very thinly sliced
1 teaspoon caraway seeds
2 teaspoons brown sugar
1½ tablespoons paprika
1 teaspoon basil
½ teaspoon oregano
2 teaspoons parsley
½ teaspoon sage
½ teaspoon marjoram
½ teaspoon thyme
1 teaspoon salt
½ teaspoon freshly ground black pepper
1 bay leaf
3 tablespoons tomato paste
2 tablespoons worcestershire sauce
1 tablespoon balsamic vinegar
3 cups beef or chicken broth
1 (16 ounce) package spätzle
1 (8 ounce) container sour cream
Cornstarch, *for thickening if desired**

Bring a large pot of water to boil. *You'll need it later to prepare the spätzle.*

In a separate, large pot, heat *1 tablespoon* vegetable oil over medium-high heat. Brown the meat on all sides, for about 5 minutes, stirring continuously. Remove meat from pot, and set aside.

Then, add 2 *tablespoons* vegetable oil and sauté the onion, garlic, red bell peppers, carrots, caraway seeds, and brown sugar until tender, about 5 minutes. Add the paprika, basil, oregano, parsley, sage, marjoram, thyme, salt, freshly ground black pepper, and bay leaf. Sauté 1 minute more, and add the tomato paste, worcestershire sauce, balsamic vinegar, and chicken broth.

Add the stew meat and bring to a boil. Then, reduce heat to medium low and cook until tender, about 45 minutes, stirring occasionally.

Meanwhile, prepare the spätzle according to package directions. Return noodles to pot and stir briefly. Place spätzle in a deep serving dish or bowl, top with goulash, and serve with a generous portion of sour cream.

**If sauce is too thin, mix a few tablespoons of cornstarch with enough water to form a paste. Bring sauce to a boil and add the paste, stirring vigorously until desired thickness.*

Italian Sausage

2 pounds Italian sausage
4 cloves garlic, minced
1 medium onion, sliced
2 green bell pepper, sliced
1 large tomato, cut into wedges
3 tablespoons olive oil
1 teaspoon hot sauce

In a large pot, bring 3 to 4 quarts water to a boil, add sausage and cook for 20 to 30 minutes. Remove sausage, drain, and set aside.

In a large heavy skillet, heat 2 tablespoons olive oil over medium high heat. Sauté garlic, pepper, hot sauce, tomato and onion until tender, about 5 to 10 minutes.

Place each piece of sausage on an individual serving plate. Top with peppers and tomatoes, and serve.

Kathy's Legendary Lasagna

"My mom's lasagna recipe has certainly evolved over the years, mainly for convenience. She used to can or freeze tomatoes, and make her own tomato sauce, but eventually began using Hunt's Spaghetti Sauce as a time saving measure. Similarly, my wife and I now typically use no-boil lasagna noodles."

2 (26.5 ounce) cans Hunt's Traditional Spaghetti Sauce
1 pound ground beef
3 cloves garlic, minced
Salt and freshly ground black pepper, to taste
24 ounces ricotta cheese
1¼ cups mozzarella cheese, shredded
2 (8 ounce) packages lasagna noodles

Preheat the oven to 350 degrees F.

In a large heavy skillet, brown the ground beef over medium heat. Then, drain the excess fat, and add garlic, salt, pepper, and 1 can of Hunt's Traditional Spaghetti Sauce. Then reduce the heat to low and let simmer.

Cook lasagna according to package directions. *You can also use no-boil lasagna noodles. However, you'll probably have to add about a cup of red wine to compensate for the moisture that the noodles will absorb.*

In a 13" x 9" greased baking dish, spread 1/3 of the spaghetti sauce.

Alternate layers of lasagna noodles, ground beef mixture, and ricotta cheese. The last layer of lasagna noodles should be topped with roughly 2/3 a can of spaghetti sauce and mozzarella cheese. Cover with parchment paper and foil.

Bake for 45 minutes. Then, carefully remove foil and parchment paper, and bake for an additional 15 minutes to allow the cheese to brown. Remove from oven, and let lasagna stand at least 15 minutes before serving.

Macaroni & Cheese

1 (16 ounce) package elbow macaroni
2 tablespoons vegetable oil
2 medium onions, cut in half and very thinly sliced
2 cloves garlic, minced
1 red bell pepper, cut into thin 2 inch long strips
1 teaspoon parsley
Salt and freshly ground black pepper, to taste
1 cup milk
10 ounces velveeta cheese, cut in ½ inch pieces
1 pound fully cooked bratwurst, cut into ½ inch pieces
½ (10 ounce) package frozen chopped spinach, *thawed and drained*
¼ cup pine nuts, *optional*
Smoked paprika, for garnish

Bring a large pot of water to boil. Cook the macaroni according to package directions. Then, using a colander, drain the noodles, return to pot, and cover.

In a medium saucepan, heat the vegetable oil over medium-high heat. Add the onions and sauté for 5 to 7 minutes. Then, add garlic, red bell pepper, parsley, salt, and freshly ground black pepper. Cook for an additional 3 to 5 minutes.

Add the milk and velveeta to the macaroni, and stir *constantly*, over medium heat, until the cheese melts. Now, add the onion mixture, bratwurst, spinach, and pine nuts. Sprinkle with smoked paprika, and serve immediately.

Meat Pie

"This savory pie contains ground beef, onions, and mushrooms. It's an old recipe my great-grandmother used to make."

Pie Filling Ingredients:
½ pound lean ground beef
1 medium onion, chopped
2 cloves garlic, minced
8 ounces mushrooms, sliced
¼ cup dry white wine
2 hard boiled eggs
2 tablespoons tomato paste
½ teaspoon paprika
Salt, and freshly ground black pepper, to taste

Pie Crust Ingredients:
2½ cups unbleached flour
1 teaspoon salt
¾ cup butter, softened
2/3 cup milk

To prepare the pie filling, place eggs in a medium saucepan and add cold water, at least an inch above the egg shells. Cover, and bring to a boil. As soon as the water comes to a full boil, remove from heat and let stand in hot water for 10 to 12 minutes. Drain water. Then, cover with cold water and ice cubes. Let stand in cold water until completely cooled. Peel and chop the eggs.

In a large skillet, brown the ground beef over medium heat. Then, drain any excess fat, and add onion, garlic, mushrooms, white wine, hard boiled eggs, tomato paste, paprika, salt, and freshly ground black pepper. Cook for 3 to 5 minutes. Set aside.

To prepare the pie crust, in a medium mixing bowl, combine the flour and salt. Cut-in butter using a pastry blender. Mixture should resemble coarse meal. Gradually add the milk, stirring all the while, until a dough forms.

Turn-out onto a floured work surface, and knead until smooth. Add just enough flour to keep the dough from sticking. Then, divide the dough into two equal parts, and roll into 2 (12 inch) circles, about 1/8 inch thick.

Preheat oven to 375 degrees F.

Use a metal spatula to carefully place one of the 12 inch circles onto a 9 inch pie pan, gently pressing the dough into the corners and using your fingertips to create a rim around sides of the pan. Now, spoon-in the ground beef mixture.

Gently place the second 12 inch circle on top. Pinch the dough together, and trim any excess (leaving about a ¾ inch overhang). Then, fold the dough under, and crimp the edges using your thumb and forefinger. Cut slits to allow steam to escape when baking.

Bake for 30 to 35 minutes, or until crust begins to brown. Let stand for 15 minutes before serving.

Kathy's Magnificent Meatloaf

"A family favorite of ours, this recipe calls for two pounds of ground beef, veal, and pork; which is commonly referred to as meatloaf mix and is available at most local butchers or supermarket meat departments. My mom used to add a layer of sliced, raw potatoes at the bottom of a large oval roasting pan before she formed the mixture into a loaf, covered it with tomato sauce, and baked it. There's no need for gravy. You wouldn't want to mask the flavor."

2 pounds ground beef, veal, and pork mixture
5 garlic cloves, minced
1 onion, chopped
½ cup italian bread crumbs
¼ cup rolled oats
1 teaspoon parsley
1 teaspoon oregano
1 teaspoon paprika
1 teaspoon worcestershire sauce
¼ cup ketchup
1 (10.75 ounce) can condensed cheddar cheese soup
1 egg
1 (10.75 ounce) can condensed tomato soup

Preheat oven to 375 degrees F.

In a large mixing bowl, combine *ground beef, veal, and pork*; garlic, onion, bread crumbs, oats, parsley, oregano, paprika, worcestershire sauce, ketchup, cheddar cheese soup, and egg. Mix the meatloaf with your hands, just enough to combine. *Do not over-mix!*

Place in a greased loaf pan, and pour the tomato soup over the meatloaf. Bake *uncovered* for 1 hour, or until the juices run clear. Remove the meat loaf from oven and let cool for approximately 15 minutes before serving.

Mushroom Risotto & Tomatoes

4 medium vine-ripened tomatoes
2 tablespoons extra-virgin olive oil
1 tablespoon cajun seasoning
1 tablespoon garlic, minced
1 small onion, chopped
16 ounces mushrooms, sliced
2 cups arborio rice
8 cups chicken broth
1 tablespoon butter
1 cup freshly grated parmesan cheese
½ cup mozzarella cheese, shredded
¼ cup sweet basil leaves, chopped

Preheat oven to 400 degrees F.

Remove tomato cores, and halve lengthwise. Coat each tomato with olive oil, and dust with cajun seasoning. Place on baking sheet, and bake for 15 to 20 minutes.

In a large saucepan, heat the olive oil over medium low heat. Sauté onions and garlic about 5 to 10 minutes. Then, add mushrooms and cook for 2 minutes. Add rice, and cook for about approximately 1 minute (stirring regularly), until translucent.

Add the chicken broth. Bring to a boil. Then, reduce to low heat and simmer for 8 to 10 minutes, stirring frequently. Cover and cook rice until water is absorbed, about 15 minutes more.

Top tomatoes with mozzarella cheese, and broil for 3 to 5 minutes, or until mozzarella cheese starts to bubble.

Remove rice from heat, and let stand covered for 10 minutes. Add butter and parmesan cheese, and mix well. Serve tomatoes over rice, and enjoy!

Paprikash

"Paprikash is similar to goulash since it's a meat stew that's made with paprika, and is typically served with spätzle or egg noodles. However, paprikash is made with chicken or pork, rather than beef. Paprikash characteristically includes sour cream as well."

1 large, whole chicken, cut into pieces
2 tablespoons extra-virgin olive oil
2 medium onions, thinly sliced
2 cloves garlic, minced
1 red bell pepper, sliced
1 medium carrot, peeled and sliced
1 (8 ounce) can tomato sauce
2 teaspoons hot sauce
1 tablespoon paprika
1 teaspoon basil
1 teaspoon oregano
1 teaspoon parsley
1 teaspoon salt
¼ teaspoon pepper
1 (14 ounce) can chicken broth
¼ cup sour cream

1 (16 ounce) package spätzle
¼ cup melted butter

Bring a large pot of water to boil. *You'll need it later to prepare the spätzle.*

Rinse the chicken with cold water and pat it dry with a paper towel. Remove the skin, and cut the chicken into pieces.

In a large pot, heat olive oil over medium high heat. Sauté onions, garlic, red bell pepper, carrot, tomato sauce, hot sauce, paprika, basil, oregano, parsley, salt, and pepper; about 5 minutes. Add chicken broth, and let simmer for 2 to 3 minutes longer.

Now, add the chicken, and bring to a boil over medium heat. Reduce heat to medium low, cover, and cook until the meat falls off the bone, about 1½ hours. Then, mix-in the sour cream, and let simmer, approximately 5 minutes.

Prepare spätzle according to package directions. Return noodles to pot, add melted butter, and stir briefly.

To serve, place spätzle in a deep serving dish or bowl. Top with chicken, then with sauce.

Pierogies

2 dozen frozen potato & cheddar pierogies
4 large onions, cut in half and thinly sliced
½ cup dry white wine
3 cloves garlic, minced
Salt and freshly ground black pepper, to taste
1 (16 ounce) container sour cream
Vegetable oil, for pan frying

Heat approximately 2 tablespoons of vegetable oil in a medium frying pan. Sauté the onions until soft and translucent, about 5 to 7 minutes. Add the white wine, and cook until the onions begin to caramelize. Then, add the garlic, salt, and freshly ground black pepper; and cook for an additional 2 to 3 minutes. Remove from heat, and set aside.

In a large skillet, heat approximately ½ inch of vegetable oil over a medium flame. Sauté the pierogies until browned, about 3 to 4 minutes on each side. Serve with caramelized onions and plenty of sour cream.

Polenta with Spinach & Feta Cheese

"This is a unique dish. It's part my mother's, and part my wife, Silvia's recipe. You see, my mom used to prepare polenta using the swiss chard she grew in her garden. Silvia, on the other hand, used to prepare polenta with feta cheese and pork. We eventually decided to use frozen spinach though, since it's available year-round."

½ pound bacon scraps or end pieces, chopped
1 (10 ounce) packages frozen chopped spinach, *thawed and drained*
3 cloves garlic, minced
1 teaspoon salt
2 cups milk
1½ cups yellow cornmeal
4½ cups boiling water
2 tablespoons parmesan cheese, grated
½ cup butter, softened
1 teaspoon smoked paprika
½ cup melted butter
1 cup feta cheese, crumbled

Sauté bacon scraps in heavy skillet, until crisp. Remove bacon, and set aside to drain on paper towel. Reserve approximately 1 tablespoon bacon fat, and discard the rest. Add spinach and garlic, and sauté over medium heat for 2 to 3 minutes.

In a large saucepan, combine salt and milk. Gradually whisk in cornmeal until blended. Then, whisk in boiling water. Bring to a boil over high heat. Then reduce the heat to medium low, and simmer, partially covered, for 20 minutes whisking continually. Remove from heat, and mix-in parmesan cheese and butter. Let stand for approximately 5 minutes. After polenta has thickened, transfer to a greased 9 x 13 inch baking dish.

Now, in a small mixing bowl, use a whisk to combine the smoked paprika and melted butter. Drizzle over top of polenta, while gently stirring. Sprinkle feta cheese and bacon over top, and serve immediately.

Pulled Pork

"Slow cookers are so practical but for some reason, we only use ours to make pulled pork. At any rate, this is Silvia's preferred method for preparing pulled pork."

1 (2 - 3 pound) center cut, boneless pork loin roast
Salt and freshly ground black pepper, to taste
1 large onion, sliced
3 cloves garlic, halved
1 (12 ounce) bottle of beer
1 (16 ounce) bottle barbecue sauce

Season the pork loin with salt and pepper, trimming any excess fat if necessary. Then, place onion, garlic, pork roast, and beer in a 3½ quart slow cooker. Cover, and cook on the 'Low' setting for 5 to 6 hours, or until a meat thermometer inserted into the thickest part of the roast reads 160 degrees F.

Remove pork roast, and set aside. When cool enough to handle, use a fork to pull the pork apart. Discard the remaining contents of the slow cooker, and return pulled pork to slow cooker. Mix-in the barbecue sauce, cover and cook on the 'High' setting for an additional 1 hour. Serve on whole wheat buns, or with baked beans and brown bread.

Potato Dumplings

"This is my great-grandmother's potato dumpling recipe. If you prefer, you can fill the dumplings with cheese, sauerkraut, smoked sausage, or even freshly made croutons. Dumplings make a tasty, filling meal, especially during the winter months."

Mashed Potatoes:
6 medium potatoes
1 teaspoon salt

Dumplings:
1 cup butter
1 small onion, finely grated
4 eggs
5 cups flour
2½ teaspoons baking powder
1½ teaspoons salt

To make the potatoes, in a large pot, combine potatoes, salt, and just enough cold water to cover the potatoes. Bring to a boil over high heat. Then reduce the heat to medium low, and simmer until fork tender, about 45 minutes.

To make the dumplings, peel the potatoes and mash with a potato masher. *While still hot*, add butter, and cream mashed potato/butter mixture. Add onion to mashed potatoes. Mix in eggs, flour, baking powder, and salt.

Bring a large pot of water to boil.

Divide into tablespoon-sized balls of dough, and knead the dough until smooth. *If you'd like to fill the dumplings with sauerkraut, for instance, shape each ball into a flat circle, place about 1 tablespoonful of sauerkraut or other filling in the center of each circle, and wrap the dough around the filling, carefully pinching the dough to close the seams.*

Drop into boiling water, cook for 10 to 12 minutes, and transfer to paper towel to drain.

Heat approximately 1 tablespoon of vegetable oil in a heavy skillet, over moderately high heat. Sauté dumplings for 2 to 3 minutes per side, or until golden brown.

Serve with butter and sour cream.

Red Beans & Rice

Red Beans Ingredients:
1 cup dried red beans
¾ cup vegetable oil
1 medium onion, chopped
3 cloves garlic, minced
1 medium celery stalk (with leaves), finely chopped
1½ teaspoons chicken soup base
½ teaspoon freshly ground black pepper
4 cups water

Rice Ingredients:
4 cups water
1 teaspoon salt
2 cups long-grain white rice

Place the beans in a medium saucepan. Add enough water to cover by approximately 2 inches, and soak overnight. Drain, rinse thoroughly, and set aside.

To prepare the beans, in a large pot, heat the vegetable oil over a medium-high flame. Sauté the onion, garlic, and celery until soft, about 3 to 5 minutes. Add the chicken soup base, freshly ground black pepper, and red beans, and cook for an additional 2 minutes, stirring regularly. Now, add the water to the rice mixture, and bring to a boil. Reduce to low heat and simmer, cover, and cook until the beans are tender, *about 3 to 4 hours*.

To prepare the rice, after approximately 3½ hours, bring 4 cups of water and 1 teaspoon of salt to a boil in a medium saucepan. Add 2 cups of long-grain white rice and return to a boil. Then, reduce heat to low and let simmer for 8 to 10 minutes. Cover, and cook until water is absorbed, about 15 minutes more. Remove pan from heat, and let stand for 15 minutes. *Serve red beans over cooked rice.*

Slovenian Rice Sausage & Sauerkraut

"Before he immigrated to the United States, my great-grandfather lived in Brezje, a small village near Bled, Slovenia, which later became part of Yugoslavia after World War I. He was exceptionally good at making fresh sausage, particularly rice sausage. Thankfully, it's still relatively easy to find in the Greater Cleveland area. For instance, Rudy's Quality Meats Inc. makes a similar rice sausage from ground pork, rice, onions, garlic, pork liver, sage, marjoram, and other spices."

1 (16 ounce) can of sauerkraut, drained and rinsed
½ (12 ounce) bottle of beer
1 medium onion, cut in half and thinly sliced
4 slices bacon, chopped
1 teaspoon caraway seeds
½ teaspoon paprika
1 pound Slovenian Rice Sausage

Preheat oven to 350 degrees F.

Place the sauerkraut, beer, onion, bacon, caraway seeds, paprika, and rice sausage in a greased 9 x 13 inch baking dish.

Cover, and bake for 40 to 45 minutes, or until heated throughout.*

*An even better approach would be to use a slow cooker. To do so, place combined ingredients in a 3½ quart slow cooker, cover, and cook on 'high' for approximately 4 hours.

Ricotta & Feta Spinach Pie

1 (10 ounce) package frozen chopped spinach, *thawed and drained*
1 tablespoon bread crumbs
3 eggs
½ cup heavy cream
1 cup ricotta cheese
1/3 cup crumbled feta cheese
2 cloves garlic, minced
½ teaspoon nutmeg
½ teaspoon salt
¼ teaspoon freshly ground black pepper

Preheat the oven to 350 degrees F.

Place spinach in a medium colander. Let stand for about 1 hour. Drain thoroughly, and pat dry using a paper towel.

Now, lightly coat a 9 inch pie pan with cooking spray, and sprinkle with bread crumbs.

In a medium mixing bowl, combine the eggs, heavy cream, ricotta cheese, feta cheese, garlic, nutmeg, salt, freshly ground black pepper, and spinach. Pour into the 9 inch pie pan, and bake for 30 to 45 minutes, or until the middle sets.

Roast Beef with Yorkshire Puddings

"Yorkshire Puddings are a lot like popovers, but are typically baked in roast beef drippings. They're most often served with roast beef, but can also be served with roast chicken or sausage."

1 (2 - 3 pound) top sirloin or rump roast
Salt and freshly ground black pepper, to taste
2 tablespoons vegetable oil
2 medium onions, quartered
4 cloves garlic, peeled and halved
2 medium stalks celery (*including celery leaves*)
2 whole carrots, peeled
½ teaspoon parsley
½ teaspoon sage
½ teaspoon rosemary
½ teaspoon thyme
1 tablespoon unbleached flour
2/3 cup dry red wine

Preheat oven to 450 degrees F.

In a large roasting pan, heat the vegetable oil over a medium-high flame. Season the beef with salt and pepper, and brown on all sides. Add the onions, garlic, celery and carrots around the perimeter of the pan. Add the parsley, sage, rosemary, and thyme; cover, and cook for 1½ hours. Remove and discard the onions, garlic, celery, and carrots. Also, reserve ½ cup pan drippings for later use.

Now, use a wooden spoon to skim off any excess fat. Pour the drippings from the roasting pan into a medium saucepan, and set to medium-high heat. Be sure to reserve the brown bits that typically remain on the bottom of the pan, and whisk the flour into the drippings, stirring continuously as it thickens to prevent lumps. Add the red wine, and bring to a simmer. Season with salt and pepper if necessary, and simmer for approximately 5 minutes. Then, strain to remove any small particles before serving.

Yorkshire Puddings

3 eggs
¾ cup milk
¾ cup unbleached flour
½ teaspoon salt
½ cup pan drippings

Preheat the oven to 450 degrees F.

In a medium mixing bowl, beat eggs and milk until light and foamy. Then, gradually add flour and salt. Mix just enough to blend well. Set aside.

Distribute the roast beef drippings in a greased muffin tin. Place the tin in the oven, and heat until smoking hot. Fill the muffin cups approximately 2/3 full with batter, and cook until light and airy, about 15 to 20 minutes.

White Bean & Tomato Rotini

2 tablespoons extra-virgin olive oil
2 cloves garlic, minced
6 medium tomatoes, diced
1 (15 ounce) can white beans, drained and rinsed
½ cup fresh basil leaves, chopped
1 (16 ounce) package rotini (spiral pasta)
½ cup freshly grated parmesan cheese
Salt, and freshly ground black pepper, to taste

Bring a large pot of salted water to boil.

In a large mixing bowl, combine olive oil, garlic, tomatoes, white beans, chopped basil leaves, salt, and freshly ground black pepper. Toss to coat well. Let stand at room temperature for at least 30 minutes to enhance flavor.

Cook the rotini according to package directions. Drain, but *do not rinse*. Return pasta to pot, add about a tablespoon of extra-virgin olive oil, stir briefly, and set aside.

To serve, place rotini in a serving bowl. Top with freshly grated parmesan cheese and white bean sauce.

Salmon Patties & Creamed Peas

"Most of the time my mom used canned salmon to make this recipe, but in the unlikely event we actually had leftover grilled salmon, she'd use that as well. My mom perfected this recipe while my father was stationed at Fort Bragg and they were living in Fayetteville, North Carolina."

Salmon Patties, Ingredients:

1 (16 ounce) can salmon, drained and flaked
4 slices stale whole-wheat bread, cut into ½ inch cubes
2 eggs
1 small onion, diced
1/4 cup chicken broth
The juice of 1 lemon
½ teaspoon freshly ground pepper

Creamed Peas, Ingredients:

2 tablespoons butter
2 tablespoons unbleached flour
½ teaspoon dill
½ teaspoon salt
¼ teaspoon freshly ground pepper
1 cup milk
1 (16 ounce) package frozen peas

Cook peas in boiling, salted water for 10 to 15 minutes. Drain well, and set aside. Heat a large skillet, with approximately 1 inch of vegetable oil, over a medium heat.

Combine salmon, bread cubes, eggs, diced onion, chicken broth, lemon juice, and freshly ground pepper. If the mixture's too wet, add more bread cubes.

Form into 3 inch patties, approximately 1 inch thick. Fry 3 to 4 minutes on each side, or until golden brown. Let oil drain on a paper towel.

In medium saucepan, melt butter. Add flour, dill, salt, and pepper. Stir constantly, until mixture is smooth and bubbly. Gradually add milk and chicken broth, stirring constantly until mixture comes to a boil and thickens.

Gently stir in peas and heat throughout. Serve over salmon patties.

Salmon with Dill Sauce

¼ cup sour cream
¼ cup mayonnaise
¼ seedless cucumber, peeled and grated
1 clove garlic, minced
1 teaspoon dill
1 teaspoon lemon juice
Salt and freshly ground black pepper, to taste
4 medium, skinless salmon fillets
1 tablespoon extra-virgin olive oil

In a medium mixing bowl, combine sour cream, mayonnaise, cucumber, garlic, dill, lemon juice, salt, and freshly ground black pepper. Cover with plastic wrap and *refrigerate for at least 1 hour*.

Preheat gas grill burners on high, covered for 10 minutes. Then, reduce heat to medium. Coat grill with non-stick cooking spray.

Brush salmon with extra-virgin olive oil and season with salt and freshly ground black pepper. Grill for 5 to 6 minutes, turning fillets halfway through. Serve salmon topped with dill sauce.

Sauerbraten

"Swabian Sauerbraten is typically marinated in water, vinegar, salt, and a variety of spices. Although it's traditionally served with spätzle, my mom always served it with red cabbage."

2 pounds rump roast
1 cup water
1¼ cups dry red wine
¾ cups red wine vinegar
2 medium onions, quartered
3 medium celery stalks (*with leaves*), finely chopped
1 tablespoon salt
1 tablespoons brown sugar
½ tablespoon mustard seeds
¼ teaspoon nutmeg
1 teaspoon whole cloves
1 teaspoon crushed peppercorns
2 sprigs fresh parsley
1 bay leaf
1 tablespoon butter
½ teaspoon corn starch

In a large mixing bowl, combine water, red wine, red wine vinegar, onions, celery, salt, brown sugar, mustard seeds, nutmeg, whole cloves, crushed peppercorns, parsley, and bay leaves. Add rump roast, cover, and let marinate in refrigerator for 4 days, turning occasionally.

On the fifth day, remove the roast from the marinade, and pat dry with paper towel (*reserve the marinade*). Generously season the rump roast with salt and pepper.

In a large pot, heat butter over medium high heat. Add the meat and brown on all sides; about 5 minutes, stirring all the while.

Add the reserved marinade, reduce the heat to medium low, and simmer covered, for 3½ to 4 hours, or until the roast is tender. Transfer to a cutting board, strain the marinade, and skim off any excess fat.

Transfer ½ cup of the marinade to a medium saucepan, bring to a boil, and stir in the corn starch and the remaining marinade, a little at a time, stirring continuously. Bring to a boil, and continue stirring until thickened. Add salt and pepper, to taste. Serve with red cabbage.

Seafood Gumbo

4 cups water
2 cups long-grain white rice
¾ cup vegetable oil
¾ cup unbleached flour
1 medium onion, cut in half and very thinly sliced
1 medium red bell pepper, cut into thin 2-inch long strips
1 medium celery stalk, thinly sliced
1 teaspoon paprika
1 teaspoon cayenne pepper
1 teaspoon garlic powder
1½ teaspoons salt
½ teaspoon freshly ground black pepper
½ teaspoon oregano
½ teaspoon thyme
3 bay leaves
2 quarts (8 cups) vegetable stock
1 pound cod, haddock, or halibut, *cut into bite sized pieces*
1 pound frozen ready-to-eat shrimp, *thawed*
2 (8 ounce) cans phillips crabmeat
1 (10 ounce) can whole baby clams
1 small bunch fresh parsley, chopped
Cornstarch, *for thickening if desired**

In a medium saucepan, bring 4 cups water and 1 teaspoon salt to a boil. Add 2 cups long-grain white rice and cook, stirring repeatedly, until water returns to a boil. Reduce to low heat and simmer for 8 to 10 minutes. Cover pan, and cook rice until water is absorbed, about 15 minutes more. Remove pan from heat, and let stand.

Heat the vegetable oil in a large pot, over medium-high heat. Whisk in the flour, and stir continuously for about 15 minutes, to form a dark brown roux. Add the onion, red bell pepper, celery, paprika, cayenne pepper, garlic powder, salt, freshly ground black pepper, oregano, thyme, and bay leaves. Cook for approximately 12 minutes. Then, add the vegetable stock and let simmer for 1 hour, stirring occasionally.

Add the fish pieces and cook for an additional 30 minutes. Then, add the shrimp, crabmeat, clams, and parsley and cook for another 3 to 5 minutes. Remove from heat, and add the cornstarch if necessary. To serve, place the gumbo in a bowl, and add a generous portion of rice in the center of the gumbo.

*If sauce is too thin, mix a few tablespoons of cornstarch with enough water to form a paste. Bring sauce to a boil and add the paste, stirring vigorously until desired thickness.

Shepherd's Pie

"I suppose a better name for this dish would be 'Cottage Pie.' 'Shepherd's Pie' is typically made with lamb, but lamb's kind of expensive, and I never did care for it very much anyway."

5 pounds yukon gold potatoes
½ cup milk
½ cup butter
½ teaspoon salt
¼ teaspoon freshly ground black pepper
2 pounds lean ground beef
2 medium onions chopped
3 cloves garlic, minced
2 medium celery stalks (*with leaves*), finely chopped
3 medium carrots, *very* thinly sliced
1 tablespoon worcestershire sauce
½ teaspoon thyme
½ teaspoon rosemary
1 (8 ounce) package frozen peas, thawed
2 tablespoons unbleached flour
1 cup grated jack or white cheddar cheese

Preheat oven to 400 degrees F.

In a large pot, combine potatoes, 1 teaspoon salt, and just enough cold water to cover the potatoes. Bring to a boil over high heat. Then reduce the heat to medium low, and simmer until fork tender, about 45 minutes. Peel the potatoes. Mash the potatoes with a potato masher while they're still warm, gradually adding the milk, butter, salt, and pepper. Set aside.

In a large skillet, brown the ground beef over medium heat. Then, drain the excess fat, and add onions, garlic, celery, carrots, worcestershire sauce, thyme, and rosemary. Sauté over medium heat until tender; 5 to 7 minutes. Add the peas, stir-in the flour, and cook for an additional 3 minutes, stirring constantly.

Transfer ground beef mixture to a greased 11 x 15 inch baking dish. Spread mashed potatoes on top. Then, sprinkle grated cheese and paprika on top, and bake for 30 to 35 minutes, or until golden brown. Serve with onion gravy.

Onion Gravy:

1 medium onion, cut in half and thinly sliced
1 tablespoon vegetable oil
2 cloves garlic, minced
1½ tablespoons unbleached flour
1½ cups beef broth
1 tablespoon worcestershire sauce
¼ teaspoon freshly ground black pepper

To make the onion gravy, in a large skillet, heat vegetable oil over medium flame. Sauté onion and garlic until tender, about 7 to 9 minutes. Stir in flour. Then, add beef broth, worcestershire sauce, and freshly ground black pepper. Let simmer, stirring continuously, until gravy is thickened, approximately 8 to 10 minutes.

Spaghetti & Italian Sausage

"My great-grandmother used condensed tomato soup to make spaghetti sauce; most likely, to save money. My mom, on the other hand, liked to use Hunt's spaghetti sauce, mainly because the twenty-six ounce cans used to be so affordable. Just about any brand of tomato sauce or spaghetti sauce will do though."

1 (16 ounce) package spaghetti
1 pound Italian sausage
2 tablespoons butter
2 medium onions, thinly sliced
1 medium celery stalk (*with leaves*), finely chopped
1 red bell pepper, chopped
2 cloves garlic, minced
1 teaspoon oregano
Salt and freshly ground black pepper, to taste
1 (10.5 ounce) can condensed tomato soup
1 (14.5 ounce) can diced tomatoes
1 teaspoon lemon juice
½ cup grated parmesan cheese, *optional*

Bring a large pot of water to boil. Cook the spaghetti according to package directions. Then, drain the noodles in colander, and rinse with cool water to stop the cooking process and help prevent sticking. Return to pot, and cover.

In a separate pot, bring 3 to 4 quarts water to a boil, add Italian sausage, and cook for 20 to 30 minutes. Then, brown sausage in a medium skillet until crisp on all sides, turning once or twice; about 4 minutes. Remove sausage, and let stand for 15 minutes before cutting into ½ inch, bite sized pieces. Set aside.

In a medium saucepan, heat butter over medium-high heat. Add onions and celery, and sauté for 5 to 7 minutes. Then, add red bell pepper, garlic, oregano, salt, and freshly ground black pepper. Cook for an additional 3 to 5 minutes.

Add tomato soup, diced tomatoes, and lemon juice. Bring to boil. Then, reduce heat to medium-low and simmer, stirring occasionally, for about 20 minutes.

Toss spaghetti with sauce. Add sausage, transfer to a serving dish, top with grated parmesan cheese, and serve immediately.

Spaghetti & Meatballs

"'On top of spaghetti, all covered with cheese, I lost my poor meatball when somebody sneezed...' This is undoubtedly one of my dad's favorite dishes."

1 pound spaghetti, cooked according to package directions

Meatball Ingredients:
1½ pounds ground beef, veal, and pork mixture
1 small onion, minced
4 cloves garlic, minced
½ teaspoon crushed red pepper flakes
1 cup unseasoned bread crumbs
¼ cup seasoned bread crumbs
1 small bunch fresh parsley, chopped
¼ cup freshly grated parmesan cheese
Salt and freshly ground black pepper, to taste
2 eggs
¾ cup water
¼ cup vegetable oil, for pan frying

Sauce Ingredients:
2 tablespoons extra-virgin olive oil
1 medium onion, finely chopped
4 cloves garlic, minced
1 teaspoon parsley
½ teaspoon oregano
½ teaspoon basil
Salt and freshly ground black pepper, to taste
½ cup dry red wine
2 (28 ounce) can crushed tomatoes, or plum tomatoes in puree, chopped

To prepare the spaghetti, bring a large pot of water to boil. Cook the spaghetti according to package directions. Then, drain the noodles in colander, and rinse with cool water to stop the cooking process and help prevent sticking. Return to pot, and cover.

To prepare the meatballs, in a large mixing bowl, combine ground beef, veal, and pork; onion, garlic, crushed red pepper flakes, bread crumbs, parsley, grated parmesan cheese, salt, freshly ground black pepper, eggs, and water. Gently mix with your hands, just enough to combine. Then, shape mixture into 2 inch meatballs.

In a large skillet, heat the vegetable oil over medium-high heat. Then, reduce heat to medium-low, and brown the meatballs on all sides. Gently turn with a spatula, and cook for approximately about 10 to 12 minutes. Let drain on paper towels, and discard remaining vegetable oil.

To prepare the sauce, in a large skillet, heat the olive oil over medium-high heat. Add the onion, garlic, parsley, oregano, basil, salt, and freshly ground black pepper, and sauté for 5 to 7 minutes. Then, add the red wine, and crushed tomatoes. Cook until most of the liquid evaporates; an additional 3 to 5 minutes. Now, add the meatballs to the sauce. Cover, and let simmer on *low* heat for 25 to 30 minutes, or until the meatballs are cooked throughout. Serve meatballs on top of spaghetti, with freshly grated parmesan cheese.

Spanish Rice

"When we were kids, my mom used Mason jars to preserve tomatoes. So, she'd use her own stewed tomatoes to make Spanish Rice. Since we don't can or freeze our own tomatoes, we simply use a can of diced tomatoes instead."

1 pound lean ground beef
½ teaspoon oregano
½ teaspoon parsley
¼ teaspoon chipotle powder
2 teaspoons hot sauce
Salt and Pepper to taste
1½ teaspoons chicken soup base
1 medium onion, chopped
2 cloves garlic, minced
1 red bell pepper, chopped
2 cups long-grain, white rice
1 (14.5 ounce) can diced tomatoes, drained (reserve juice)
3 ¾ cups water (in addition to approximately ¼ cup reserved juice)
1½ cups grated jack or white cheddar cheese

In a large pot, brown the ground beef over medium heat. Then, drain the excess fat, and add onion, garlic, red bell pepper, oregano, parsley, chipotle powder, hot sauce, salt, and pepper; stirring all the while. Cook until tender.

Add rice, and cook for approximately 1 minute (*stirring regularly*), until translucent.

Drain the juice from the tomatoes into a liquid measuring cup. Then, fill the can with water, and add enough to equal 4 cups of liquid. Add the liquid and diced tomatoes to the rice mixture, and bring to a boil.

Reduce to low heat and simmer for 8 to 10 minutes, stirring repeatedly. Cover and cook rice until water is absorbed, about 15 minutes more.

Remove from heat, and let stand covered for 5 minutes. Fluff with a fork and serve. Top with grated jack or white cheddar cheese.

Stuffed Cabbage

1 large head of cabbage
½ pound ground beef
½ pound ground pork
1 cup long-grain white rice
1 medium onion, finely chopped
2 cloves garlic, minced
1 tablespoon parsley
1 teaspoon paprika
1 teaspoon cumin
Salt and freshly ground pepper, to taste
1 egg
2 tablespoons extra-virgin olive oil
1 large onion, chopped
4 cloves garlic, minced
1 teaspoon freshly ground black pepper
1 tablespoon smoked paprika
2 teaspoons hot sauce
1 (14 ounce) can tomato sauce
2 cups chicken broth

In a medium saucepan, bring 2 cups water and 1 teaspoon salt to boil over medium-high heat. Add rice, stir, and reduce to low heat. Cover and cook for about 10 minutes. Set aside to cool.

Fill a large pot with approximately 4 quarts of water, and bring to a boil over high heat. Place the whole head of cabbage in the pot, reduce the heat to medium-low and simmer, partially covered, until the leaves begin to separate. Once you're able to remove 6 to 8 cabbage leaves, return the leaves to the pot, and cook them for an additional 3 to 5 minutes. Drain water, and carefully remove the thick, tough part of the stem.

Preheat oven to 325 degrees F. In a medium mixing bowl, combine ground beef, ground pork, cooked rice, onion, garlic, parsley, paprika, cumin, salt, pepper, and egg. Mix well, and form ¼ cup sized servings. Place ¼ cup stuffing in the middle of each cabbage leaf. Then, tightly roll the cabbage leaf from bottom to the top, while folding-in the sides.

In a large heavy skillet, heat the olive oil over medium high heat. Sauté onion, garlic, salt, and freshly ground black pepper, about 5 to 10 minutes. Then, add the paprika, hot sauce, tomato sauce, and chicken broth. Simmer 2 to 3 minutes longer.

Grate the remaining cabbage, and spread it on the bottom of a large casserole dish. Place each stuffed cabbage, with its seam facing downward, on top of the shredded cabbage. Generously cover with sauce, and bake covered for 1 hour. Add more liquid if necessary.

Uncover, *bake for another hour*, and serve with a generous portion of sour cream.

Stuffed Peppers

"Many Donauschwäbische recipes, such as this stuffed peppers recipe, were influenced by the various neighboring regions governed by the Austro-Hungarian Empire."

2 tablespoons butter
1 medium onion, chopped
1 clove garlic, minced
2 (15 ounce) cans crushed tomatoes
2 tablespoons tomato paste
2 teaspoons hot sauce
1 tablespoon brown sugar
½ cup water
1 teaspoon salt
¼ teaspoon pepper
1 cup long-grain white rice
1 slice crusty bread
½ pound lean ground beef
1 bunch fresh, finely chopped parsley
½ teaspoon paprika
3 large red bell peppers

To prepare the sauce, in a large saucepan, melt butter over medium heat. Sauté ½ onion, and garlic, then add crushed tomatoes, tomato paste, hot sauce, brown sugar, water, salt, and pepper. Bring to a boil, cover, and cook over low heat for 15 minutes.

To prepare the rice, in a separate pan, bring 2 cups water and 1 teaspoon salt to boil over medium-high heat. Add rice, stir, and reduce to low heat. Cover and cook for about 10 minutes, or until the rice absorbs most of the water.

To prepare the stuffing, soak bread in a little milk or water, and immediately wring it out. Then, mash it with a fork. In a medium mixing bowl, combine bread, ½ onion, ground beef, parsley, paprika, ½ teaspoon salt, and ¼ teaspoon pepper. Add rice and mix well.

Now, cut peppers in half (*lengthwise*) and remove seeds. Stuff peppers with mixture, and place in above-mentioned, large sauce pan. Place a plate, just smaller than the circumference of the saucepan, over the peppers to keep them from floating to the top.

Cover and simmer, adding water if the sauce becomes too thick. If the sauce is too thin, add some flour and cook uncovered, stirring continuously until thickened.

Cook over medium heat for 45 to 60 minutes, or until peppers are tender. Spoon remaining sauce over peppers, and serve with a generous portion of sour cream.

Three Beans & Rice

2 tablespoons extra-virgin olive oil
1 medium onion, chopped
3 cloves garlic, minced
2 teaspoons parsley
1 teaspoon ancho chili powder
1 teaspoon hot sauce, *optional*
Salt and pepper to taste
2 cups long-grain, white rice
3½ cups chicken broth
1 (15 ounce) can red kidney beans, drained and rinsed
1 (15 ounce) can garbanzo beans, drained and rinsed
1 (15 ounce) can black beans, drained and rinsed
1 (14.5 ounce) can stewed tomatoes, quartered
1 (4 ounce) can green chilies, chopped
1 (10 ounce) package frozen green peas, thawed
½ cup spanish pimento-stuffed olives, drained and sliced

Preheat oven to 375 degrees F.

In a five quart dutch oven, heat extra-virgin olive oil over medium high heat. Cook onion until tender, about 3 to 5 minutes, stirring occasionally. Add garlic, parsley, ancho chili powder, hot sauce, salt, pepper, and rice. Cook for about 1 minute more (*stirring continuously*), until rice grains are translucent.

Add the kidney beans, garbanzo beans, black beans, stewed tomatoes, green chilies, and chicken broth. Bring to a boil over high heat. Then, bake for 45 minutes.

Add peas and olives, return to oven, and bake until heated throughout (about 15 minutes more).

Three Sisters Stew

"In Native American mythology, beans, corn, and squash are known as of the 'three sisters;' hence the name of this longstanding recipe. My mom's version is a little spicy, and she added ½ a bottle of beer. Not sure why, but this is undoubtedly one of my favorites."

Stew Ingredients:

½ cup dried pinto beans
½ cup dried baby lima beans
½ cup dried great northern beans
½ cup dried black beans
1 tablespoon vegetable oil
1 medium onion, chopped
3 cloves garlic, minced
1 red bell pepper, chopped
1 carrot, very thinly sliced
1 jalapeno pepper, *seeded and chopped*
2 teaspoons chili powder

1 teaspoon paprika
1 teaspoon ground cumin
1/8 teaspoon cayenne pepper
1/8 teaspoon chipotle powder
½ teaspoon freshly ground black pepper
1 (14.5 ounce) can diced tomatoes, *with juice*
½ (12 ounce) bottle of beer
2 quarts chicken broth
2 cups frozen whole kernel corn, *thawed and drained*
1 medium zucchini, thinly sliced
1 medium yellow summer squash, thinly sliced

Dumpling Ingredients:

1 egg, *lightly beaten*
1/3 cup milk
1 tablespoon melted butter
½ cup yellow cornmeal
½ cup unbleached flour
2 teaspoons baking powder
½ teaspoon salt
½ cup frozen whole kernel corn, *thawed and drained*

Place the beans in separate bowls. Add enough water to cover by approximately 2 inches, and soak overnight. Drain, rinse thoroughly, and set aside. Now, to prepare the stew, in a large pot, heat the vegetable oil over a medium-high flame. Sauté the onion, garlic, red bell pepper, carrot, and jalapeno pepper until soft, about 3 to 5 minutes. Add the chili powder, paprika, ground cumin, cayenne pepper, chipotle powder, and freshly ground black pepper; and cook for an additional 3 minutes. Then, add the diced tomatoes and beer, and let simmer for 15 minutes. Add the chicken broth and beans, and bring to a boil. Reduce the heat, and let simmer until the beans are tender, approximately 1½ to 2 hours. Add the corn, zucchini, and yellow summer squash, and cook for an additional 10 minutes. Serve with Dumplings.

To prepare the dumplings, in a medium mixing bowl, combine the egg, milk, and melted butter. In a separate mixing bowl, use a whisk to combine the cornmeal, flour, baking powder, and salt. Add to the egg mixture, and mix just enough to blend well. Then, gently fold in the corn, and drop the batter (*about a tablespoon at a time*) into the simmering stew. Cover, and cook about 15 to 20 minutes, or until a toothpick inserted into the center of the dumplings is clean when removed. Serve immediately.

Baked Tilapia

"This was actually one of my mom's favorite ways to prepare catfish, but it's an ideal recipe for tilapia as well. It's tender and moist...the best baked fish I've ever had."

¼ cup butter
1 medium onion, chopped
3 cloves garlic, minced
1 medium red bell pepper, chopped
1 medium celery stalk (*with leaves*), finely chopped
1 teaspoon parsley
2 tablespoons dry white wine
½ teaspoon hot sauce
1 pound boneless, skinless tilapia fillets
Salt and freshly ground black pepper, to taste
Juice of one lemon

Preheat oven to 350 degrees F. Then, rinse the tilapia with cold water and pat it dry with a paper towel.

In a large heavy skillet, melt the butter over medium-high heat. Sauté the onion, garlic, red bell pepper, celery, and parsley for 3 to 5 minutes. Then, add the wine and hot sauce, and cook for 1 minute more.

Season the tilapia with salt and pepper, and place the fillets in a 9 x 13 inch baking dish. Add the fresh lemon juice, and spoon the sautéed vegetables over the fish. Bake for 20 to 30 minutes, or until the catfish flakes easily with a fork.

Tuna Casserole

"This is my great-grandmother's tuna casserole recipe. It's ideal for potlucks and family gatherings, and can be served in the ceramic pottery or casserole dish it's prepared in."

1 (12 ounce) package egg noodles
2 tablespoons extra-virgin olive oil
1 medium onion, chopped
2 cloves garlic, minced
1 medium celery stalk, finely chopped
1 carrot, very thinly sliced
1 teaspoon oregano
1 teaspoon basil
Salt and freshly ground black pepper, to taste
2 (6 ounce) cans albacore tuna, drained and flaked
2 (10¾ ounces) cans cream of mushroom soup
1 cup mayonnaise
2 cups milk
1 cup mushrooms, sliced
1 cup bread crumbs
¼ cup butter, melted

Bring a large pot of water to boil. Cook egg noodles according to package directions. Drain noodles in colander, *but do not rinse.* Return noodles to pot, drizzle with olive oil, stir briefly, and set aside.

Preheat oven to 350 degrees F.

In a large skillet, sauté onion, garlic, celery, carrot, oregano, basil, salt, and pepper in 1 tablespoon olive oil over medium-low heat until tender, about 3 to 5 minutes. Add tuna, cream of mushroom soup, mayonnaise, milk, and mushrooms. Cook for an additional 3 to 5 minutes.

In a small mixing bowl, combine bread crumbs and melted butter.

In a 9 x 13 inch greased baking dish, combine egg noodles and tuna mixture. Toss lightly, top with bread crumbs, and bake for 25 to 30 minutes or until golden brown.

Veal Parmesan

8 thin veal cutlets
1 cup unbleached flour
2 eggs, beaten (*add a little milk if necessary*)
2 cups plain bread crumbs
½ cup vegetable oil
1 tablespoon olive oil
1 medium onion, cut in half and thinly sliced
3 cloves garlic, minced
½ teaspoon parsley
½ teaspoon basil
½ teaspoon oregano
Salt and freshly ground black pepper, to taste
1 (15 ounce) can crushed tomatoes
1 tablespoon tomato paste
¾ cup shredded mozzarella cheese
¼ cup grated parmesan cheese

Pound the veal cutlets to approximately 1/8 inch thickness. Trim excess fat and gristle if necessary. Then, season the cutlets with salt and freshly ground black pepper.

Place flour, eggs, and bread crumbs in 3 separate bowls. Coat each veal cutlet with flour, dip in egg wash, and thoroughly cover with bread crumbs.

Heat vegetable oil in large skillet, over medium flame. Cook veal cutlets for approximately 2 to 3 minutes on each side, or until golden brown. Let oil drain on a paper towel.

Preheat oven to 350 degrees F.

In a separate heavy skillet, heat olive oil over medium-high heat. Sauté onion, garlic, parsley, basil, oregano, salt, and freshly ground black pepper; about 3 minutes. Add crushed tomatoes and tomato paste, and let simmer for approximately 5 minutes.

Pour approximately ½ the sauce into a greased 9 x 13 inch baking dish, and arrange the veal cutlets over top, slightly overlapping them if necessary. Pour the remaining sauce on top, and add the mozzarella and parmesan cheeses. Cover with parchment paper and foil, and bake until heated throughout, about 20 minutes.

Carefully remove foil and parchment paper, and bake for an additional 10 minutes to allow the cheese to brown. Remove from oven, and let stand 5 minutes before serving.

Vegetable Beef Casserole

"This is my mom's vegetable beef casserole recipe. Sometimes she'd leave out the potatoes, and serve it over egg noodles or with mashed potatoes."

1 tablespoon vegetable oil
1 pound beef stew meat, *cut into 1 inch pieces*
2 tablespoons butter
1 onion, cut in half and thinly sliced
1 carrot, very thinly sliced
1 medium eggplant, peeled and cut into ½ inch pieces
1 zucchini, cut into thin 2 inch long strips
½ pint cherry tomatoes, halved
1 red bell pepper, cut into thin 2 inch long strips
2 cloves garlic, minced
1 teaspoon oregano
Salt and freshly ground black pepper, to taste
3 pounds yukon gold or red potatoes, cut into ½ inch pieces
2½ cups beef stock

Using a paper towel, lightly coat the inside of a large pot with vegetable oil. Brown the beef on all sides over medium-high heat, for about 7 minutes, stirring continuously. Set aside.

In a heavy skillet, melt the butter over a medium-low flame. Sauté the onion, carrot, eggplant, and zucchini for about 10 minutes, or until tender. Add the cherry tomatoes, red bell pepper, garlic, oregano, salt, and freshly ground black pepper; and cook for an additional 3 minutes.

Now, add the mixed vegetables, potatoes, and beef stock to the pot, cover, and cook over medium heat for 30 minutes.

Vegetarian Chili

"This is my mom's vegetarian chili recipe, a favorite of mine. She always served this with freshly baked cornbread because she believed that the combination formed a complete protein; same with beans and rice, and baked beans with brown bread. I'm not sure if that's a myth or not, but it definitely made for a great meal!"

2 tablespoons vegetable oil
2 medium onions, chopped
1 red bell pepper, chopped
1 rib celery, chopped
2 cloves garlic, minced
2 tablespoons chili powder
2 teaspoons cumin
Salt and pepper, to taste
1 teaspoon hot sauce*
2 (14.5 ounce) cans diced tomatoes, *do not drain*
2 (15 ounce) cans red kidney beans, drained and rinsed

In a medium saucepan, heat vegetable oil over medium flame. Sauté onions, red bell pepper, celery, and garlic until tender, about 3 to 5 minutes. Add chili powder, cumin, salt, pepper, and hot sauce. Cook for 1 minute more. Add diced tomatoes and 1 can of red kidney beans.

Place the other can of kidney beans in a food processor, and grind into a paste. Stir into saucepan, cover. Then reduce heat to medium low, and let simmer for 30 minutes, adding water if needed.

*My mom used to grow red cayenne chili peppers. Usually, she'd let them dry and add ¼ or ½ a chili pepper to her chili instead of using hot sauce.

Vegetarian Lasagna

2 (16 ounce) cans crushed tomatoes
2 teaspoons oregano
2 teaspoons basil
Salt and freshly ground black pepper, to taste
3 cloves garlic, minced
2/3 cup red wine
1 cup water
2 eggs, beaten
24 ounces ricotta cheese
1/3 cup freshly grated parmesan cheese
2 (8 ounce) packages lasagna noodles
2 cups mozzarella cheese, shredded

Preheat the oven to 350 degrees F.

Cook lasagna according to package directions. You can also use no-boil lasagna noodles for this recipe. However, you'll probably have to add water to compensate for the moisture that the noodles will absorb.

In a medium mixing bowl, combine the crushed tomatoes, oregano, basil, salt, pepper, garlic, red wine, and water.

In a separate, medium mixing bowl, combine eggs, ricotta cheese, and parmesan cheese.

In a 15" x 11" greased baking dish, spread ¼ of the tomato sauce.

Reserve 1 cup of mozzarella cheese for topping.

Alternate layers of lasagna noodles, sauce, and cheese. The last layer of lasagna noodles is topped with tomato sauce and the reserved mozzarella cheese. Cover with parchment paper, then foil.

Bake for 1 hour. Remove from oven, and carefully take off the foil and parchment paper. Let lasagna stand at least 5 minutes before serving.

Wiener Schnitzel

"Schnitzel, the German word for cutlet, is typically thought of as thin, boneless slice of veal that's been breaded and fried. However, other types of schnitzel are common as well, including pork schnitzel (schweine schnitzel), chicken schnitzel (haehnchen schnitzel), and even turkey schnitzel (puten schnitzel)."

1 pound veal cutlet or other, tender cut such as the boneless shoulder
1 cup unbleached flour
2 eggs, beaten (add a little milk if necessary)
2 cups plain bread crumbs
½ cup vegetable oil
Salt and freshly ground black pepper, to taste

Pound the veal cutlets to approximately 1/8 inch thickness. Trim excess fat and gristle if necessary. Then, season the veal cutlets with salt and freshly ground black pepper.

Place flour, eggs, and bread crumbs in 3 separate bowls. Coat each veal cutlet with flour, dip in egg wash, and thoroughly cover with bread crumbs.

Heat vegetable oil in large skillet, over medium flame. Cook veal cutlets for approximately 2 to 3 minutes on each side, or until golden brown. Let oil drain on a paper towel.

Miscellaneous

Butter Tea

"Butter Tea, also known as Tibetan Tea, is made of black tea, butter, milk, and salt, and is normally served in bowls rather than cups. It's ideal on a cold winter's day. Rumor has it that Tibetans traditionally prepare Butter Tea with yak butter. Good luck finding that at the local farmer's market!"

1 cup water
1 tea bag (*preferably an oolong tea*)
¼ teaspoon salt
¼ cup milk
2 teaspoons butter

Using a kettle or teapot, bring freshly drawn water to boil, and brew tea for approximately 5 minutes. Add honey, milk, and butter. Stir until butter has completely dissolved, and serve immediately.

Chai Tea

"This typically strong, Indian black tea steeped with milk, honey, and various spices. Mulling spices usually include cinnamon, cloves, allspice, and nutmeg. They're convenient, and work well with this recipe. Though, you'll get even better results if you use spices that contain cardamom. Also, adding a few black peppercorns will produce a slightly hot/spicy flavor if desired."

2 cups water
2 assam or ceylon tea bags
1 cinnamon stick
1 teaspoon mulling spices
¼ teaspoon ginger
½ teaspoon black peppercorns (*optional*)
2½ cups milk
½ cup honey

In a small saucepan, combine water, tea bags, cinnamon stick, mulling spices, ginger, and if you prefer, peppercorns. Bring to a boil over high heat. Then, reduce to medium-low heat and simmer for 5 minutes.

Add milk. Return to boil, and let simmer for another 2 to 3 minutes. Strain, and discard the tea bags and spices. Add honey, and serve.

Custard Frosting

1 cup milk
5 tablespoons unbleached flour
1 cup butter
1 cup sugar
1 teaspoon vanilla extract

In a medium saucepan, heat milk and flour over medium flame until mixture thickens. Let cool.

In a medium mixing bowl, beat butter, sugar, and vanilla extract until light and fluffy. Gradually add milk and flour mixture, and beat until thick enough to spread.

Easy Fudge Icing

2 cups powdered sugar
½ cup cocoa powder
1 tablespoon melted butter
3 tablespoons hot, strong coffee

In a medium mixing bowl, use a whisk to combine the powdered sugar and cocoa powder. Add the melted butter and coffee (*a tablespoon at a time*), and beat until smooth.

Face Soap

"My great-grandmother, like most people at the time, used to make her own soap out of lye and lard. Her recipe was for 'face soap.' It's important to wear an apron, gloves, and safety goggles when making soap, since it can cause chemical burns."

1 (12 ounce) can lye
3 pints warm (*not hot*) water
5½ pounds clean lard
1 cup borax powder
1 cup ammonia
1 ounce oil of sassafras

In a large stainless steel* container, add lye to water. Let stand for two to three hours.

In a large pot, heat lard over low flame until fat melts and forms a uniform mixture.

In a separate stainless steel container, combine lard, borax powder, ammonia, and oil of sassafras. Pour the lard mixture into the lye mixture, and stir continuously for 20 to 30 minutes, until the lye has completely dissolved.

Pour mixture into plastic molds and let stand at room temperature for 24 hours.

*Do not use aluminum. It reacts with lye.

Hot Toddy

"Believed to cure the common cold; at the very least, a hot toddy is an ideal nightcap during the winter months."

1 cup water
1 assam or ceylon tea bag
1 tablespoon honey
Juice of ½ lemon
2 tablespoons dark rum

Using a kettle or teapot, bring freshly drawn water to boil and brew tea for approximately 5 minutes. Add honey, lemon juice, and rum. Stir until honey has completely dissolved, and serve immediately.

Kimmel

"Kimmel (Kümmel, in German) is a type of caraway schnapps that is relatively common in northern Germany. My great-grandmother believed that kimmel supported digestion; helped to relieve cramps and migraine headaches. Kimmel is best when served chilled. You can also add fennel seeds and cumin seeds if you prefer."

¾ cup sugar
¼ cup water
1½ tablespoons caraway seeds
¾ (750 ml) bottle of vodka

In a small saucepan, combine the sugar and water. Bring to a boil over medium-high heat. Once the sugar has completely dissolved, remove from heat and let cool to room temperature.

Using a funnel, add the caraway seeds to a *three-quarters-full* bottle of vodka. Then, add the syrup, cap the bottle, and turn it upside down a few times to completely dissolve the syrup.

Allow to steep at room temperature for 8 to 10 days. Then, strain the liquor, and place in the freezer for at least two hours before serving.

Lemon Cheese Filling

This filling can be used to make pastries such kolachky cookies, &c.

1 cup ricotta cheese
1/3 cup sugar
1 egg yolk
1 teaspoon lemon zest
½ teaspoon vanilla extract

Beat ricotta cheese, sugar, egg yolk, lemon zest, and vanilla extract in food processor until smooth and creamy.

Poppy Seed Filling

This is my mom's poppy seed filling recipe. It can be used in place of 1 (12 ounce) can poppy seed filling, to make all sorts of pastries including poppy seed squares, strudel, scones, kolachky cookies, coffee cake, custard pie, bundt cake, cheesecake, &c.

1 cup poppy seeds
¾ cup milk
1/3 cup honey
½ cup brown sugar
2 tablespoons butter
½ cup sun dried raisins, chopped *(optional)*
1 teaspoon vanilla extract
1 teaspoon lemon juice
1 teaspoon lemon zest
2 eggs, *slightly beaten*

In a small saucepan, combine poppy seeds, milk, honey, brown sugar, butter, and raisins. Bring to boil over medium heat. Reduce heat, and let simmer for approximately 15 to 20 minutes (*stirring frequently*), until most of the liquid is absorbed.

Remove from heat, and let stand 30 minutes. Then, add vanilla extract, lemon juice, and lemon zest. In a separate bowl, beat eggs, and slowly whisk into poppy seed mixture. *Refrigerate for at least 2 hours before using.*

Roasted Almonds

"There's nothing quite like the taste of freshly roasted almonds on a cold winter's night; the aroma and incredible roasted almond flavor…"

12 to 16 ounces raw almonds
1 tablespoon vegetable oil
1 teaspoon salt

Preheat oven to 325 degrees F.

In a medium mixing bowl, combine the almonds, vegetable oil, and salt. Toss gently, and transfer to a baking sheet with sides, or a rim about ½ inch high.

Roast the almonds until they brown evenly, about 20 minutes. *Stir occasionally.* Let cool to room temperature before serving.

Root Beer

"My great-grandfather made his own root beer. He kept it in the basement, along with his homemade wine. Other popular beverages among the Banater Schwaben include mulberry, rhubarb, and dandelion wine; fruit brandy or schnapps, kummel bier, coffee, and herbal tea."

1 cup brown sugar
¼ teaspoon active dry yeast
1 plastic (2 liter) bottle, *with cap*
1 tablespoon root beer extract
2 liters cold tap water

In a small mixing bowl, use a whisk to combine 1 cup brown sugar and ¼ teaspoon active dry yeast.

Then, using a funnel, transfer the sugar/yeast mixture to a plastic 2 liter bottle. Add the root beer extract and 1 liter of cold tap water.

Turn the bottle upside down a few times to help dissolve the sugar and add approximately 1 liter of cold tap water, leaving about an inch of head space at the top.

Cap the bottle, and once again, turn it upside down a few times to make sure the sugar has completely dissolved.

Store at room temperature for three or four days, or until the bottle is firm. *If the bottle is still somewhat elastic and yields when you press it, the yeast needs more time to ferment.*

Finally, refrigerate overnight, and be sure to *slowly release the pressure before serving*.

Royal Icing (No Egg Whites):

1½ cups powdered sugar
2¼ teaspoons meringue powder
1/8 teaspoon vanilla extract
2 tablespoons warm water

In a medium mixing bowl, use a whisk to combine the powdered sugar and meringue powder. Add the vanilla extract and water (*a little at a time*), and beat until stiff peaks form, about 5 to 7 minutes. If necessary, add more powdered sugar or water. *The icing must be used immediately because it hardens when exposed to air.* Cover with plastic wrap when not in use.

Tomato Sauce

"This is one of my mom's tomato sauce recipes. It's made with plum tomatoes, onion, garlic, parsley, and basil, and is ideal for pasta."

16 plum tomatoes, chopped
1 teaspoon salt
1 tablespoon extra-virgin olive oil
1 onion, cut in half and thinly sliced
3 cloves garlic, minced
½ teaspoon freshly ground pepper
½ teaspoon red pepper flakes
½ teaspoon brown sugar
½ cup fresh parsley, chopped
1 cup fresh basil leaves

In a strainer, combine the chopped tomatoes and salt. *Let stand for approximately 30 minutes.* Drain any excess liquid.

Now, in a heavy skillet, heat the olive oil over medium-high heat. Sauté the onion, garlic, freshly ground black pepper, red pepper flakes, and brown sugar. Cook over low heat until very soft, about 10 minutes.

Add the tomatoes, parsley, and basil, and increase heat to medium-high. Cook for 5 to 10 minutes, or until sauce begins to thicken.

Whipped Marshmallow Cream Frosting

1 cup sugar
6 tablespoons water
1 tablespoon plain gelatin
1/3 cup cold water
4 egg whites
1/8 teaspoon salt
1/8 teaspoon cream of tartar
1 cup powdered sugar
1 teaspoon flavoring

Boil sugar and 6 tablespoons water until sugar is dissolved. Soak gelatin in 1/3 cup water and dissolve in hot syrup. Let cool to room temperature. Then, beat egg whites, salt, and cream of tartar until stiff. Alternately add powdered sugar and gelatin. Mix-in vanilla extract, and chill until frosting stiffens slightly. Cover cake with frosting, and refrigerate for at least 4 hours before serving.

Muffins & Stuff

Apple Cinnamon Muffins

2 cups unbleached flour
1 tablespoon baking powder
½ teaspoon salt
1/3 cup brown sugar
1¼ teaspoons cinnamon, divided
¾ cup milk
1 egg
¼ cup butter, melted
1 cup apples, peeled, cored, and chopped
2 tablespoons granulated white sugar

Preheat oven to 400 degrees F.

Coat the inside of a muffin tin with butter or shortening, or use paper liners if you prefer.

In large mixing bowl, combine flour, baking powder, salt, brown sugar and 1 teaspoon cinnamon. Add milk, egg, and butter. Then, stir-in chopped apples. Mix just enough to blend well. *Do not over-mix!*

Fill greased muffin cups 2/3 full with batter. Mix remaining ¼ teaspoon cinnamon with 2 tablespoons granulated white sugar, and sprinkle over muffins.

Bake for 25 to 30 minutes, or until lightly browned.

Blueberry Muffins

"This is my great-grandmother's recipe for blueberry muffins; one of my grandmother's favorites. My grandmother used to grow her own blueberries as well, so fresh blueberries were readily available."

¼ cup butter, softened
½ cup sugar
1 egg
½ teaspoon vanilla extract
1 tablespoon baking powder
½ teaspoon salt
2 cups unbleached flour
1 cup milk
1 cup fresh blueberries

Preheat oven to 350 degrees F. Grease muffin cups, or use muffin liners if you prefer.

In a medium mixing bowl, beat butter and sugar until light and fluffy. Add egg and vanilla extract, and beat until well mixed. Then, gradually add baking powder, salt, flour, and milk (*a little at a time*). Fold in blueberries, and gently mix.

Fill greased muffin cups 2/3 full with batter, *sprinkle with coarse granulated sugar*, and bake for 12 to 15 minutes.

Bran Muffins

"These are ideal when served with warmed honey or maple syrup."

3 tablespoons butter, softened
¼ cup brown sugar
¼ cup molasses
1 egg
1 cup bran flakes
¾ cup buttermilk
1 cup unbleached flour
1 teaspoon baking powder
½ teaspoon baking soda
½ teaspoon salt
½ cup sun dried raisins

Preheat oven to 400 degrees F. Coat the inside of a muffin tin with butter or shortening, or use paper liners if you prefer.

In a small bowl, combine raisins with about ¼ cup water, and set aside to soak.

In a large mixing bowl, beat together butter, brown sugar, molasses, and egg. Mix well. Add bran flakes, buttermilk, and *drained* raisins.

Combine flour, baking powder, soda, and salt in a medium mixing bowl.

Gradually add the flour mixture to the egg mixture, and mix just enough to blend well. *Do not over-mix!*

Fill greased muffin cups 2/3 full with batter. Bake for 25 to 30 minutes.

Ice Cream Cone Cupcakes

1 (18.25 ounce) package chocolate cake mix
24 *"kiddie cup"* flat-bottom ice cream cones

Frosting Ingredients:
1 cup butter, *at room temperature*
1½ (8 ounce) packages cream cheese, *at room temperature*
2 cups powdered sugar
1 teaspoon vanilla extract

Preheat oven to 350 degrees F.

To prepare the cake batter, follow the package directions. Then, carefully place the ice cream cones on a baking sheet or mini muffin tin, and fill each cone approximately ¾ full of batter.

Bake for 25 to 30 minutes, or until a toothpick inserted near the center of the cupcake comes out clean. Let cool to room temperature.

To prepare the frosting; in a medium mixing bowl, beat the butter, cream cheese, powdered sugar, and vanilla extract until smooth and creamy.

Now, transfer the frosting to a gallon freezer bag, and cut the corner (*about ½ inch*) off the bottom of the bag. Hold the bag tightly, and pipe the frosting in a spiral fashion (*starting at the outer edges and working your way towards the center*) to form the shape of an ice cream cone. Top with red, white, and blue sprinkles.

Lemon Poppy Seed Muffins

½ cup vegetable oil
¾ cup sugar
2 eggs
1 cup sour cream
2 tablespoons milk
½ teaspoon vanilla extract
1 teaspoon lemon extract
2 tablespoons poppy seeds
1 teaspoon baking powder
1 teaspoon baking soda
¼ teaspoon salt
2 cups unbleached flour

Preheat oven to 400 degrees F. Grease mini-muffin cups, or use muffin liners if you prefer.

In a medium mixing bowl, beat together the vegetable oil, sugar, eggs, sour cream, milk, vanilla extract, and lemon extract. Add the poppy seeds, baking powder, baking soda, salt, and flour. *Mix just enough to blend well.*

Fill greased muffin cups 2/3 full with batter, and bake for 15 to 18 minutes, or until a toothpick comes out clean. Let stand 10 minutes before removing.

Maple Walnut Cupcakes

"Silvia's maple walnut cupcakes are ideal for children's birthday parties but they're so good, you might not want to wait for a special occasion."

Cupcake Ingredients:
¾ cup sugar
½ cup butter, *at room temperature*
2 eggs
1½ teaspoons maple extract
¾ cup unbleached flour
1 teaspoon baking powder
2 tablespoons corn starch
1/8 teaspoon salt
½ cup walnuts, chopped
¼ cup milk

Maple Cream Frosting:
1 (8 ounce) package cream cheese, *at room temperature*
½ stick butter, *at room temperature*
1 cup powder sugar
3 tablespoons pure maple syrup
1 teaspoon maple extract

Preheat oven to 350 degrees F. Prepare muffin cups, using muffin liners.

To make the cupcakes, in medium mixing bowl, beat sugar and butter until light and fluffy. Add egg and maple extract, and beat until well mixed. Then, gradually add flour, baking powder, corn starch, salt, walnuts, and milk. Mix just enough to blend well. *Do not over-mix!*

Fill muffin cups 2/3 full with batter, and bake for 20 to 25 minutes, or until golden brown.

To make the maple cream frosting, in a medium mixing bowl, combine cream cheese, butter, powdered sugar, maple syrup, and maple extract, and beat until smooth.

Once cupcakes have cooled to room temperature, spread a thin layer of frosting on top of each cupcake, and serve.

Morning Glory Muffins

1 cup vegetable oil
1 cup brown sugar
3 eggs
2 teaspoons vanilla extract
2 teaspoons baking soda
¼ teaspoon salt
2 teaspoons cinnamon
2 cups unbleached flour
4 medium carrots, finely shredded
½ cup chopped raisins
½ cup chopped walnuts
½ cup sweetened coconut flakes
1 apple, peeled, cored, and shredded

Preheat oven to 350 degrees F. Grease muffin cups, or use muffin liners if you prefer.

In a medium mixing bowl, combine the vegetable oil, brown sugar, eggs, and vanilla extract. Add the baking soda, salt, cinnamon, and flour. Then, stir in the shredded carrots, chopped raisins, chopped walnuts, coconut flakes, and shredded apple.

Fill greased muffin cups 2/3 full with batter and bake for 20 to 25 minutes, or until a toothpick inserted into the center of a muffin is clean when removed.

Peanut Butter Cupcakes

"This is my great-grandmother's peanut butter cupcake recipe. They're delicious and easy to make. I'd definitely recommend using a natural peanut butter, like Smucker's."

Cupcake Ingredients:
1 cup brown sugar
1/3 cup butter
2 eggs
1 teaspoon vanilla extract
½ cup creamy peanut butter
2 cups unbleached flour
2½ teaspoons baking powder
½ teaspoon salt
¾ cup milk

Frosting Ingredients:
2 tablespoons butter
3 cups powdered sugar
½ teaspoon vanilla extract
¼ cup creamy peanut butter
¼ cup milk
¼ cup peanuts, chopped

Preheat oven to 375 degrees F. Coat the inside of a muffin tin with butter or shortening, or use paper liners if you prefer.

To make the cupcakes, in medium mixing bowl, beat brown sugar and butter until light and fluffy. Add eggs, vanilla extract, and peanut butter. Beat until well mixed. Then, gradually add flour, baking powder, salt, and milk.

Fill greased muffin cups 2/3 full with batter. Bake for 25 to 30 minutes. Remove from oven and let cool to room temperature.

To make the frosting, in a medium mixing bowl, cream butter, powdered sugar, and vanilla extract. Mix in peanut butter, and add just enough milk (*about 1 tablespoon at a time*) until frosting is light and fluffy.

Frost the top of the cupcakes, and sprinkle with chopped peanuts before serving.

Popovers

"Bar Harbor was the ideal, romantic getaway for my parents. My mom enjoyed stopping by Jordan Pond House at Acadia National Park for afternoon tea and popovers."

2 eggs
1 cup milk, *divided*
1 cup unbleached flour
¼ teaspoon baking soda
¼ teaspoon salt
½ cup butter, softened
Smucker's Strawberry Preserves

Preheat oven to 425 degrees F.

In a large mixing bowl, use a whisk to beat the eggs on high speed until a uniform consistency is achieved, about 3 to 5 minutes. Now, at the slowest speed, add *½ cup milk* and beat until well incorporated.

Gradually add the flour, baking soda, and salt, and mix just enough to blend well. At medium speed, add the remaining *½ cup milk*, and beat for 2 minutes. Increase to high speed, and beat for 5 to 7 minutes; until smooth.

Pour the popover mixture into large, greased muffin tins, about ¾ full. *If you prefer large popovers, fill the tins to the top.*

Place the muffin tins on the center rack of oven, and bake for 15 minutes. *Be sure not to the open oven door!*

Reduce the oven temperature to 350 degrees, and cook for an additional 15 to 20 minutes, until brown and glossy. Serve immediately, with butter and strawberry preserves.

Zucchini Muffins

2 eggs
½ cup vegetable oil
1½ cups unbleached flour
1 cup brown sugar
½ teaspoon baking powder
½ teaspoon baking soda
½ teaspoon salt
½ teaspoon cinnamon
2 cups shredded zucchini
1 cup chopped walnuts
½ cup raisins

Preheat oven to 350 degrees F.

In a medium mixing bowl, combine the eggs and vegetable oil. In a separate mixing bowl, use a whisk to combine the flour, brown sugar, baking powder, baking soda, salt, and cinnamon. Gradually blend the flour mixture into the egg mixture. Then, mix in the zucchini, chopped walnuts, and raisins. *Do not over-mix!*

Coat the inside of a muffin tin with shortening, or use paper liners if you prefer. Fill the tin three-fourths full with batter.

Bake for 20 to 25 minutes, or until a toothpick inserted into the center of the muffin is clean when removed. Let stand for approximately 5 minutes before removing from tin.

Pies

Apple Pie

Pie Filling:
½ cup brown sugar
½ cup white sugar
¼ cup unbleached flour
1 tablespoon corn starch
1 teaspoon cinnamon
4 large apples, peeled, cored, and thinly sliced
2 tablespoons melted butter

Pie Crust:
2 cups unbleached flour
1 teaspoon salt
¾ cup shortening
¼ cup cold water
Egg wash (*made by beating 1 egg white lightly, with 2 teaspoons water*)

To make the pie filling, in a medium bowl, use a whisk to combine the brown sugar, white sugar, flour, corn starch, and cinnamon. Add sliced apples and melted butter, and mix well. Set aside.

To make the pie crust, in a medium mixing bowl, combine flour and salt. Cut-in shortening using a pastry blender. Mixture should resemble coarse meal. Gradually add cold water, stirring all the while, until a dough forms.

On a lightly floured work surface, knead dough until smooth. Add just enough flour to keep the dough from sticking. Then, divide the dough into two equal parts, and roll into 2 (12 inch) circles, about 1/8 inch thick.

Preheat oven to 375 degrees F.

Use a metal spatula to carefully place one of the 12 inch circles onto a 9 inch pie pan, gently pressing the dough into the corners and using your fingertips to create a rim around sides of the pan. Now, spoon-in the apple pie filling.

Gently place the second 12 inch circle on top. Pinch the dough together, and trim any excess (*leaving about a ¾-inch overhang*). Then, fold the dough under, and crimp the edges using your thumb and forefinger. Cut slits to allow steam to escape when baking, and sprinkle a little sugar over the pie crust.

Place the pie on a baking sheet lined with parchment paper and bake for *30 minutes* at 375 degrees F. Then, reduce oven temperature to 325 degrees F, and bake for an additional *30 minutes*. Brush lightly with egg wash, and bake for an additional *30 minutes*, or until golden brown. Serve warm with vanilla ice cream.

Blueberry Pie

Pie Filling:
1 cup sugar
¼ cup unbleached flour
1 tablespoon corn starch
½ teaspoon cinnamon
2 pounds fresh blueberries
2 tablespoons melted butter

Pie Crust:
2 cups unbleached flour
1 teaspoon salt
¾ cup shortening
¼ cup cold water

To make the pie filling, in a medium bowl, use a whisk to combine the sugar, flour, corn starch, and cinnamon. Add blueberries and melted butter, and mix well. Set aside.

To make the pie crust, in a medium mixing bowl, combine flour and salt. Cut-in shortening using a pastry blender. Mixture should resemble coarse meal. Gradually add cold water, stirring all the while, until a dough forms.

On a lightly floured work surface, knead dough until smooth. Add just enough flour to keep the dough from sticking. Then, divide the dough into two equal parts, and roll into 2 (12 inch) circles, about 1/8 inch thick. Cover loosely with plastic wrap, and *refrigerate for 1 hour*.

Preheat oven to 400 degrees F.

Use a metal spatula to carefully place one of the 12 inch circles onto a 9 inch pie pan, gently pressing the dough into the corners and using your fingertips to create a rim around sides of the pan. Now, spoon-in the blueberry pie filling.

Gently place the second 12 inch circle on top. Pinch the dough together, and trim any excess (*leaving about a ¾-inch overhang*). Then, fold the dough under, and crimp the edges using your thumb and forefinger. Cut slits to allow steam to escape when baking, and sprinkle a little sugar over the pie crust.

Place the pie on a baking sheet lined with parchment paper and bake for 20 minutes at 400 degrees F. Then, reduce oven temperature to 350 degrees F, and *bake for an additional 20 minutes*, or until golden brown. Serve warm with vanilla ice cream.

Cherry Pie

Pie Filling:
1½ cups white sugar
¼ cup unbleached flour
¼ cup corn starch
2 pounds cherries, pitted
¼ teaspoon almond extract
2 tablespoons melted butter

Pie Crust:
2 cups unbleached flour
1 teaspoon salt
¾ cup shortening
¼ cup cold water

To make the pie filling, in a medium bowl, use a whisk to combine the sugar, flour, and corn starch. Add cherries, almond extract, and melted butter, and mix well. Set aside.

To make the pie crust, in a medium mixing bowl, combine flour and salt. Cut-in shortening using a pastry blender. Mixture should resemble coarse meal. Gradually add cold water, stirring all the while, until a dough forms.

On a lightly floured work surface, knead dough until smooth. Add just enough flour to keep the dough from sticking. Then, divide the dough into two equal parts, and roll into 2 (12 inch) circles, about 1/8 inch thick. Cover loosely with plastic wrap, and *refrigerate for 1 hour*.

Preheat oven to 400 degrees F.

Use a metal spatula to carefully place one of the 12 inch circles onto a 9 inch pie pan, gently pressing the dough into the corners and using your fingertips to create a rim around sides of the pan. Now, spoon-in the cherry pie filling.

Gently place the second 12 inch circle on top. Pinch the dough together, and trim any excess (*leaving about a ¾-inch overhang*). Then, fold the dough under, and crimp the edges using your thumb and forefinger. Cut slits to allow steam to escape when baking, and sprinkle a little sugar over the pie crust.

Place the pie on a baking sheet lined with parchment paper and bake for 25 minutes at 400 degrees F. Then, reduce oven temperature to 350 degrees F, and *bake for an additional 30 minutes*, or until golden brown. Serve warm with vanilla ice cream.

Key Lime Pie

"Named after the key limes that are common throughout the Florida Keys, Key Lime Pie was one of my mom's favorite desserts."

3 eggs, separated
1½ cups sugar, *divided*
1/3 cup cornstarch
½ teaspoon salt, *divided*
2 cups water
2 tablespoons butter
1/3 cup key lime juice
1 tablespoon grated lime peel
3 drops of green food coloring *(optional)*
1 (9 inch) graham cracker pie shell
¼ teaspoon cream of tartar

Preheat oven to 350 degrees F.

In a medium mixing bowl, beat the *egg yolks* until light and fluffy, about 2 to 3 minutes. Set aside.

In a medium saucepan, use a whisk to combine *1¼ cups sugar*, cornstarch, *¼ teaspoon salt*, and water. Bring to a boil over medium heat and cook for 2 minutes, stirring all the while. Then, remove from heat and *let cool to room temperature*.

Add the egg yolks, butter, and key lime juice; and return to a boil. Cook for an additional 2 minutes, stirring continuously. Remove from heat, add grated lime peel and green food coloring, and pour into a (9 inch) graham cracker pie shell. Set aside.

Now, in a separate mixing bowl, use a whisk to beat the *egg whites*, cream of tartar, and remaining *¼ teaspoon salt* until light and foamy. Add the remaining *¼ cup sugar*, and continue beating until the sugar dissolves and stiff peaks form, at least 5 to 7 minutes.

Spread the meringue on top of the pie filling, carefully using a rubber spatula to form peaks in the topping.

Place the pie on a baking sheet lined with parchment paper and bake for 12 minutes, or until lightly browned. Remove from oven, and *refrigerate overnight before serving*.

Mulberry Pie

"My grandmother used to have a great big mulberry tree in her front yard. In fact, my great-grandfather planted the tree. It produced a dark purple (almost black) fruit that was great for making jam, wine, and a variety of baked goods. My sister, Mary, and I used to enjoy picking mulberries. Though, I don't think my mom enjoyed the fact that the fruit stained our hands, our mouths, and sometimes even our clothes."

Pie Filling:
1¼ cups sugar
¼ cup unbleached flour
1 tablespoon corn starch
½ teaspoon cinnamon
1½ pounds fresh mulberries
2 tablespoons melted butter

Pie Crust:
2 cups unbleached flour
1 teaspoon salt
¾ cup shortening
¼ cup cold water

To make the pie filling, in a medium bowl, use a whisk to combine the sugar, flour, corn starch, and cinnamon. Add mulberries and melted butter, and mix well. Set aside.

To make the pie crust, in a medium mixing bowl, combine flour and salt. Cut-in shortening using a pastry blender. Mixture should resemble coarse meal. Gradually add cold water, stirring all the while, until a dough forms.

On a lightly floured work surface, knead dough until smooth. Add just enough flour to keep the dough from sticking. Then, divide the dough into two equal parts, and roll into 2 (12 inch) circles, about 1/8 inch thick. Cover loosely with plastic wrap, and *refrigerate for 1 hour*.

Preheat oven to 375 degrees F.

Use a metal spatula to carefully place one of the 12 inch circles onto a 9 inch pie pan, gently pressing the dough into the corners and using your fingertips to create a rim around sides of the pan. Now, spoon-in the mulberry pie filling.

Gently place the second 12 inch circle on top. Pinch the dough together, and trim any excess (*leaving about a ¾-inch overhang*). Then, fold the dough under, and crimp the edges using your thumb and forefinger. Cut slits to allow steam to escape when baking, and sprinkle a little sugar over the pie crust.

Place the pie on a baking sheet lined with parchment paper and bake for 15 minutes at 400 degrees F. Then, reduce oven temperature to 350 degrees F, and *bake for an additional 30 minutes*, or until golden brown. Serve warm with vanilla ice cream.

Peach Pie

Pie Filling:
½ cup brown sugar
½ cup white sugar
¼ cup unbleached flour
2 tablespoons corn starch
½ teaspoon cinnamon
¼ teaspoon nutmeg
8 peaches, *peeled, pitted, and sliced*
2 tablespoons melted butter

Pie Crust:
2 cups unbleached flour
1 teaspoon salt
¾ cup shortening
¼ cup cold water

To make the pie filling, in a medium bowl, use a whisk to combine the brown sugar, white sugar, flour, corn starch, cinnamon, and nutmeg. Add sliced peaches and melted butter, and mix well. Set aside.

To make the pie crust, in a medium mixing bowl, combine flour and salt. Cut-in shortening using a pastry blender. Mixture should resemble coarse meal. Gradually add cold water, stirring all the while, until a dough forms.

On a lightly floured work surface, knead dough until smooth. Add just enough flour to keep the dough from sticking. Then, divide the dough into two equal parts, and roll into 2 (12 inch) circles, about 1/8 inch thick. Cover loosely with plastic wrap, and *refrigerate for 1 hour*.

Preheat oven to 400 degrees F.

Use a metal spatula to carefully place one of the 12 inch circles onto a 9 inch pie pan, gently pressing the dough into the corners and using your fingertips to create a rim around sides of the pan. Now, spoon-in the peach pie filling.

Gently place the second 12 inch circle on top. Pinch the dough together, and trim any excess (*leaving about a ¾-inch overhang*). Then, fold the dough under, and crimp the edges using your thumb and forefinger. Cut slits to allow steam to escape when baking, and sprinkle a little sugar over the pie crust.

Place the pie on a baking sheet lined with parchment paper and bake for 20 minutes at 400 degrees F. Then, reduce oven temperature to 350 degrees F, and *bake for an additional 20 minutes*, or until golden brown. Serve warm with vanilla ice cream.

Poppy Seed Custard Pie

"One of my great-grandmother's many uses for poppy seed."

Filling Ingredients:

1 egg
3 egg yolks
1/3 cup sugar
2 teaspoons lemon zest
½ cup frozen orange juice concentrate, thawed
1½ cups milk
1 (12 ounce) can poppy seed filling
1 (9 inch) graham cracker pie shell

Meringue Ingredients:

3 egg whites
¼ teaspoon salt
¼ teaspoon cream of tartar
1 teaspoon vanilla extract
1/3 cup sugar

Preheat oven to 300 degrees F.

In a medium mixing bowl, combine egg, egg yolks, with sugar, lemon zest, and orange juice concentrate. Gradually add milk, then poppy seed filling, and mix well. Pour into pie shell. Bake for 75 minutes.

After an hour has passed; in a medium mixing bowl, beat egg whites until stiff peaks form, about 10 minutes. Use a whisk to add salt, cream of tartar, and vanilla extract. Beat until peaks form. Gradually add sugar, and beat until smooth.

Once pie is done, increase oven temperature to 325 degrees F.

Spread meringue over pie filling, place the pie on a baking sheet lined with parchment paper, and bake approximately 15 minutes, or until lightly browned.

Rhubarb Custard Pie

"This is my mom's rhubarb custard pie recipe. Yet another way she made use of the rhubarb growing near the side of our house."

Pie Filling:
3 cups rhubarb, chopped
2 tablespoons butter, softened
2 eggs, beaten
2 cups brown sugar
3 tablespoons unbleached flour
½ teaspoon salt
½ teaspoon nutmeg

Pie Crust:
2 cups unbleached flour
1 teaspoon salt
¾ cup shortening
¼ cup cold water

To make the pie filling, in a medium mixing bowl, combine rhubarb, butter, eggs, brown sugar, flour, salt, and nutmeg. Set aside.

To make the pie crust, in a separate mixing bowl, combine flour and salt. Cut-in shortening using a pastry blender. Mixture should resemble coarse meal. Gradually add cold water, stirring all the while, until a dough forms.

On a lightly floured work surface, knead dough until smooth. Add just enough flour to keep the dough from sticking. Then, divide the dough into two equal parts, and roll into 2 (12 inch) circles, about 1/8 inch thick. Cover loosely with plastic wrap, and *refrigerate for 1 hour*.

Preheat oven to 400 degrees F.

Use a metal spatula to carefully place one of the 12 inch circles onto a 9 inch pie pan, gently pressing the dough into the corners and using your fingertips to create a rim around sides of the pan. Now, spoon-in the rhubarb pie filling.

Gently place the second 12 inch circle on top. Pinch the dough together, and trim any excess (*leaving about a ¾-inch overhang*). Then, fold the dough under, and crimp the edges using your thumb and forefinger. Cut slits to allow steam to escape when baking, and sprinkle a little sugar over the pie crust.

Place the pie on a baking sheet lined with parchment paper and bake for 30 minutes at 400 degrees F. Then, reduce oven temperature to 350 degrees F, and *bake for an additional 30 minutes*, or until golden brown. Serve warm with vanilla ice cream.

Strawberry Pie

Pie Filling:
1 cup sugar
¼ cup unbleached flour
1 tablespoon corn starch
2 pounds strawberries, quartered
2 tablespoons melted butter

Pie Crust:
2 cups unbleached flour
1 teaspoon salt
¾ cup shortening
¼ cup cold water

To make the pie filling, in a medium bowl, use a whisk to combine the sugar, flour, and corn starch. Add strawberries and melted butter, and mix well. Set aside.

To make the pie crust, in a medium mixing bowl, combine flour and salt. Cut-in shortening using a pastry blender. Mixture should resemble coarse meal. Gradually add cold water, stirring all the while, until a dough forms.

On a lightly floured work surface, knead dough until smooth. Add just enough flour to keep the dough from sticking. Then, divide the dough into two equal parts, and roll into 2 (12 inch) circles, about 1/8 inch thick. Cover loosely with plastic wrap, and *refrigerate for 1 hour*.

Preheat oven to 400 degrees F.

Use a metal spatula to carefully place one of the 12 inch circles onto a 9 inch pie pan, gently pressing the dough into the corners and using your fingertips to create a rim around sides of the pan. Now, spoon-in the strawberry pie filling.

Gently place the second 12 inch circle on top. Pinch the dough together, and trim any excess (*leaving about a ¾-inch overhang*). Then, fold the dough under, and crimp the edges using your thumb and forefinger. Cut slits to allow steam to escape when baking, and sprinkle a little sugar over the pie crust.

Place the pie on a baking sheet lined with parchment paper and bake for 20 minutes at 400 degrees F. Then, reduce oven temperature to 350 degrees F, and *bake for an additional 20 minutes*, or until golden brown. Serve warm with vanilla ice cream.

Salads, Fruits & Vegetables

Applesauce

"My mom didn't purée her applesauce. She preferred large chunks of apple instead. Most often we'd have applesauce in the fall, as an accompaniment to pork chops or occasionally with potato pancakes. Of course, it's great with most breakfast foods as well."

8 medium apples, peeled, cored, and cut into ½ inch pieces
1 cup water
1 cup brown sugar
2 tablespoons lemon juice
1 teaspoon cinnamon
½ teaspoon nutmeg
¼ cup dark rum or apple brandy, *optional*

In a medium saucepan or dutch oven, combine the apples, water, brown sugar, lemon juice, cinnamon, and nutmeg.

Cover, and bring to a boil over high heat. Then reduce the heat to low and simmer, covered, for 15 minutes; stirring occasionally.

Remove the lid and simmer for an additional 30 minutes, until most of liquid has evaporated. Add the rum and simmer for 1 minute more, stirring all the while. Set aside, and let cool.

Baked Beans

"Rather than use dried navy beans, my mom would sometimes prepare this 'Cliffs Notes' version of Boston Baked Beans. It was always well received at pot lucks and family gatherings."

2 (16 ounce) cans baked beans
1 medium onion, finely chopped
3 cloves garlic, thinly sliced
¼ cup molasses
1 tablespoon maple syrup
1 tablespoon brown sugar
2 teaspoons dijon mustard
½ teaspoon paprika
2 slices bacon, diced

Preheat oven to 350 degrees F.

In a large mixing bowl, combine beans, onion, garlic, molasses, maple syrup, brown sugar, mustard, and paprika. Mix well. Pour mixture into an 8 x 8 inch baking dish, and top with bacon.

Bake covered for 30 minutes. Then, remove cover and bake for an additional 30 minutes. Let stand approximately 15 minutes before serving.

Baked Pumpkin & Roasted Pumpkin Seeds

"A medium (5 pound) pumpkin should yield about 1½ cups of mashed pumpkin or pumpkin puree."

1 medium (5 pound) pumpkin

To bake the pumpkin, preheat the oven to 375 degrees F.

Cut the pumpkin in half, and discard the stem and pulp. *Be sure to reserve the seeds for later use.* Place both halves face-down in a large baking dish, add enough water to cover the bottom of the baking dish, and cover with foil. Bake for approximately 1½ hours, or until the skin is tender and gives easily.

Let stand for 15 minutes. Then, using a large spoon, scoop out the flesh and mash the pumpkin with a potato masher. For a smooth pulp, use a handheld blender to puree the mashed pumpkin.

To roast the pumpkin seeds, reduce oven temperature to 300 degrees F.

In a medium mixing bowl, combine the pumpkin seeds, melted butter, and salt. Toss gently to coat, and spread the seeds (in a single layer) on an ungreased baking sheet. Bake for 45 minutes or until golden brown, stirring occasionally.

Beets

2 pounds beets
1 cup water
1 teaspoon salt

Cut off all but 2 inches of the beet tops, leaving the root attached. Wash thoroughly, and place the beets in a medium saucepan. Add salt and water (about an inch above the beets). Cover, and bring to a boil.

Reduce heat to medium low and cook until tender, allowing approximately 60 to 90 minutes for young beets; 2 to 3 hours for large beets. Drain. Rub off tops, skins, and roots. Then, slice and season to taste.

Black Bean Salad

"My mom's black bean salad; undoubtedly one of my favorites. It's ideal for a picnic, potluck, or other social gathering."

Salad Ingredients:
2 (16 ounce) cans black beans
8 slices bacon
3 cups frozen sweet corn
2 avocados, pitted, peeled and chopped

Dressing Ingredients:
1 teaspoon oregano
1 teaspoon cilantro
½ teaspoon cumin
¼ teaspoon cayenne pepper
1½ teaspoons ancho chili powder
1 teaspoon salt
½ teaspoon freshly ground black pepper
1 tablespoon brown sugar
3 tablespoons water
1 medium onion, diced
3 cloves chopped garlic
¼ cup lemon juice
1/3 cup vegetable oil
3 tablespoons red wine vinegar

To prepare the salad, drain and rinse the black beans in a strainer or colander. Then, sauté the bacon in a heavy skillet, until crisp. Remove the bacon, and set aside to drain on a paper towel. Now, in a medium saucepan, bring 2 quarts of water to a boil. Add the corn, and cook for 6 minutes. Drain thoroughly, and place the corn and beans in a large mixing bowl. Set aside.

To prepare the dressing, in a medium mixing bowl, use a whisk to combine the oregano, cilantro, cumin, cayenne pepper, ancho chili powder, salt, freshly ground black pepper, and brown sugar. Add 3 tablespoons of water, and mix well. Now, add the onion, garlic, lemon juice, vegetable oil, and red wine vinegar. Whisk vigorously, and pour the dressing over the beans salad, *stirring all the while*. Add the avocado, crumble bacon over top, and *refrigerate for at least two hours before serving.*

Black-Eyed Peas

1 pound dried black-eyed peas
¼ cup butter
1 medium onion, cut in half and thinly sliced
2 cloves garlic, minced
1 red bell pepper, cut into thin 2 inch long strips
1 teaspoon salt
½ teaspoon freshly ground black pepper

Soak the black-eyed peas overnight in cold water. The next day, rinse, pick-over, and drain the peas.

In a large skillet, melt the butter over medium-high heat. Add the onion and garlic, and cook until tender; about 3 to 5 minutes. Add the black-eyed peas, cover, and increase to high heat. Cook for an additional 8 minutes.

Transfer the black-eyed pea and onion mixture to a large pot, adding just enough water to cover, about 3 to 4 cups.

Bring to a boil, and add the red bell pepper, salt, and freshly ground black pepper. Reduce heat to medium, and cook for 1 hour, or until tender.

Broccoli Salad

4 slices bacon
1 head fresh broccoli, *cut into bite-size pieces*
¼ cup chopped walnuts
1 small red onion, very thinly sliced
½ cup frozen peas, thawed
¼ cup sun dried raisins
½ cup mayonnaise
1 tablespoon vinegar
2 tablespoons honey

In a heavy skillet, sauté bacon until crisp. Remove bacon, and set aside to drain on paper towel.

In a large pot, combine 4 to 6 quarts cold water and 1 teaspoon salt. Bring to boil over high heat, add the broccoli, and cook for *2 minutes*. Drain, and rinse with cold water to stop the cooking process.

In a large mixing bowl, combine the broccoli, chopped walnuts, red onion, peas, and raisins. Then, in a separate bowl, use a whisk to combine the mayonnaise, vinegar, and honey. Pour the dressing over the broccoli salad, and crumble bacon on top. Mix well, and *refrigerate for at least 2 hours before serving.*

Coleslaw

"This is my mom's coleslaw recipe. It's tasty and light; ideal for a summer picnic or family get-together."

2 tablespoons granulated white sugar
½ teaspoon salt
¼ teaspoon freshly ground black pepper
½ cup mayonnaise
¼ cup milk
¼ cup buttermilk
2 tablespoons fresh lemon juice
1 tablespoon white vinegar
½ medium green cabbage, cored and shredded
½ medium red cabbage, cored and shredded
2 medium carrots, peeled and finely grated
1 small red onion, cut in half and very thinly sliced

To prepare the dressing, in a small mixing bowl, use a whisk to combine the sugar, salt, freshly ground black pepper, mayonnaise, milk, buttermilk, fresh lemon juice, and white vinegar.

In a separate mixing bowl, combine the green cabbage, red cabbage, carrot, red onion, and dressing. Mix well, and refrigerate for at least 1 hour before serving.

Compote

"My great-grandmother used to make compote with cherries, apples, and pears; in order to preserve the fruit my great-grandfather tended to. It makes a tasty dessert, and is also an ideal complement to breakfast foods such as crepes, pancakes, and waffles."

1/3 cup brown sugar
2/3 cup water
1 tablespoon fresh lemon juice
½ teaspoon cinnamon
¼ teaspoon nutmeg
1 cup (*about ½ pint*) rainier cherries, pitted and quartered
2 medium apples, peeled, cored, and sliced
3 medium pears, peeled, cored, and sliced
1 teaspoon vanilla extract
¼ cup dark rum or apple brandy, *optional*

In a medium saucepan, combine the brown sugar, water, and lemon juice. Bring to a boil over high heat, stirring continuously. Once the brown sugar has completely dissolved, reduce the heat to medium-low and let simmer until a syrup forms, approximately 7 to 9 minutes. Add the cinnamon, nutmeg, cherries, apples and pears, and return to boil. Now, add the vanilla extract and rum, remove from heat, and let cool to room temperature before serving.

Creamed Parsnips

1½ pounds parsnips, peeled, cored, and chopped
2 tablespoons extra-virgin olive oil
1/8 teaspoon nutmeg
Salt and freshly ground black pepper, to taste
1 cups water

Preheat oven to 400 degrees F.

Line a shallow baking pan with aluminum foil. Arrange the parsnips in a single layer, and drizzle olive oil over top.

Season with nutmeg, salt, and freshly ground pepper, and bake until lightly golden; about 20 to 25 minutes. *Be sure to turn the parsnips over after 10 or 15 minutes.*

In a blender or food processor, combine parsnips and water. Puree.

Creamed Spinach

3 tablespoons extra-virgin olive oil
3 (10 ounce) packages frozen chopped spinach, *thawed and drained*
2 cloves garlic, minced
½ cup heavy cream
½ teaspoon nutmeg
¼ cup freshly grated parmesan cheese
Salt and freshly ground black pepper, to taste

In a large skillet, heat olive oil over medium heat. Add spinach and garlic, and cook until tender, about 5 to 7 minutes. Remove from heat, place in a colander, and drain thoroughly.

Now, heat spinach, heavy cream, and nutmeg over medium heat. Cook for an additional 5 to 7 minutes. Then, add parmesan cheese, season with salt and pepper, and cook until cheese is melted; 2 to 3 minutes. Serve immediately.

Cucumber Salad

3 medium cucumbers, *peeled and sliced*
1 teaspoon salt
½ cup sour cream
½ bunch fresh dill, chopped
2 teaspoons lemon juice
Freshly ground black pepper, to taste

In a medium colander, sprinkle sliced cucumbers with salt. Let stand for about 1 hour. Drain thoroughly, and pat dry using a paper towel.

In a medium mixing bowl, combine sour cream, dill, and lemon juice. Season with freshly ground black pepper, and mix well.

Add cucumbers and toss gently. Cover and refrigerate for at least 4 hours before serving.

Curried Bean Salad

"My mom's curried bean salad is an enticing take on a more conventional three bean salad. It's a great side dish, one you'll want to bring along on a family picnic."

½ cup cider vinegar
¼ cup vegetable oil
4 cloves garlic, minced
2 teaspoons oregano
Salt and freshly ground black pepper, to taste
½ teaspoon ground cumin
½ teaspoon curry powder
1 (16 ounce) can kidney beans, *rinsed and drained*
1 (15 ounce) can pinto beans, *rinsed and drained*
1 (15 ounce) can garbanzo beans, *rinsed and drained*
1½ cups frozen whole kernel corn, *thawed*
3 medium celery stalks, finely chopped
1 medium red onion, finely chopped

To prepare the dressing, in a small mixing bowl, use a whisk to combine the cider vinegar, vegetable oil, garlic, oregano, salt, freshly ground black pepper, cumin, and curry powder.

To prepare the salad, in a separate mixing bowl, combine the kidney beans, pinto beans, garbanzo beans, corn, celery, and red onion.

Pour the dressing over the bean mixture and toss gently to coat. Cover, and *refrigerate overnight*.

Dandelion Salad with Vinegar & Oil Dressing

"Not a lot of people realize that dandelion greens can be eaten, cooked or raw. Actually, they have a slightly bitter taste, and are pretty similar to mustard greens. Young leaves are usually eaten raw, while the older leaves are cooked. My great-grandfather used to make dandelion wine with the flowers as well."

3 slices bacon
1 medium onion, cut in half and thinly sliced
2 cloves garlic, minced
Salt and freshly ground black pepper, to taste
2 teaspoons brown sugar
2 teaspoons dijon mustard
¼ cup balsamic vinegar
½ cup extra-virgin olive oil
1 large bunch dandelion greens, chopped
1 small bunch fresh dill, chopped
2 hard boiled eggs, chopped

Place eggs in a medium saucepan and add cold water, at least an inch above the egg shells. Cover, and bring to a boil. As soon as the water comes to a full boil, remove from heat and let stand in hot water for 10 to 12 minutes. Drain water. Then, cover with cold water and ice cubes. Let stand in cold water until completely cooled. Peel and chop the eggs.

Sauté bacon in skillet until crisp. Remove bacon, and set aside to drain on paper towel. Reserve 2 to 3 tablespoons of drippings.

In a medium saucepan, add bacon drippings, onion, garlic, salt, and black pepper. Stir, and let the mixture cook for a minute or two.

Add brown sugar, dijon mustard, balsamic vinegar, and olive oil. Cook over low heat for an additional 1 to 2 minutes. *Set aside, and let cool to room temperature.*

In a large mixing bowl, combine dandelion greens, dill, and hard boiled eggs. Crumble bacon, and sprinkle on top. Pour dressing over salad and gently toss together.

Dandelion Salad

Salad Ingredients:
1 large bunch dandelion greens, chopped
1 red onion, sliced
1 bunch fresh dill, chopped
3 hard boiled eggs, chopped
3 slices bacon

Dressing Ingredients:
1½ tablespoons unbleached flour
1 teaspoon salt
2 tablespoons brown sugar
1 egg
¼ cup cider vinegar
2 cups milk
Bacon drippings

Place eggs in a medium saucepan and add cold water, at least an inch above the egg shells. Cover, and bring to a boil. As soon as the water comes to a full boil, remove from heat and let stand in hot water for 10 to 12 minutes. Drain water. Then, cover with cold water and ice cubes. Let stand in cold water until completely cooled. Peel and chop the eggs.

Sauté bacon in skillet until crisp. Save approximately 2 - 3 tablespoons drippings. Set aside.

In a large mixing bowl, combine dandelion greens, red onion, dill, and eggs. Crumble bacon, and sprinkle on top. Toss together.

In a separate mixing bowl, combine flour, salt, and brown sugar together. Add egg, cider vinegar, and milk, and mix well.

Heat bacon drippings over low flame. Add flour and egg mixture to bacon drippings, and cook until thickened, stirring all the while. Let stand to cool.

Pour dressing over salad and toss gently.

Fried Green Tomatoes

"A great way to make use of un-ripened tomatoes at the end of the season, just before the first frost; fried green tomatoes make an ideal side dish."

1½ cups milk
1 tablespoon white vinegar
1 cup cornmeal
1 cup unbleached flour
1 teaspoon garlic powder
½ teaspoon paprika
2 teaspoons salt
½ teaspoon freshly ground black pepper
4 large green tomatoes, thinly sliced
Vegetable oil, for pan frying

In a small mixing bowl, combine the milk and vinegar, and let stand for approximately 10 minutes.

In a separate mixing bowl, use a whisk to combine the cornmeal, flour, garlic powder, paprika, salt, and freshly ground black pepper.

Dip each tomato slice in sour milk, and thoroughly cover with cornmeal mixture. Then, heat approximately ½ inch of vegetable oil in a heavy skillet. When the oil is hot, fry until golden brown and crispy, about 3 to 4 minutes on each side. Drain on paper towels, and serve with lemon wedges.

German Potato Salad

½ cup bacon scraps or end pieces, chopped
2 tablespoons unbleached flour
1 teaspoon salt
¼ teaspoon black pepper
1 tablespoon brown sugar
½ cup cider vinegar
1 tablespoon Dijon mustard
1¼ cups water
6 medium potatoes
½ cup celery, thinly sliced
1 medium onion, cut in half and thinly sliced
2 tablespoons chopped spinach

Wash the potatoes. Then, place the potatoes in a medium pot, and cover with water and add 1 teaspoon salt. Boil for about 20 minutes, or until tender. Drain excess water, peel potatoes, and let stand. Once cool, cut each potato in half lengthwise, then in thirds. *If you don't like to peel potatoes, be sure to choose red-skinned potatoes!*

Sauté bacon scraps in skillet until crisp. Save 2 to 3 tablespoons drippings. Set aside.

In a medium saucepan, add bacon drippings, flour, salt, and black pepper. Stir, and let the mixture cook for a minute or two. Then, add the brown sugar, cider vinegar, mustard, and water. Bring to boil, and simmer for 1 to 2 minutes.

Add celery, and onion. Cook over low heat until vegetables are tender. Add potatoes, spinach, and bacon scraps.

Company Green Beans

1 pound *fresh* green beans, *ends trimmed; cut into 2-inch pieces*
1/3 cup chopped walnuts
3 tablespoons butter
1 medium onion, cut in half and thinly sliced
1 clove garlic, minced
2 teaspoons dijon mustard
Salt and freshly ground black pepper, to taste.

Preheat oven to 350 degrees F.

Bring a large pot of water to boil. Cook green beans for approximately 4 to 5 minutes. Drain the beans in a colander, rinse with cold water, and set aside.

Toast walnuts for approximately 10 minutes, stirring occasionally.

In a medium saucepan, melt butter and sauté onion for approximately 2 to 3 minutes. Add garlic, dijon mustard, salt, and freshly ground black pepper. Then, add green beans and chopped walnuts.

Cook over medium heat until tender, about 10 minutes, or until the mixture is hot throughout.

Dutch-Style Green Beans

1 pound *fresh* green beans, *ends trimmed; cut into 2-inch pieces*
3 slices bacon
1 medium onion, cut in half and thinly sliced
2 teaspoons corn starch
¼ teaspoon dry mustard
Salt and freshly ground black pepper, to taste
½ cup chicken broth
1 tablespoon cider vinegar
1 tablespoon brown sugar

Bring a large pot of water to boil. Cook green beans for approximately 4 to 5 minutes. Drain the beans in a colander, rinse with cold water, and set aside.

In a medium saucepan, sauté bacon until crisp. Remove bacon, and set aside to drain on paper towel. Reserve approximately 2 tablespoons bacon fat, and discard the rest.

Add onion and sauté in bacon fat for approximately 2 to 3 minutes. Then, add corn starch, dry mustard, salt, freshly ground black pepper, and chicken broth. Bring to a boil. Then, add cider vinegar, brown sugar, and green beans.

Cook over medium heat until tender, about 10 minutes. Crumble bacon over top, and serve immediately.

Sweet & Sour Green Beans with Bacon

1 pound *fresh* green beans, *ends trimmed; cut into 2-inch pieces*
3 slices bacon
1 medium onion, cut in half and thinly sliced
1 tablespoon cider vinegar
1½ teaspoons brown sugar
½ teaspoon salt
½ teaspoon freshly ground black pepper

Bring a medium pot of water to boil. Cook green beans for approximately 4 to 5 minutes. Drain the beans in a colander, rinse with cold water, and set aside.

In a medium saucepan, sauté bacon until crisp. Remove bacon, and set aside to drain on paper towel. Reserve approximately 2 tablespoons bacon fat, and discard the rest.

Add onion and sauté in bacon fat for approximately 2 to 3 minutes. Then, add beans, cider vinegar, brown sugar, salt, and freshly ground black pepper. Cook over medium heat until tender, about 10 minutes. Crumble bacon over top, and serve immediately.

Sweet & Sour Green Beans with Pimentos

1 pound *fresh* green beans, *ends trimmed; cut into 2-inch pieces*
2 (2 ounce) jars pimentos, drained and chopped
¼ cup cider vinegar
3 tablespoons vegetable oil
2 tablespoons brown sugar
½ teaspoon salt
½ teaspoon freshly ground black pepper

Bring a large pot of water to boil. Cook green beans for approximately 4 to 5 minutes. Drain the beans in a colander, rinse with cold water, and set aside.

In a medium saucepan, add beans, chopped pimentos, cider vinegar, vegetable oil, brown sugar, salt, and freshly ground black pepper. Cook over medium heat until tender, about 10 minutes.

Kohlrabi & Dill

"The word "kohlrabi" comes from the German "kohl," meaning cabbage and "rabi," meaning turnip. It's kind of like a potato, except it's crisp and juicy."

3 to 4 young, tender bulbs kohlrabi
2 tablespoons butter
¼ teaspoon dill
¼ teaspoon parsley
1 teaspoon lemon juice
Salt and freshly ground black pepper, to taste

Peel kohlrabi, and cut into ½ inch cubes.

Place kohlrabi in a medium saucepan and add enough water to cover. Bring to a boil over high heat.

Reduce heat to medium low, and simmer *uncovered* until fork-tender, about 40 to 45 minutes.

Drain water and add butter, dill, parsley, lemon juice, salt, and freshly ground black pepper.

Note: Kohlrabi is sweet and tender when harvested small, but will become tough and chewy if left to grow too large. Avoid using kohlrabi that's much larger than the size of a baseball.

Mushy Peas

"Inspired by a small pub in Swansea, this recipe's great served with fish and chips, and of course, a good brown ale, such as Newcastle."

1 (10 ounce) package frozen green peas
¼ cup heavy cream
1 tablespoon butter
Salt and freshly ground black pepper, to taste

In a medium saucepan, combine the frozen green peas and just enough water to cover. Bring to boil. Then, reduce heat, cover, and let simmer for 10 to 12 minutes, or until tender. Drain thoroughly, and set aside.

Now, combine the peas, heavy cream, butter, salt, and freshly ground black pepper in a food processor, and grind into a puree. Serve immediately.

Pasta Salad

1 (16 ounce*) package rotini pasta
1 (6-ounce) jar marinated artichoke hearts, drained and sliced
2 tablespoons artichoke marinade, *reserved*
8 ounces baby bella mushrooms, sliced
1 cup cherry tomatoes, halved
1 cup kalamata olives, pitted and chopped
½ bunch fresh parsley, chopped
1 teaspoon basil
1 teaspoon oregano
3 cloves garlic, minced
¾ cup vegetable oil
¼ cup white vinegar
¾ cup freshly grated parmesan cheese
Salt and freshly ground black pepper, to taste

Bring a large pot of salted water to boil. Cook rotini according to package directions. Drain noodles in colander, and gently rinse with cold water.

In a large mixing bowl, combine rotini, artichoke hearts, artichoke marinade, mushrooms, tomatoes, kalamata olives, parsley, basil, oregano, garlic, vegetable oil, white vinegar, parmesan cheese, salt and freshly ground black pepper. Mix well, and refrigerate.

* The rule of thumb is 2 ounces of dry pasta per person for a first course or side dish, and 3 to 4 ounces per person for a main course.

Potato Salad

"My mom didn't necessarily have a recipe for potato salad. Instead, she used fresh vegetables from the garden; whatever was available at the time. So, this recipe is an approximation of what her potato salad typically included."

6 large yukon gold potatoes
2 hard boiled eggs, chopped
2 cups miracle whip
1 pint cherry tomatoes, halved
1 green bell pepper, chopped
½ bunch fresh parsley, chopped
1 small onion, cut in half and thinly sliced
Salt and freshly ground black pepper, to taste

In a large pot, combine potatoes, 1 teaspoon salt, and just enough cold water to cover the potatoes. Bring to a boil over high heat. Then reduce the heat to medium low, and simmer until fork tender, about 45 minutes. Peel the potatoes. Then, slice each potato lengthwise, then crosswise, into ½ inch pieces. Set aside to cool.

Place eggs in a medium saucepan and add cold water, at least an inch above the egg shells. Cover, and bring to a boil. As soon as the water comes to a full boil, remove from heat and let stand in hot water for 10 to 12 minutes. Drain water. Then, cover with cold water and ice cubes. Let stand in cold water until completely cooled. Peel and chop the eggs.

In a large mixing bowl, combine potatoes, hardboiled eggs, miracle whip, cherry tomatoes, bell pepper, fresh parsley, onion, salt, and freshly ground black pepper. Toss lightly, and *refrigerate for at least 2 hours before serving.*

Red Cabbage

"Also known as red kraut or blue kraut, red cabbage was one of my mom's favorite side dishes. Though, the raw form can also be used for salads and coleslaw."

2 small red cabbages, quartered
1 medium onion, peeled and thinly sliced
2 apples, peeled, cored, and sliced
¼ cup firmly packed brown sugar
Salt and freshly ground black pepper, to taste
½ cup red wine vinegar
2 cups chicken stock

Preheat oven to 350 degrees F.

Place the cabbage, onions, and apples in a greased 9 x 13 inch baking dish. Then, in a small saucepan, combine the brown sugar, salt, freshly ground black pepper, red wine vinegar, and chicken stock. Heat until the brown sugar has completely dissolved. Pour over the cabbage, cover, and bake for 1 hour, or until the cabbage is soft and tender.

Mashed Rutabaga

2 pounds rutabaga*
¼ cup butter
¼ teaspoon nutmeg
Salt and freshly ground black pepper, to taste

Peel rutabaga, and cut into ½ inch cubes.

Place rutabaga in a medium saucepan and add 1 teaspoon salt and enough water to cover, about 2 quarts. Bring to a boil over high heat.

Reduce heat to medium low, and simmer uncovered until fork-tender, about 40 to 45 minutes.

Drain water, and cook for an additional 2 to 3 minutes. Add butter, nutmeg, salt, and pepper, and mash with a potato masher while still warm.

Rutabaga should be harvested when approximately 3 to 4 inches in diameter; weighing no more than 2 to 3 pounds.

Spaghetti Squash

1 medium spaghetti squash
½ cup parmesan cheese
¼ cup butter, melted
½ teaspoon basil
½ teaspoon oregano
Salt and freshly ground black pepper, to taste

Preheat oven to 375 degrees F.

Cut the spaghetti squash in half, lengthwise. Remove and discard the seeds. Then, place the squash (*cut side down*) in a 9 x 13 inch baking dish, adding enough water to cover the bottom of the baking dish. Bake for 1 hour, or until the skin is tender and gives easily.

Now, using a fork, rake the inside of the squash, separating it into thin strands that resemble spaghetti. In a medium casserole dish, toss the spaghetti squash with the parmesan cheese, melted butter, basil, and oregano. Season with salt and pepper, and serve immediately.

Spinach Marie

4 eggs
¼ teaspoon salt
1/8 teaspoon freshly ground black pepper
2¾ cups heavy cream
1 (10 ounce) package frozen chopped spinach, *thawed and drained*
2 cups white cheddar cheese, shredded
2/3 cup unseasoned bread crumbs
2 tablespoons butter
2 teaspoons paprika

Preheat oven to 375 degrees F.

In a medium mixing bowl, beat the eggs until light and foamy. Add the salt, freshly ground black pepper, and heavy cream. Mix well. Now, add the spinach and cheddar cheese. Pour into a greased 9 x 9 inch baking dish, and top with bread crumbs and butter. Sprinkle with paprika, and bake at for 40 to 45 minutes.

Stuffed Squash

Stewed Tomatoes:
1 (14.5 ounce) can stewed tomatoes, quartered
¼ cup vegetable oil
1 medium onion, chopped
2 cloves garlic, minced
1 medium celery stalk, finely chopped
1 medium red bell pepper, chopped
1 tablespoon brown sugar
1 teaspoon parsley
½ teaspoon thyme
Salt and freshly ground black pepper, to taste

Stuffed Squash:
2 medium yellow summer squash
1 medium zucchini, chopped
½ cup butter
1 medium onion, finely chopped
2 cloves garlic, minced
1½ teaspoons chicken soup base
1 cup plain bread crumbs
¾ cup freshly grated parmesan cheese
½ bunch fresh parsley, chopped
Salt and freshly ground black pepper, to taste
¼ cup water

To prepare the stewed tomatoes, in a medium saucepan, heat the vegetable oil over a medium flame. Add the onion, garlic, celery, red bell pepper, stewed tomatoes, brown sugar, parsley, thyme, salt, and freshly ground black pepper. Cook for 10 to 12 minutes, or until tender.

To prepare the squash, cut the squash in half, lengthwise. Remove the interior, and chop the remnants into small pieces. *The hollow squash exterior should remain intact.*

Now, in a medium mixing bowl, combine the chopped squash remnants and zucchini, and set aside. *Preheat the oven to 350 degrees F.*

In a small saucepan, melt the butter over a medium-low flame. Sauté, the onion, garlic, chopped squash, and zucchini for 5 to 7 minutes, or until tender. Add the chicken soup base, and cook for an additional 3 minutes. Then, add the bread crumbs, parmesan cheese parsley, salt, and freshly ground black pepper. Remove from heat, and set aside.

Stuff each squash, and place in a 9 x 13 inch baking dish. Add ¼ cup water, cover with foil, and bake for 20 minutes, or until tender. Serve with stewed tomatoes and fresh corn bread.

Summer Squash

"One of my mom's recipes. She used to prepare freshly grown zucchini, summer squash, and tomatoes as a side dish, especially during late summer/early fall."

3 tablespoons extra-virgin olive oil
2 medium zucchini, thinly sliced
2 medium yellow summer squash, thinly sliced
2 cloves garlic, minced
1 cup cherry tomatoes, quartered
1 small bunch fresh dill, chopped
1 teaspoon salt
½ teaspoon freshly ground black pepper

In a large heavy skillet, heat the olive oil over medium-high heat. Add zucchini and summer squash, and increase to high heat. Sauté, stirring frequently, until tender, 15 to 20 minutes.

Add the garlic, cherry tomatoes, dill, salt, and pepper. Cook for another 3 to 5 minutes.

Swiss Chard with Cream Sauce

¼ cup butter
1 medium onion, chopped
1 clove garlic, chopped
1 small carrot, finely grated
2 medium red potatoes, cut into ¼ inch cubes
1½ pounds swiss chard
½ cup heavy cream
Salt and pepper to taste

Separate swiss chard leaves from stalks and cut both into thin strips, crosswise.

In a large skillet, heat butter over medium flame. Sauté onion, garlic, carrot, potatoes, and stalks until tender.

Add swiss chard leaves, and with salt and pepper. Cover and cook over low heat until tender, about 10 minutes. Add heavy cream, and simmer uncovered for 2 to 3 minutes longer.

Beaner's Favorite Three Bean Salad

"When I was born, one of the nurses said I looked just like a tiny little bean, and as a result the nickname 'beaner' was born as well. This is my favorite kind of bean salad, made from green beans, yellow wax beans, and kidney beans. If you can't find wax beans, you can substitute garbanzo beans. However, it's my opinion that doing so will change the flavor substantially."

¼ cup vegetable oil
1/3 cup cider vinegar
¼ cup brown sugar
1 teaspoon parsley
½ teaspoon salt
½ teaspoon freshly ground black pepper
1 (16 ounce) can green beans, rinsed and drained
1 (16 ounce) can yellow wax beans, *rinsed and drained*
1 (16 ounce) can kidney beans, *rinsed and drained*
1 medium red onion, cut in half and thinly sliced

To prepare the dressing, in a small mixing bowl, use a whisk to combine the vegetable oil, cider vinegar, brown sugar, parsley, salt, and freshly ground black pepper.

To prepare the salad, in a separate mixing bowl, combine the green beans, yellow wax beans, kidney beans, and red onion.

Pour the dressing over the bean mixture and toss gently to coat. Cover, and *refrigerate overnight*.

Tomato Salad

"My mom used to make this tomato salad all the time. It's a great way to enjoy ripe tomatoes from the garden. More often than not, she used fresh, homegrown herbs as well."

4 large vine-ripened tomatoes
1 small, red onion, chopped
1 clove garlic, minced
¼ cup vegetable oil
2 tablespoons cider vinegar
½ teaspoon dill
½ teaspoon marjoram
1 teaspoon thyme or basil
½ teaspoon salt
½ teaspoon freshly ground black pepper
2 small heads of green leaf lettuce, *optional*

Dice tomatoes and place in medium mixing bowl. Add red onion and garlic. Set aside.

In a small mixing bowl, use a whisk to combine the vegetable oil, cider vinegar, dill, marjoram, thyme, salt, and freshly ground black pepper. Pour over tomatoes, and toss gently. Let marinate for 30 to 45 minutes. Serve over a bed of chopped leaf lettuce.

Wilted Lettuce Salad

"My mom used to make this salad (and several variants that included arugula, radicchio and endive) using various different types of loose-leaf lettuce she produced in her vegetable garden."

3 slices bacon
½ cup cider vinegar
3 tablespoons brown sugar
Salt and freshly ground black pepper, to taste
2 tablespoons unbleached flour
½ cup water
1 medium bunch red leaf lettuce, chopped
1 small red onion, very thinly sliced
1 clove garlic, minced
2 hard boiled eggs, chopped

Place eggs in a medium saucepan and add cold water, at least an inch above the egg shells. Cover, and bring to a boil. As soon as the water comes to a full boil, remove from heat and let stand in hot water for 10 to 12 minutes. Drain water. Then, cover with cold water and ice cubes. Let stand in cold water until completely cooled. Peel and chop the eggs.

In a large skillet, cook bacon over medium heat until crisp. Remove bacon and place on paper towels to drain, reserving about 2 tablespoons bacon fat.

Add cider vinegar, brown sugar, salt, freshly ground black pepper, flour, and water to reserved fat. Let simmer for approximately 3 to 5 minutes. Set aside.

In a large salad bowl, combine leaf lettuce, red onion, garlic, and hard boiled eggs. Pour dressing over salad; Crumble bacon over top, toss, and serve.

Wurst Salad

"Wurst salad, or sausage salad, is really easy to prepare. In theory, it should contain more sausage than potatoes but I think you'll enjoy this recipe."

½ pound cooked bratwurst, *cut in ¼ inch pieces*
6 medium red potatoes, *cooked and cut into ¼ inch pieces*
¼ cup cider vinegar
2 tablespoons vegetable oil
3 cloves garlic, minced
1 small onion, cut in half and thinly sliced
1 medium tomato, chopped
2 teaspoons parsley
1 teaspoon dill
Salt and freshly ground black pepper, to taste

In a medium mixing bowl, combine bratwurst, red potatoes, vinegar, vegetable oil, garlic, onion, tomato, parsley, dill, salt, and pepper. Mix well. Cover loosely with plastic wrap, and refrigerate for at least 2 hours before serving.

Mother's Zucchini

"This recipe was passed down to my great-grandmother by her mother (my 2nd great-grandmother), Anna Beer."

2 slices bacon
1 medium onion, chopped
1 medium tomato, peeled and chopped
3 small zucchini, cut in half (lengthwise) then cut in ½ inch pieces
4 slices muenster cheese
Salt and freshly ground black pepper, to taste

Sauté bacon in a heavy, 11-inch skillet until crisp. Remove bacon, and set aside to drain on paper towel. Reserve approximately 2 tablespoons bacon fat, and discard the rest.

Add onions and zucchini, and sauté in bacon fat for 2 to 3 minutes, being careful not to brown or caramelize the onions. Add tomato, salt, and freshly ground black pepper. Cover, and cook until tender, about 10 minutes.

Add cheese, cover, and cook until cheese is melted; 2 to 3 minutes. Crumble bacon over top if desired. Serve immediately.

Sandwiches

Black Bean Veggie Burgers

1 (15 ounce) can black beans
1 egg
1 (4 ounce) can green chilies
1 cup bread crumbs
1 teaspoon ancho chili powder
1 tablespoon cornmeal
2 tablespoons vegetable oil
2 tablespoons mayonnaise
5 whole-wheat hamburger buns
5 leaves red leaf lettuce
5 tomato slices
5 onion slices

Puree black beans in food processor, and place in medium mixing bowl. Add egg, chilies, bread crumbs and ancho chili powder. Mix thoroughly.

Place cornmeal in separate bowl. Shape bean mixture into 5 (½ inch-thick) patties, and thoroughly coat each patty with cornmeal.

Heat vegetable oil in large skillet over medium flame. Cook patties for 5 to 6 minutes on each side, or until crisp.

Spread mayonnaise on whole wheat buns. Place leaf lettuce, bean patties, tomato, and onion on bun and serve.

Bratwurst & Kraut Sandwich

"Sometimes my mom would add sliced apples to sauerkraut, giving it a pleasant, mild flavor. Hickory smoked bacon is also a great choice for this recipe."

1 (16 ounce) can of sauerkraut, *drained and rinsed*
1 medium onion, cut in half and thinly sliced
3 medium apples; peeled, cored, and sliced
1 tablespoon brown sugar
Salt and freshly ground black pepper, to taste
3 slices bacon, chopped
½ (12 ounce) bottle of beer
1 pound bratwurst links
1 bunch fresh parsley, chopped
6 to 8 rye or pumpernickel buns
1 (5 ounce) jar bavarian style mustard

Optional: Use a fork to pierce each bratwurst link in several places. Then, in a large mixing bowl combine bratwurst with about 2 cups of milk. Cover with plastic wrap, and refrigerate overnight.

Preheat oven to 350 degrees F.

Place sauerkraut, onion, apples, brown sugar, salt, freshly ground pepper, chopped bacon, beer, and bratwurst in a greased casserole dish. Mix sauerkraut gently.

Cover the casserole dish and bake for 40 to 45 minutes, or until heated thoroughly.*
Remove from heat and stir in fresh parsley.

Serve on bun, topped with sauerkraut and mustard.

* An even better approach would be to use a slow cooker. To do so, place combined ingredients in a 3½ quart slow cooker, cover, and cook on 'high' for approximately 4 hours.

Cheeseburger

"My first job was working as a dishwasher at Fant's Steakhouse, in Richmond Park apartments, Richmond Heights. I began working as a prep cook shortly afterwards though. Fant's burgers were very popular and this is, to the best of my recollection, how they were prepared."

1 pound ground beef
½ medium onion, finely chopped
2 teaspoons worcestershire sauce
1 tablespoon A1 steak sauce, *optional*
1 tablespoon tomato juice
½ teaspoon garlic powder
½ teaspoon oregano
½ teaspoon salt
¼ teaspoon freshly ground black pepper
1 egg
4 slices american cheese, *optional*
2 tablespoons mayonnaise
4 hamburger buns
4 onion slices
4 leaves romaine or leaf lettuce
4 tomato slices

Prepare grill for high heat.

In a large mixing bowl, use your hands to combine the ground beef, onion, worcestershire sauce, A1 steak sauce, tomato juice, garlic powder, oregano, salt, freshly ground black pepper and egg. Divide the meat (*about ½ cup per serving*) into hamburger patties, tossing from one hand to the other.

Reduce grill to medium heat, and lightly oil the grill. Place hamburger patties on the grill, and cook for 4 to 5 minutes per side, or until medium-well. *Top with cheese, and cook for an additional 2 to 3 minutes.*

Let rest 2 to 3 minutes before serving. Spread mayonnaise on toasted buns. Place sliced onion, lettuce, tomato, and burger on bun, and serve with ketchup and mustard.

Chicken Salad

½ cup mayonnaise
1 teaspoon lemon juice
1 teaspoon dijon mustard
½ teaspoon parsley
½ teaspoon dill
½ teaspoon thyme
Salt and freshly ground pepper, to taste
1 pound cooked chicken breast, cut into ½ inch pieces
1 small onion, finely chopped
1 medium celery stalk, finely chopped
1 carrot, finely shredded

In a medium mixing bowl, use a whisk to combine the mayonnaise, lemon juice, dijon mustard, parsley, dill, thyme, salt, and freshly ground pepper. Add the chicken, onion, celery, and carrot, and mix well. Serve as a sandwich, on whole-wheat or multi-grain bread.

Egg Salad

8 eggs
¼ cup mayonnaise
1 tablespoons dijon mustard
1 teaspoon dill
½ teaspoon paprika
1 small onion, chopped
1 medium celery stalk, finely chopped
Salt and freshly ground pepper, to taste

Place eggs in a medium saucepan and add cold water, at least an inch above the egg shells. Cover, and bring to a boil. As soon as the water comes to a full boil, remove from heat and let stand in hot water for 10 to 12 minutes. Drain water. Then, cover with cold water and ice cubes. Let stand in cold water until completely cooled. Peel and chop the eggs.

In a large mixing bowl, combine the eggs, mayonnaise, mustard, dill, paprika, onion, celery, salt, and pepper. Mix well.

Serve as a sandwich on whole-wheat or multi-grain bread.

Fried Eggplant Sandwich with Pesto Sauce

1½ cups unbleached flour
2 eggs, beaten (*add a little milk if necessary*)
1½ cups seasoned bread crumbs
1 medium eggplant, peeled and sliced ¼ inch thick
¼ cup vegetable oil
1 medium onion, sliced
4 ounces sliced mozzarella cheese
1 (3.5 ounce) jar pesto sauce
Eight slices multigrain bread, toasted
4 leaves red leaf lettuce
4 tomato slices

Place flour, egg, and bread crumbs in 3 separate bowls.

Coat each slice of eggplant with flour, dip in egg wash, and thoroughly cover with bread crumbs.

In a large skillet, heat the vegetable oil over a medium flame. Cook the eggplant for approximately 3 minutes on each side, or until golden brown. Then, let the oil drain on a paper towel.

Add the sliced onion and mozzarella cheese. Cover the skillet, and cook for additional 2 minutes, or until the cheese melts.

Spread pesto sauce on multigrain bread. Place leaf lettuce, tomato, and eggplant between two pieces of bread, and serve.

Ham Salad

1 pound baked ham, diced
1 small onion, finely chopped
1 medium celery stalk, finely chopped
1/3 cup mayonnaise
1 teaspoon parsley
2 teaspoons dijon mustard
½ teaspoon freshly ground black pepper

In a medium bowl, combine ham, onion, celery, mayonnaise, parsley, mustard, and black pepper. Mix well.

Serve as a sandwich on whole-wheat or multi-grain bread.

Lobster Rolls

4 medium hoagie rolls
¼ cup melted butter
1/3 cup mayonnaise
1 tablespoon extra-virgin olive oil
2 teaspoons lemon juice
Salt and freshly ground black pepper, to taste
1 stalk celery, chopped
1 small onion, chopped
1 clove garlic, minced
1 bunch fresh parsley, chopped
1 tablespoon dill
1 pound lobster meat*, cut into bite size pieces
4 leaves red leaf lettuce
2 medium vine-ripened tomatoes, sliced

Preheat broiler. Brush the inside of each roll with melted butter, place on baking sheet, and lightly toast under the broiler. This should only take a minute; two at the most.

In a medium mixing bowl, combine the mayonnaise, olive oil, lemon juice, salt, and pepper. Then, add the celery, onion, garlic, parsley, and dill. Mix well, and gently fold in the lobster.

Divide leaf lettuce, tomatoes, and lobster salad evenly among the hoagie rolls, and serve.

If lobster isn't affordable, you can substitute with imitation crab meat. Just be sure to tear it into bite-size pieces.

Portobello Burgers with Pesto Sauce

Seasoning Ingredients:
2 teaspoons salt
½ teaspoon freshly ground black pepper
¼ teaspoon onion powder
¼ teaspoon garlic powder
1 teaspoon paprika
1/4 teaspoon cayenne pepper
1/8 teaspoon coriander
1/8 teaspoon turmeric
2 tablespoons extra-virgin olive oil

Portobello Burger Ingredients:
4 large portobello mushroom caps
¼ cup balsamic vinegar
4 slices mozzarella cheese

Pesto Sauce Ingredients:
1 cup fresh basil
½ cup fresh parsley
3 tablespoon capers
¼ cup pine nuts
2 cloves garlic
1 tablespoon lemon juice
¼ cup extra-virgin olive oil
Salt and freshly ground black pepper, to taste
½ cup freshly grated parmesan cheese

Additional Ingredients:
4 wholegrain hamburger buns
4 onion slices
4 leaves romaine or leaf lettuce
4 tomato slices

To prepare the seasoning, in a small mixing bowl, use a whisk to combine the salt, freshly ground black pepper, onion powder, garlic powder, paprika, cayenne pepper, coriander, and turmeric. Set aside

To prepare the portobello burgers, in a heavy skillet, heat the olive oil over a medium-high flame. Season the portobello mushrooms with prepared mixture, and cook for 2 to 3 minutes. Turn the mushrooms cap side down, and drizzle balsamic vinegar over mushrooms. When the vinegar has completely evaporated (another 2 to 3 minutes), turn the mushrooms cap side up and cover with a slice of mozzarella cheese. Remove skillet from heat, cover with foil, and let stand.

To prepare the pesto sauce, combine the basil, parsley, capers, pine nuts, garlic, and lemon juice in a food processor, and grind into a paste. Mix in the olive oil, salt, freshly ground black pepper, and parmesan cheese, and set aside.

Spread the pesto sauce on toasted wholegrain hamburger buns. Place sliced onion, lettuce, tomato, and portobello mushroom on each bun, and serve immediately.

Reuben Sandwich

"A reuben is typically made with corned beef, sauerkraut, swiss cheese, and thousand island dressing. Although my mom loved guggisberg baby swiss, I prefer muenster cheese instead of swiss cheese, and mayonnaise instead of thousand island dressing."

2 teaspoons mayonnaise
2 slices dark rye bread
1 slice muenster cheese
3 to 4 slices of shaved corned beef
1/3 cup sauerkraut
1 tablespoon butter

Spread mayonnaise on one slice of rye bread. Top with muenster cheese, corned beef, sauerkraut, and a second slice of bread. Lightly butter the outside of the sandwich (*both sides*), and cook on a non-stick griddle, over medium-high heat, until the bread is toasted and the cheese has completely melted, about 3 minutes on each side.

Sloppy Joes

"If I'm not mistaken, a Sloppy Joe is essentially a 1930s depression-era food. However, its popularity increased significantly when canned preparations such as Manwich became widely available. Nevertheless, this is my great-grandmother's take on Sloppy Joes."

1 pound ground beef
1 medium onion, chopped
1 clove garlic, minced
1 tablespoon flour
1 cup chicken broth
2 teaspoons worcestershire sauce
¾ cup ketchup
½ teaspoon freshly ground black pepper
2 tablespoons mayonnaise
8 leaves romaine or red leaf lettuce
8 tomato slices
8 whole-wheat buns, toasted

Brown ground beef in large skillet over medium flame. Drain any excess fat, and add onion, garlic, and flour; stirring occasionally. Cook until tender, 3 to 5 minutes.

Add chicken broth, worcestershire sauce, ketchup, and freshly ground black pepper. Simmer, stirring occasionally, for 15 to 20 minutes.

Spread mayonnaise on whole wheat buns. Place leaf lettuce, tomato, and ground beef mixture on bun and serve.

Tuna Salad

1 (6 ounce) can tuna packed in water, *drained*
½ small onion, finely chopped
1 medium celery stalk, finely chopped
1 small carrot, finely shredded
½ teaspoon dill
½ teaspoon parsley
¼ cup mayonnaise
½ teaspoon freshly ground black pepper

In a small mixing bowl crumble tuna with a fork. Toss with the onion, celery, carrot, dill, and parsley. Add the mayonnaise, and freshly ground black pepper. Combine all ingredients, and mix well.

Serve as a sandwich on whole-wheat or multi-grain bread.

Turkey Burgers

1 pound ground turkey
1 medium onion, finely chopped
1 clove garlic, minced
1 carrot, finely shredded
½ small zucchini, finely shredded
½ teaspoon thyme
Salt and freshly ground black pepper, to taste
1 tablespoon extra-virgin olive oil
4 whole-wheat buns, toasted
2 tablespoons mayonnaise
4 leaves romaine or red leaf lettuce
4 tomato slices

In a medium mixing bowl, combine ground turkey, onion, garlic, carrot, zucchini, thyme, salt, and freshly ground black pepper. Shape into 4 patties, and brush with olive oil.

Heat a nonstick pan over medium-high heat, and use a paper towel to lightly coat the pan with vegetable oil. Cook the turkey burgers for 6 to 7 minutes on each side, or until medium-well.

Spread mayonnaise on whole-wheat buns. Place leaf lettuce, turkey burgers, and tomato slices on buns and serve immediately.

Veggie Burgers

1 tablespoon extra virgin olive oil
2 cups zucchini, shredded
1 medium onion, chopped
1 clove garlic, minced
1 cup mushrooms, chopped
¼ teaspoon basil
¼ teaspoon marjoram
¼ teaspoon oregano
¼ teaspoon sage
Salt and freshly ground black pepper, to taste
1 cup seasoned bread crumbs
1 egg
3 tablespoons tomato sauce
1 cup shredded mozzarella cheese
2 tablespoons vegetable oil
2 tablespoons mayonnaise
6 whole-wheat club or onion rolls
6 leaves romaine or red leaf lettuce
6 tomato slices

In a heavy skillet, heat the olive oil over a medium-low flame. Sauté the zucchini, onion, garlic, mushrooms, basil, marjoram, oregano, sage, salt, and freshly ground black pepper; about 3 to 5 minutes. Remove from heat, and let stand for 10 minutes.

In a medium mixing bowl, combine sautéed vegetables, seasoned bread crumbs, egg, and tomato sauce in medium mixing bowl. Add cheese and mix thoroughly. Shape into 6 patties.

Now, heat vegetable oil in large skillet over a medium flame. Cook veggie burgers for 5 to 6 minutes on each side, or until crisp.

Spread mayonnaise on whole-wheat club or onion rolls. Place leaf lettuce, veggie burgers, and tomato slices on buns and serve immediately.

Scones

Bannock

"Bannock is a traditional Scottish cake/flat bread similar to a large scone. The oldest and arguably most well known type of bannock is Selkirk Bannock, which is the inspiration for this recipe."

1 cup sun dried raisins
2 packages (*about 1½ tablespoons*) quick-rise yeast
¼ cup warm water
1/3 cup unbleached flour
1 tablespoon sugar
1 teaspoon salt
¼ cup milk
1/3 cup butter, softened
¼ cup shortening
½ cup sugar
1¾ cups unbleached flour
1 egg
2 tablespoons water

In a small bowl, combine the raisins with about ½ cup water, and set aside to soak.

Dissolve the yeast in ¼ cup warm water, with a pinch of sugar. Let stand 5 minutes. Then, in a large mixing bowl, combine the yeast mixture with 1/3 cup flour, 1 tablespoon sugar, 1 teaspoon salt, and ¼ cup milk. Set aside, and let stand for an additional 15 minutes.

In a separate bowl, cream the butter, shortening, and ½ cup sugar. Add the yeast mixture and 1¾ cups flour. Add a little more flour if necessary, enough to make a dough that's firm but elastic. *Knead the dough until smooth*, about 3 to 5 minutes. Then, place the dough in greased bowl, cover loosely with plastic wrap, and *let rise in a warm place for 30 minutes.*

Drain the raisins and add them to the dough, little by little, kneading as you go. This might take a while. Once again, place the dough in greased bowl, cover loosely with plastic wrap, and *let rise in a warm place for about 30 minutes.*

Now, shape the dough into a round bun, and place it in a greased 8 inch round cake pan. The dough should not touch the sides of the pan. *Let rise in a warm place for about 45 minutes.*

Preheat oven to 350 degrees F, and bake for 20 minutes. Then, using 1 egg and 2 tablespoons water, make an egg wash solution. Brush the bannock with the egg wash, and return to oven for an additional 5 minutes, or until golden brown.

Blueberry Scones

"My mom thought the Great Harvest Bread Company in Mentor made the best scones, and eventually adopted their approach to making them. They'd use whatever fresh fruit happened to be available. Even though this recipe calls for blueberries, feel free to substitute whatever fruit you like. If you prefer, you can also use dried fruit such as raisins, currants, and dates. Scones are great served with tea and Devonshire Cream."

1 cup whole-wheat flour
2 cups unbleached white flour
1 teaspoon salt
1 tablespoon baking powder
¼ cup brown sugar*
1/3 cup butter *or shortening*
1 egg
¾ cup milk
1 cup blueberries

Preheat oven to 425 degrees F.

In a medium mixing bowl, combine the wheat flour, white flour, salt, baking powder, and brown sugar. Cut in the butter using a pastry blender, *and gently mix in the blueberries.*

In a separate, small mixing bowl, beat the egg and milk together. Now, add the egg mixture to the flour mixture. Mix just enough to blend well. *Do not over-mix!*

Roll the dough into an 8 inch circle, and cut into 8 equal pie-shaped pieces. *Repeat if necessary.*

Place the scones on a greased baking sheet, and bake for 20 to 25 minutes.

*If you'd like to make sugar-free blueberry scones, substitute ½ cup Splenda.

Cheese Scones

4 slices bacon, chopped
1 medium onion, very finely chopped
3 cups unbleached flour
1 tablespoon baking powder
1 tablespoon sugar
1½ teaspoons salt
½ teaspoon freshly ground black pepper
½ cup butter
1½ cups sharp cheddar cheese, grated
1 cup buttermilk
¼ cup melted butter

Preheat the oven to 400 degrees F.

In a medium skillet, cook the bacon until crisp, about 5 minutes. Remove bacon, and set aside to drain on paper towel. Reserve approximately 2 tablespoons bacon fat, and discard the rest. Sauté onion in bacon fat for approximately 3 to 5 minutes, until tender. Set aside.

In a medium mixing bowl, use a whisk to combine the flour, baking powder, sugar, salt, and freshly ground black pepper. Using a pastry blender, cut in butter, cheese, onion, and bacon until mixture is crumbly.

Gradually add buttermilk, mixing just enough to blend well. Add more buttermilk if the dough is too dry. *Do not over-mix!*

Turn-out the dough onto a floured work surface, and knead until smooth. Then, roll the dough into 2 (8 inch) circles, and cut each into 8 equal pie-shaped pieces.

Place scones on a greased baking sheet, brush with melted butter, and bake for 20 to 25 minutes, or until golden brown. Remove from oven, brush with remaining melted butter, and serve.

Lemon Poppy Seed Scones

Poppy Seed Scones Ingredients:
2/3 cup butter, softened
2/3 cup granulated white sugar
2 eggs
1 tablespoon + *1 teaspoon* baking powder
1 teaspoon baking soda
½ teaspoon salt
2 tablespoons poppy seeds
Zest of 1 lemon
4 cups unbleached flour
1 cup buttermilk
2 tablespoons fresh lemon juice

Lemon Glaze Ingredients:
1 tablespoon melted butter
½ cup powdered sugar
1 teaspoon lemon extract
2 to 3 tablespoons milk

Preheat oven to 425 degrees F.

To prepare the scones, in a medium mixing bowl, beat butter and sugar until light and fluffy. Add eggs and beat until well mixed. Add baking powder, baking soda, salt, poppy seeds, lemon zest, flour, and buttermilk, *a little at a time*. Mix just enough to blend well. *Do not over-mix!*

On a lightly floured work surface, knead dough until smooth and elastic. Then, roll the dough into an 8 inch circle, and cut into 8 equal pie-shaped pieces. *Repeat if necessary.*

Place the scones on a greased baking sheet, and bake for 12 to 15 minutes, or until golden brown. Drizzle lemon juice over top of scones.

To prepare the glaze, in a medium mixing bowl, use a whisk to combine the melted butter, powdered sugar, and lemon extract. Add the milk (*a tablespoon at a time*), and blend until the mixture forms a thick syrup. Let scones cool to room temperature, drizzle glaze over top, and serve with lemon curd or orange marmalade.

Maple Walnut Scones

"My mom loved Chardon's annual Maple Festival, which celebrates the local maple syrup trade. It's important to use pure maple syrup (not imitation or maple-flavored syrup) for this recipe."

Topping Ingredients:
2 tablespoons brown sugar
2 tablespoons finely chopped walnuts

Maple Walnut Scones Ingredients:
2 cups unbleached flour
2 teaspoons baking powder
¼ teaspoon salt
2 tablespoons brown sugar
½ cup butter
½ cup chopped walnuts
1 egg
2 tablespoons milk
1/3 cup pure maple syrup

Preheat oven to 400 degrees F.

To make the topping, in a small mixing bowl, use a whisk to combine the brown sugar and chopped walnuts. Set aside.

To make the maple walnut scones, in a medium mixing bowl, combine the flour, baking powder, salt, and brown sugar. Cut in the butter; until mixture resembles fine crumbs. Now, add chopped walnuts.

In a separate mixing bowl, combine the egg, milk, and maple syrup. Gradually add the egg mixture to the flour mixture; just enough to blend well. *Do not over-mix!*

Roll the dough into an 8 inch circle, and cut into 8 equal pie-shaped pieces (*repeat if necessary*). Then, brush with additional maple syrup, and sprinkle with brown sugar and walnut mixture.

Place scones on a greased baking sheet, and bake for 16 to 18 minutes. Serve immediately.

Pumpkin Scones

½ cup dried cranberries
1 cup whole wheat flour
2 cups unbleached white flour
1 teaspoon salt
1 tablespoon baking powder
½ cup brown sugar
1 teaspoon cinnamon
1/8 teaspoon ground cloves
¼ teaspoon ginger
¼ teaspoon freshly ground nutmeg
1/3 cup butter
1 egg
½ cup milk
1 teaspoon vanilla extract
1 cup pumpkin puree

Preheat oven to 425 degrees F.

In a small bowl, combine the cranberries with about ½ cup water, and set aside to soak.

In a medium mixing bowl, combine the whole wheat flour, unbleached white flour, salt, baking powder, brown sugar, cinnamon, ground cloves, ginger, and nutmeg. Cut in the butter, until mixture resembles coarse meal.

In a separate, small mixing bowl, beat the egg, milk, vanilla extract, and pumpkin puree together. Add the *drained* cranberries.

Then, add the egg mixture to the flour mixture. Mix just enough to blend well. *Do not over-mix!*

Roll the dough into an 8 inch circle, and cut into 8 equal pie-shaped pieces. *Repeat if necessary.*

Place the scones on a greased baking sheet, and bake for 20 to 25 minutes.

Irish Soda Scones

1 cup whole wheat flour
2 cups unbleached white flour
1 tablespoon sugar
1 teaspoon baking soda
1 teaspoon salt
1½ cups buttermilk
¼ cup melted butter
1 cup raisins

Preheat oven to 425 degrees F.

In a small bowl, combine raisins with 1 cup water, and set aside to soak.

In a medium mixing bowl, use a whisk to combine the whole wheat flour, unbleached white flour, sugar, baking soda, salt, and *drained* raisins. Gradually add the buttermilk, until you have a soft, moist dough. Mix just enough to blend well. *Do not over-mix!*

Turn-out the dough onto a floured work surface, and knead until smooth. Then, roll the dough into an 8 inch circle, and cut into 8 equal pie-shaped pieces. *Repeat if necessary.*

Place scones on a greased baking sheet, brush with melted butter, then dust with a little flour and bake for 20 to 25 minutes, or until a toothpick inserted into the center is clean when removed. Remove from oven, brush with remaining melted butter, and serve warm, with butter and jam.

Snacks & Desserts

Almond Biscotti

"Biscotti are a traditional twice-baked Italian biscuit, typically served with espresso or cappuccino. Biscotti can be stored for long periods of time and make ideal gifts."

1½ cups sugar
4 eggs
¼ cup melted butter
2 teaspoons vanilla extract
3¾ cups unbleached flour
1 teaspoon baking soda
¼ teaspoon salt
¼ teaspoon cinnamon
1 cup sliced, toasted almonds
6 ounces baking chocolate

Preheat the oven to 375 degrees F.

In medium mixing bowl, beat sugar, and eggs until light and fluffy. Add melted butter and vanilla extract, and beat until well mixed. Then, gradually add flour, baking soda, salt, cinnamon, and toasted almonds, to form a heavy dough.

Roll the dough* into 2 logs, each about 12 inches long and 2 inches wide. Arrange the logs on a parchment paper-lined baking sheet, and bake for 30 minutes, or until slightly firm to the touch. Remove from oven, and let stand for 5 minutes.

Cut biscotti diagonally into ½ inch pieces. Then, return the biscotti to a parchment paper-lined baking sheet, reduce oven temperature to 325 degrees F, and bake for an additional 6 to 10 minutes on each side, or until crisp.

In a small saucepan, melt baking chocolate over low heat, *stirring continuously*. Now, using a wooden spoon, drizzle the melted chocolate in a zigzag pattern over the biscotti. Let stand until chocolate is firm.

*If the dough becomes too soft to work with, place it in the freezer for a few minutes to firm up.

Apple Date Squares

"This is my great-grandmother's apple date square recipe; another family favorite with an undeniably natural sweetness."

½ cup butter, softened
¾ cup sugar
1 egg
1 teaspoon vanilla extract
1½ cups unbleached flour
1 teaspoon baking soda
¼ teaspoon salt
3 medium apples, peeled, cored and finely chopped
½ cup dates, chopped
¼ cup brown sugar
1 teaspoon cinnamon
¾ cup chopped walnuts

Preheat oven to 350 degrees F.

In medium mixing bowl, beat butter and sugar until light and fluffy. Add egg and vanilla extract, and beat until well mixed. Then, gradually add flour, baking soda, salt, apples, and dates. Spread dough on bottom of a greased 8 x 8 inch baking dish.

In a small mixing bowl, combine brown sugar, cinnamon, and walnuts. Sprinkle on top of dough. Bake for 30 to 35 minutes, or until golden brown. *Let cool to room temperature, and cut into squares before serving.*

Apple Dumplings

Dumpling Ingredients:
½ cup sugar
¼ teaspoon cinnamon
2 cups unbleached flour
2 teaspoons baking powder
1 teaspoon salt
½ cup shortening
2/3 cup milk
8 small apples, peeled, cored, and *very thinly sliced*
2 tablespoons butter, *softened and divided*

Sauce Ingredients:
¾ cup brown sugar
1/3 cup butter
¼ teaspoon nutmeg
¼ teaspoon cinnamon
1 1/3 cups hot water

Preheat oven to 450 degrees F.

In a small mixing bowl, combine ½ cup sugar and ¼ teaspoon cinnamon. Set aside.

To make the dumplings, in a separate, medium mixing bowl, combine flour, baking powder and salt. Cut-in shortening until mixture resembles coarse meal. Add milk, *a little at a time*.

On a lightly floured work surface, roll-out the dough to about a 1/8 inch thickness, and cut rounds using a small, floured drinking glass or cookie cutter (approximately 2 inches in diameter).

Place about 1 tablespoonful of sliced apples, a pinch of sugar/cinnamon mixture, and about 1 teaspoon of butter in the center of each round. Wrap the dough around the filling, carefully pinching the dough to close the seams. Arrange dumplings in well greased dutch oven, allowing for space in between.

To make the sauce, in a separate mixing bowl, combine the brown sugar, butter, nutmeg, cinnamon, and hot water. Pour over top of dumplings, and bake for 10 minutes. Then, reduce oven temperature to 400 degrees F and bake for an additional 20 minutes, or until apples are tender.

Helen's Apple Fritters

"Like Della, Helen's technically my first cousin, once removed, but she was more like an aunt to me. This is her apple fritter recipe."

1 cup unbleached flour
1 ½ teaspoons baking powder
3 tablespoons powdered sugar
¼ teaspoon salt
1/3 cup milk
1 egg, well beaten
3 medium apples, peeled, cored, and thinly sliced
¼ cup vegetable oil

In a large mixing bowl, use a whisk to combine flour, baking powder, powdered sugar, and salt. Add milk and egg, stirring all the while until a dough forms. Stir in apples, and mix well.

Heat vegetable oil in a large, heavy pot until the thermometer registers 365 degrees F.

Drop batter by spoonful into hot oil, and cook for approximately 1½ minutes on each side, or until golden brown. Transfer to paper towel to drain. Serve warm, sprinkled with powdered sugar.

Granny's Apple Kuchen

"This is another donauschwaben recipe my great-grandmother used to make. Although she used different types of fruit toppings, I liked her apple kuchen the most. This type of kuchen has a thick square, or rectangular yeast-based crust, and can be topped with apples, cherries, strawberries, or plums. Kuchen is German for 'cake.'"

Dough Ingredients:
¼ cup warm milk
1 package quick-rise yeast
½ cup butter, softened
½ cup sugar
1 egg
2 egg whites
3 cups unbleached flour
¼ cup water

Topping Ingredients:
2 tablespoons butter
½ cup honey
1 teaspoon cinnamon
6 large apples, peeled, cored, and sliced

To make the dough, In a small mixing bowl, dissolve quick-rise yeast in warm milk. Let stand for 5 minutes.

In a medium mixing bowl, cream butter and sugar, until light and fluffy. Add egg, egg whites, and yeast mixture. Then, gradually add flour and water, and stir until well mixed. The dough should be very soft, yet should have the consistency of a thick cake batter.

Place dough in a floured bowl, and cover loosely with plastic wrap. Set aside, and allow to double in size. Approximately 1½ to 2 hours.

To make the topping, peel, core, and slice the apples. Preheat oven to 375 degrees F.

In a medium saucepan, melt butter over medium heat. Add honey and cinnamon, stirring all the while. Cook for 5 minutes, or until honey is completely melted.

Use a rubber spatula to spread the dough evenly into a greased 9 x 13 inch baking dish, pushing it into the corners and using your fingertips to create about a ½ inch rim around sides of the baking dish. Place the sliced apples on top, and lightly press into the dough. Then, generously brush the honey glaze over the apples. Bake for 30 to 35 minutes, or until golden brown.

Apple Squares

"My mom's recipe actually referred to these as 'breakfast apple squares' but you can serve them anytime. It's an ideal autumn apple recipe."

3 eggs
¾ cup brown sugar
1 teaspoon vanilla extract
1½ cups unbleached flour
2 teaspoons baking powder
¼ teaspoon salt
2 teaspoons cinnamon
4 apples, peeled, cored, and sliced
½ cup sun dried raisins
½ cup chopped walnuts, *optional*

Preheat oven to 350 degrees F.

In a small bowl, combine raisins with about ½ cup water, and set aside to soak.

In medium mixing bowl, beat eggs, brown sugar, and vanilla extract until well mixed. Then, gradually add flour, baking powder, salt, and cinnamon. Add the apples *drained* raisins, and chopped walnuts, and mix just enough to blend well.

Use a rubber spatula to spread the dough evenly into a greased 9 x 13 inch baking dish, pushing it into the corners. Bake for 30 to 35 minutes, or until edges pull away from the baking dish. Let cool, and cut into squares before serving.

Apple Strudel

"'Apfelstrudel' is a traditional Austrian pastry that was very popular in the Banat, which once belonged to the Austro-Hungarian Empire."

Dough Ingredients:
1 cup unbleached flour
½ teaspoon salt
¼ cup butter, *softened*
1/3 cup warm water

Apple Filling Ingredients:
¼ cup raisins, *chopped*
2 tablespoons rum or brandy
6 large apples, *peeled, cored, and thinly sliced*
½ cup brown sugar
1½ tablespoons cornstarch
½ teaspoon cinnamon
¼ teaspoon nutmeg
1 teaspoon vanilla extract
1 teaspoon lemon juice
1/3 cup melted butter, *divided*
¼ cup walnuts, *chopped*
1 cup graham cracker crumbs (*if necessary, use a food processor to make crumbs*)

To prepare the dough, in a medium mixing bowl, combine the flour, salt, butter, and water. Mix well. On a lightly floured work surface, knead the dough with your hands until smooth. Then, cover the bowl loosely with plastic wrap and set aside for 30 minutes.

To prepare the apple filling, in a small bowl, combine the chopped raisins and rum. Set aside to soak. In a separate mixing bowl, combine the sliced apples, brown sugar, cornstarch, cinnamon, nutmeg, vanilla extract, lemon juice, 2 tablespoons melted butter, chopped walnuts, and *drained* raisins.

Preheat oven to 375 degrees F.

On a large floured tablecloth, roll out the dough to form a 16" x 24" rectangle. The dough should be nearly transparent. Then, brush the dough with melted butter, and sprinkle with graham cracker crumbs. Arrange the apple filling on the dough, in a row about 4 inches wide. Leave about 1 inch between the apple filling and the edge of the dough.

Fold the edges of the dough over the filling, and use the table cloth to roll the dough from the longer edge, starting with the filling. Roll tightly, to maintain shape and tuck-in the edges as you go.

Roll onto a greased jellyroll pan (*a baking pan with sides about ½ inch high*) with the seam on the bottom, and brush with melted butter. Make a few incisions for the steam to escape, and bake for 35 to 45 minutes, or until golden brown. *If necessary, cover with foil for the last 10 to 15 minutes, to prevent the crust from burning.*

Bavarian Dumplings with Vanilla Glaze

Dumpling Ingredients:
1 package quick-rise yeast
¼ cup lukewarm milk
3 cups unbleached flour
2 tablespoons sugar
½ teaspoon salt
¾ cup + 2 tablespoons lukewarm water
2 tablespoons + 1/3 cup melted butter
1 teaspoon vanilla extract
1 tablespoon brandy

Vanilla Glaze Ingredients:
2 tablespoons butter
2 tablespoons unbleached flour
1¼ cups milk
½ cup brown sugar
2 tablespoons brandy
1 teaspoon vanilla

To make the dumplings, dissolve the quick-rise yeast and 1 teaspoon of sugar in ¼ cup lukewarm milk. Let stand 5 minutes.

In a medium mixing bowl, combine the flour, sugar, and salt. Add the yeast mixture, lukewarm water, 2 tablespoons melted butter, vanilla extract, and brandy.

Mix just enough to blend well. Knead the dough until smooth and elastic, place in a greased bowl, cover with plastic wrap, and *let rise for 1 hour.*

Shape dough into 1 inch balls. Then, roll the dough in 1/3 cup melted butter. Arrange in a well-greased 9 inch bundt pan, forming multiple layers. *Cover loosely with plastic wrap, and let rise for 1 hour.*

To make the vanilla glaze, melt butter in a small saucepan. Gradually add flour and cook for about 1 minute, stirring constantly, until smooth. Then, add milk, stirring continuously, until glaze thickens. Add brown sugar, brandy, and vanilla extract. Mix well, and set aside.

Preheat oven to 350 degrees F. Bake for 30 to 35 minutes, or until golden brown. Pour vanilla glaze over top of dumplings. Allow dough to absorb glaze, and serve.

Porgie's Bread Pudding

"If you're looking for a tasty bread pudding recipe, you'll definitely want to try my mom's, which was actually one of my dad's favorite desserts. She served it hot, and didn't feel as though it needed any sort of rum sauce or anything like that. Also, she had a tendency to break the bread with her hands, rather than chopping it."

¾ cup raisins
½ cup honey
4 cups stale white bread cubes
1 quart milk
5 eggs
¼ cup brown sugar
¼ teaspoon salt
2 teaspoons vanilla extract
¼ teaspoon nutmeg

Preheat oven to 350 degrees F.

In a small bowl, combine the raisins with about 1 cup water. Set aside to soak.

In a medium saucepan, combine the honey and bread cubes. Cook over medium heat, and stir until the bread fully absorbs the honey; about 2 to 3 minutes.

In a medium mixing bowl, combine the milk, eggs, brown sugar, salt, and vanilla extract. Add the *drained* raisins and the egg mixture to the bread cubes, and mix well.

Pour into a greased 2 quart, deep baking dish. Sprinkle with nutmeg, and place the dish in a pan of hot water.

Bake for 1 hour, or until a knife comes out clean when inserted into the center of the bread pudding.

Brown Betty

"If I'm not mistaken, my mom got this recipe from my great-grandmother. A 'Brown Betty' is a dessert that evidently dates back to colonial times. A 'Betty' is essentially a baked pudding made with layers of fruit and bread crumbs, served with whipped cream. Though, we prefer graham cracker crumbs and vanilla ice cream."

8 medium apples, peeled, cored, and thinly sliced
1/3 cup butter, melted
1 teaspoon vanilla extract
1 teaspoon lemon juice
2 tablespoons dark rum or brandy
1 cup brown sugar
1 teaspoon cinnamon
½ teaspoon nutmeg
1 cup walnuts, chopped
1½ cups graham cracker crumbs

Preheat oven to 350 degrees F.

In a medium mixing bowl, combine the apples, melted butter, vanilla extract, lemon juice, and rum. In a separate mixing bowl, combine the brown sugar, cinnamon, nutmeg, and chopped walnuts.

Place a layer of sliced apples in a greased 8 x 8 inch baking dish, sprinkle with sugar/walnut mixture, then with bread crumb mixture. Repeat, to form layers, until all ingredients are used, saving a layer of graham cracker crumbs for the top.

Cover with foil, and bake for 40 minutes. Then, carefully remove foil and bake for an additional 20 minutes, allowing the top layer to brown. Remove from oven, and let stand at least 15 minutes before serving. Serve warm, with vanilla ice cream.

Brownies

2 eggs, separated
1/3 cup butter
¾ cup sugar
4 ounces baking chocolate, melted
1 teaspoon vanilla extract
½ cup unbleached flour
½ teaspoon baking powder
½ teaspoon salt
2 tablespoons milk
¾ cup walnuts, chopped

Preheat oven to 300 degrees F.

In a medium mixing bowl, beat egg whites until stiff peaks form, at least 5 to 7 minutes. Set aside.

In a separate mixing bowl, beat butter and sugar until light and fluffy. Add egg yolks and melted chocolate, and beat until well mixed. Add vanilla extract. Then, gradually add flour, baking powder, salt, and milk.

Use a whisk to gently fold-in the stiffly beaten egg whites and chopped walnuts. Spread into a lightly greased 8 x 8 inch baking dish, bake for 35 to 40 minutes, or until a toothpick inserted into the center of the bread is clean when removed. Cut into squares and serve immediately as the brownies will deflate quickly.

Cheese Strudel

"This austro-hungarian-style strudel recipe makes use of phyllo dough, rather than typical German strudel dough. It's also relatively quick and easy to make."

¼ cup sugar
1 (16 ounce) box frozen phyllo dough
1 ¼ cup butter, melted
1 (24 ounce) container small-curd cottage cheese
5 eggs

Allow phyllo dough to thaw in refrigerator overnight. Bring to room temperature before using.

Preheat oven to 350 degrees F.

Mix cottage cheese, sugar, and eggs. Carefully unroll the phyllo dough onto a smooth, dry surface, and divide into three equal parts, each consisting of approximately two or three sheets.

Place the *first layer* of phyllo dough on the bottom of an ungreased 9 x 13 inch baking dish, brush lightly with melted butter, and spread ½ cottage cheese mixture over top.

Place the *second layer* of phyllo dough on top, brush with melted butter, and spread remaining cottage cheese mixture over top.

Place the *third layer* of phyllo dough on top, and brush with melted butter.

Bake for 60 to 70 minutes. Let cool to room temperature, and cut into squares before serving.

Chocolaty Chocolate Biscotti

"Silvia made these one year for Christmas, and everybody loved 'em, especially my mom."

2 cups unbleached flour
½ cup cocoa powder
1 teaspoon baking soda
1 teaspoon salt
1/3 cup butter, *softened*
¾ cup sugar
2 eggs
¼ cup milk
½ cup chopped walnuts
¾ cup chocolate chips
6 ounces baking chocolate, *melted*

Preheat oven to 350°F.

In medium mixing bowl, use a whisk to combine the flour, cocoa powder, baking soda, and salt.

In a separate mixing bowl, beat the butter and sugar until light and fluffy. Add the eggs and beat until well mixed. Gradually add the flour mixture, milk, chopped walnuts, and chocolate chips.

Roll the dough into 2 logs, each about 12 inches long and 2 inches wide. Arrange the logs on a parchment paper-lined baking sheet, and bake for 35 minutes, or until slightly firm to the touch. Remove from oven, and let stand for 5 minutes.

Cut biscotti diagonally into ¾ inch slices. Then, return the biscotti to a parchment paper-lined baking sheet, and bake for an additional 10 minutes; until crisp.

In a small saucepan, melt the baking chocolate over low heat, stirring constantly. Now, using a wooden spoon, drizzle the melted chocolate in a zigzag pattern over the biscotti. Let stand until chocolate is firm.

Hilda's Cleaning Lady's Cake

"This is my Aunt Hilda's putzfrauenkuchen recipe. Putzfrauenkuchen, meaning 'cleaning lady's cake,' was inspired by German housekeepers that typically bring coffee and cake with them for their morning break."

Dough Ingredients:
½ cup butter
½ cup sugar
2 eggs
1 cup flour
1½ teaspoons baking powder

To make the dough, beat butter, sugar, and eggs together in a medium mixing bowl. Add flour and baking powder, and combine to make a soft dough. Use a spatula to spread the dough into a greased 9" x 13" baking dish.

Cream Pudding Ingredients:
2 (11 ounce) cans mandarin oranges, drained
3 egg whites
3 cups sour cream
3 egg yolks
¾ cup sugar
3 tablespoons milk
1½ tablespoons *'cook & serve' (not instant)* vanilla pudding
1½ cups sweetened coconut flakes

Preheat oven to 325 degrees F.

To make the cream pudding, evenly distribute the mandarin oranges over the top of the dough. Then, in a small mixing bowl, beat the egg whites until stiff peaks form, at least 5 to 7 minutes. Set aside.

In a separate bowl, combine sour cream, egg yolks, sugar, milk, and vanilla pudding. Use a whisk to mix in the egg whites. *Be careful not to deflate the egg whites*. Use a spatula to spread the cream pudding over the mandarin oranges.

Sprinkle coconut flakes over cream pudding, cover with parchment paper, and bake for 50 to 60 minutes. *Refrigerate overnight, and cut into squares before serving.*

Cream Cheese Cookie Tarts

Pastry Cup Ingredients:
½ cup butter, softened
1/3 cup sugar
¼ teaspoon salt
3 tablespoons milk
½ teaspoon vanilla extract
1 1/3 cups unbleached flour

Lemon Filling Ingredients:
1 (8 ounce) package cream cheese
¼ cup sugar
3 tablespoons unbleached flour
1 egg yolk
½ teaspoon grated lemon peel
2 teaspoons lemon juice
½ cup sweetened coconut flakes

To make the pastry cups, in a medium mixing bowl, beat butter, sugar, and salt until light and fluffy. Add milk and vanilla extract, and beat until well mixed. Then, gradually add flour, cover loosely with a clean kitchen towel or dish cloth, and *refrigerate for 30 minutes.*

To prepare the lemon filling, in a separate mixing bowl, combine the cream cheese, sugar, flour, and egg yolk. Add the grated lemon peel and lemon juice, and beat until well mixed.

Preheat oven to 375 degrees F. Then, lightly grease a muffin tin.

Press approximately 1 tablespoon of pastry dough into the bottom, and up the sides of each muffin cup. Then, spoon 1 tablespoon of lemon filling into each tart cup, and sprinkle with coconut flakes.

Bake for 12 to 15 minutes, or until pastry cups are light brown around the edges. Let cool slightly before removing from muffin tin.

Junior's Crescent Roll Cheesecake

"This is my granduncle, John Kleindienst's crescent roll cheesecake recipe. He made it for a graduation party, and my mom loved it, so she asked him to send the recipe via e-mail. Uncle John's e-mail address was 'thegr8johnl@aol.com.' He had a great sense of humor, which was also evident in the message's subject: 'Desert recipe, as requested. So there!'"

Topping Ingredients:
¼ cup butter
½ cup sugar
1½ teaspoons cinnamon

Filling & Crust Ingredients:
2 (8 ounce) packages cream cheese
1 cup sugar
1 teaspoon vanilla extract
2 (8 ounce) packages Pillsbury crescents

Preheat oven to 400 degrees F.

To prepare the topping, in a medium saucepan, heat butter over a medium flame, until just melting. Stir in sugar and cinnamon, remove from heat, and set aside.

To prepare the filling, in a medium mixing bowl, beat cream cheese, sugar, and vanilla until smooth. Set aside.

To prepare the crust, unroll 1 (8 ounce) package of crescent dough, and place the crescents side by side in a greased 9 x 13 inch baking dish. Pinch the seams together, to form one sheet of dough.

Bake for 10 minutes at 400 degrees F, for a firmer crust. Let cool for approximately 10 to 15 minutes.

Once the crust has cooled to room temperature, spread the cream cheese filling over top. Then, unroll the remaining package of crescent dough, and once again, place the crescents side by side, on top of the cream cheese mixture.

Use a brush to evenly distribute the melted butter topping over the top layer; *reduce the oven temperature to 350 degrees F*, and bake for an additional 30 minutes, or until golden brown. *Refrigerate overnight, and cut into squares before serving.*

Date Nut Bars

"This is another one of my great-grandmother's recipes. These date nut bars are easy to make, and are ideal for the holidays."

¼ cup unbleached flour
½ teaspoon baking powder
½ teaspoon salt
½ cup walnuts, chopped
1 cup dates, chopped
2 eggs
½ cup brown sugar

Preheat oven to 350 degrees F.

In a medium mixing bowl, beat eggs until light and fluffy. Add brown sugar.

In a separate mixing bowl, combine flour, baking powder, and salt. Add walnuts and dates, and gradually blend flour mixture into egg mixture.

Spread batter into a greased and floured 8 x 8 inch baking dish, and bake for 30 minutes, or until a toothpick inserted into the center of the bread is clean when removed. Let cool, and cut into bars, about 4 inches long x 1½ inches wide.

Date Oatmeal Squares

2 cups boiling water
2 (13 ounce) packages pitted, pressed baking dates
1 tablespoon unbleached flour
1 teaspoon vanilla extract
1 cup brown sugar
1 cup unbleached flour
1 teaspoon baking soda
3 cups rolled oats
½ cup melted butter
1 egg

Preheat oven to 375 degrees F.

In a medium saucepan, combine boiling water and dates. Add flour, and let simmer over low flame for 10 to 15 minutes, or until thickened. Remove from heat and add vanilla extract.

In a medium mixing bowl, combine the brown sugar, flour, baking soda, and rolled oats. Gradually add melted butter, stirring all the while. Add the egg and mix well.

Spread ½ oatmeal mixture in a greased 9 x 13 inch baking dish and punch it down. Then, using a spatula or large wooden spoon, gently cover with date mixture, and sprinkle with remaining oatmeal mixture.

Bake for 20 to 25 minutes, or until golden brown. Let cool to room temperature, and cut into 2" squares before serving.

Date Pudding

"This date pudding recipe was inspired by yet another visit to Ohio's Amish country. If I'm not mistaken, we might have had this for the first time at Der Dutchman, a commercial Amish family restaurant franchise of sorts. Ironic, no?"

Date Pudding Ingredients:
1 cup dates, chopped
1 tablespoon butter
1 teaspoon baking soda
1 cup boiling water
1 teaspoon vanilla
1 cup brown sugar
¼ teaspoon salt
1 egg
1 cup unbleached flour
1 cup walnuts, chopped

Syrup Ingredients:
1¼ cups brown sugar
½ cup water
1 teaspoon vanilla
Juice of ½ lemon

Preheat oven to 350 degrees F.

To make the date pudding, in a large mixing bowl, combine dates, butter, baking soda, and boiling water.

In a separate mixing bowl, beat vanilla, brown sugar, salt, and egg. Gradually add the flour and mix well. Then, add the egg/flour mixture to the date mixture, and add the chopped walnuts.

Pour into a greased 8 x 8 inch baking dish and bake for 45 - 50 minutes, or until a toothpick inserted into the center is clean when removed.

To make the syrup, in a medium saucepan, combine brown sugar, water, vanilla extract, and lemon juice. Bring to a boil over medium-high heat. Once the brown sugar has completely dissolved, remove from heat and let cool before using.

Serve date pudding warm, with simple syrup drizzled on top.

Date Sticks

1 cup sugar
2 tablespoons butter, softened
2 eggs
2 tablespoons warm milk
1 teaspoon vanilla extract
1 cup unbleached flour
1 teaspoon baking powder
1 cup dates, chopped
1/3 cup walnuts, chopped
2 tablespoons powdered sugar

Preheat oven to 350 degrees F.

In medium mixing bowl, beat sugar and butter until light and fluffy. Add eggs, milk, and vanilla extract. Beat until well mixed. Then, gradually add flour, baking powder, dates, and walnuts.

Spread dough on bottom of a greased 8 x 8 inch baking dish, and bake 25 to 30 minutes, or until golden brown. Let cool to room temperature, cut into strips, and garnish with powdered sugar.

Fruit Nut Bars

1 cup unbleached flour
2 tablespoons powdered sugar
½ cup butter, softened
2 eggs
¼ teaspoon salt
1 tablespoon whole-wheat flour
¾ cup brown sugar
2 tablespoons lemon juice
½ cup sweetened coconut flakes
¾ cup chopped walnuts
¼ cup sun dried raisins, chopped

Preheat oven to 350 degrees F.

In a small bowl, combine raisins with about ¼ cup water, and set aside to soak.

In a medium mixing bowl, use a whisk to combine the flour and powdered sugar. Then cut-in the butter to make a stiff dough, and spread on bottom of a greased 8 x 8 inch baking dish. *Bake for 10 minutes, and set aside.*

In a medium mixing bowl, beat eggs until light and foamy. Add salt, whole-wheat flour, brown sugar, lemon juice, coconut flakes, chopped walnuts, and *drained* raisins. Beat until well mixed.

Evenly distribute the egg mixture over the crust, and bake for 30 minutes or until golden brown and firm on top. *Refrigerate overnight, and cut into squares before serving.*

Gingerbread Hearts *(Lebkuchenherzen)*

"In Germany, large, elaborately decorated gingerbread hearts, known as lebkuchenherzen, are reasonably popular at festivals, especially during the holidays. They're an ideal gift for your sweetheart, often inscribed with phrases such as 'Be Mine,' 'I'm Yours,' or 'True Love.'"

Lebkuchenherzen Ingredients:
1/3 cup granulated white sugar
2 tablespoons butter, *softened*
1 egg
½ cup molasses
¼ cup honey
3¼ cups unbleached flour
1 teaspoon baking soda
1 tablespoon cocoa powder
½ teaspoon ginger
½ teaspoon cinnamon
¼ teaspoon nutmeg
1/8 teaspoon ground cloves
½ cup milk

To make the gingerbread hearts, in a medium mixing bowl, beat the sugar and butter until light and fluffy. Add the egg, molasses, and honey, and mix well.

In a separate mixing bowl, use a whisk to combine the flour, baking soda, cocoa powder, ginger, cinnamon, nutmeg, and ground cloves. Blend into the molasses mixture; *alternately with milk*. Place in a greased bowl, cover with plastic wrap, and *refrigerate for at least 3 hours*.

Preheat oven to 350 degrees F

On a floured work surface, knead the dough until smooth and workable. A slightly sticky dough is normal. Then, using a rolling pin, roll out the dough to a ¼ inch thickness. Cut-out the gingerbread hearts using a large, heart-shaped cookie cutter or template, and bake on a greased cookie sheet for 8 to 10 minutes, or until edges begin to brown. *Let cool completely before decorating with frosting.*

Frosting Ingredients:
2 cups powdered sugar
2 tablespoons butter, softened
2 tablespoons milk
½ teaspoon vanilla extract
Red food coloring, as needed

To make the frosting, in a mixing bowl, beat the powdered sugar, butter, milk, and vanilla extract until light and fluffy. Divide the mixture in half. Leaving half white, and adding a few drops of red food coloring to the other half. Now, fill a piping bag with white frosting, fill another with red frosting, and decorate the gingerbread hearts.

Indian Pudding

"This is my mom's take on indian pudding; a classic colonial american dish. Add ½ cup chopped walnuts if you like."

Pudding Ingredients:
2/3 cup cornmeal
½ teaspoon ginger
¼ teaspoon nutmeg
4 cups milk, *divided*
1 cup maple syrup
¼ cup butter
1½ cups dried cherries or raisins

Rum Sauce Ingredients:
½ cup butter, softened
1½ cup powdered sugar
2 tablespoons dark rum

Preheat oven to 300 degrees F.

To make the indian pudding, in small mixing bowl, use a whisk to combine the cornmeal, ginger, and nutmeg.

In a medium saucepan, heat *3 cups* milk and 1 cup maple syrup over a medium flame, until almost boiling. Reduce to low flame, and add ¼ cup butter. Gradually whisk in the cornmeal mixture and cook until thickened, about 5 minutes. Then, fold in the dried cherries, and spoon into a greased 8 x 8 inch baking dish. Pour the remaining *1 cup* milk over top, but *do not stir!*

Bake for 2½ hours, or until the milk has been absorbed and the top of the pudding is golden brown.

To prepare the rum sauce, in a medium mixing bowl, beat the butter and powdered sugar until light and fluffy. Then, add the rum, and beat until well mixed. Serve over top of indian pudding, with whipped cream.

Maple Nut Chews

"Maple trees flourish throughout northeastern Ohio, producing some of the finest maple syrup in the world. That's why pure maple syrup is a common sweetener in many of my mother's recipes, including Maple Nut Chews."

1/3 cup butter
¼ cup brown sugar
¼ cup maple syrup
½ teaspoon maple extract
1 egg
½ cup unbleached flour
¼ teaspoon salt
¼ teaspoon baking powder
½ cup sun dried raisins, chopped
½ cup walnuts, chopped

Preheat oven to 350 degrees F.

In a small bowl, combine raisins with about ½ cup water, and set aside to soak.

In a medium saucepan, combine butter, brown sugar, and maple syrup. Melt the butter, over medium heat, stirring all the while. Remove from heat, and *let cool to room temperature*. Add maple extract and egg.

In a medium mixing bowl, combine flour, salt, and baking powder. Add to butter mixture. Then, drain the raisins and add the raisins and walnuts to the batter. The batter should be thin enough to pour, but not runny.

Spread mixture into a 9 x 9 inch greased baking dish. Bake for 25 to 30 minutes, and let cool slightly. Cut into bars while still warm.

Aunt Mary's Mini Whiskey Cakes

"My great-grandaunt, Mary Beer used to make these mini whiskey cakes; another family favorite. She typically didn't use recipes. Instead, she'd just use a pinch of this, a dash of that, and handful the other. At any rate, this is an attempt to re-create some of her magic."

Cake Ingredients:
1 cup unbleached flour
1 cup sugar, divided
6 large eggs, separated
1 teaspoon vanilla extract
1 tablespoon water
Zest of 1 orange
3/4 teaspoon cream of tartar

Filling Ingredients:
1 cup walnuts, ground
¾ cup warm milk
¼ cup whiskey or dark rum
1 teaspoon vanilla extract
2/3 cup butter, softened
2/3 cup powdered sugar
2 teaspoons cocoa powder

Frosting Ingredients:
¼ cup butter
½ cup cocoa powder
1/3 cup + 1 tablespoon milk
1 teaspoon vanilla extract
3 cups powdered sugar
¼ cup walnuts, chopped

To make the mini cakes, preheat oven to 350 degrees F and let the eggs stand for approximately 30 minutes, in order to reach room temperature. Then, in a small mixing bowl, use a whisk to combine the flour and ¼ cup sugar. Set aside. In a separate mixing bowl, beat the egg yolks and ½ cup sugar on high speed for approximately five minutes, or until light and fluffy. Add vanilla extract, water, and orange zest. Mix well. Beat the egg whites until stiff peaks form, at least 5 to 7 minutes. Then, gradually add cream of tartar and remaining ¼ cup sugar. Use a whisk to gently mix in the flour mixture and egg whites into egg yolk mixture, just enough to incorporate. *Overmixing will deflate the batter.* Line the bottom of a 9 x 13 inch baking dish with parchment paper, and apply a light coating of nonstick cooking spray. Then, pour the batter into the baking dish and use a spatula to evenly distribute the cake batter. Bake for 30 to 35 minutes or until a toothpick inserted into the center is clean when removed. *Remove from oven and immediately invert.* Let stand for at least one hour before cutting into rounds using a floured drinking glass or a 2 inch round cookie cutter*, and *carefully splitting each cake into two horizontal layers.*

To make the filling, in a small bowl, combine the ground walnuts, warm milk, whiskey, and vanilla extract. Let stand for approximately 10 minutes, until cool. Then, in a separate mixing bowl, cream the butter, powdered sugar, and cocoa powder. Gradually add the milk and walnut mixture about 1 tablespoon at a time, and beat until well combined. *A slightly wet appearance is normal.* Place the bottom layer of a sponge cake on a serving platter, spread with filling, place second layer on top, and repeat. *Cover mini cakes with plastic wrap, and freeze overnight.*

To make the frosting, in a medium mixing bowl, beat butter and cocoa powder together. Add milk and vanilla extract, and beat until light and fluffy. Gradually blend in powdered sugar until desired consistency is achieved. Add more milk or powdered sugar if necessary. Frost the top and sides of the mini cakes, sprinkle with chopped walnuts, and *refrigerate for at least two hours before serving!*

*If you prefer, you can also reserve the excess trimmings, use a blender or food processor to grind them into coarse crumbs, and add them to the filling.

Nut Queens

Topping Ingredients:
1 egg white, *reserve yolk for cake*
1 teaspoon vanilla extract
½ cup brown sugar
½ cup walnuts, chopped

Cake Ingredients:
½ cup butter
1 cup white sugar
2 egg yolks
1 egg white
1 teaspoons vanilla extract
2 cups unbleached flour
2 teaspoons baking powder
¼ teaspoon salt
¼ - ½ cup milk

Preheat oven to 325 degrees F.

In a medium mixing bowl, beat 1 egg white until stiff peaks form, at least 5 to 7 minutes. Using a whisk, add 1 teaspoon vanilla extract, brown sugar, and chopped walnuts. Set aside.

In a separate mixing bowl, cream butter and white sugar. Add egg yolks, remaining egg white, and 1 teaspoon vanilla extract. Beat until well mixed. Then, gradually add flour, baking powder, and salt. Add just enough milk, about a tablespoon at a time, to bring the mixture to a consistency that's thin enough to spread easily.

Spread dough into a greased 8 x 8 inch baking dish, and cover with walnut mixture, using a spatula to form peaks in the topping. Bake 35 to 40 minutes, or until golden brown. Let cool, and cut into small squares.

Orange Date Squares

Cake Ingredients:
1/3 cup butter
2/3 cup sugar
2 eggs
Grated rind of 1 orange
2 cups unbleached flour
1 teaspoon baking powder
1 teaspoon salt
½ cup orange juice
1½ cup dates, finely chopped
½ cup pecans, finely chopped

Icing Ingredients:
1 tablespoon butter, melted
1¼ cups powdered sugar
2 tablespoons orange juice

Preheat oven to 350 degrees F.

To make the cake, in large mixing bowl, beat butter and sugar until light and fluffy. Add eggs, and grated orange rind. Mix well.

In a separate mixing bowl, combine flour, baking powder, and salt. Gradually add flour mixture and orange juice to egg mixture. Fold-in dates and pecans.

Spread into greased 8 x 8 inch baking dish, bake for 1 hour, and let cool to room temperature.

To make the icing, in a medium mixing bowl, blend melted butter, powdered sugar, and orange juice until light and fluffy.

Once cake has cooled to room temperature, spread with icing, *refrigerate overnight*, and cut into 2 inch squares before serving.

Orange Marmalade Bread Pudding

5 slices day-old bread, toasted
3 tablespoons butter, softened
¾ cup orange marmalade
3 eggs, slightly beaten
1¾ cups milk
1 tablespoon lemon juice
1/8 teaspoon nutmeg

Preheat oven to 300 degrees F.

Spread the slices of toast with butter and marmalade, do not remove crust. Arrange slices of toast in a greased 2 quart, deep baking dish.

In a medium mixing bowl, combine eggs, milk, brown lemon juice and nutmeg. Mix well, and pour over the toast. Let stand for 10 minutes, pressing down occasionally, into the milk mixture.

Bake for 45 minutes, or until a sharp knife inserted into the center comes out clean and the top is lightly browned. Serve warm, with cream or lemon sauce.

Peach Kuchen

"Although not a typical yeast kuchen, my great-grandmother's peach kuchen is ideal served with vanilla ice cream."

3 cups unbleached flour, *divided*
1 teaspoon salt, *divided*
1 cup butter
2 cups sour cream, *divided*
8 peaches, pitted, and sliced
2 eggs, slightly beaten
1½ cups sugar
1 teaspoon cinnamon

Preheat oven to 375 degrees F.

In a medium mixing bowl, combine 2¾ cups flour and ½ teaspoon salt. Cut-in butter, and blend until mixture resembles coarse crumbs. Add ¼ cup sour cream, and mix well.

Spread the dough evenly into a greased 9 x 13 inch baking dish, punching down the dough and pushing it into all four corners. Bake for 20 minutes. Then, place the sliced peaches on the baked crust.

In a separate mixing bowl, combine the remaining ¼ cup flour, ½ teaspoon salt, 1¾ cups sour cream, eggs, sugar, and cinnamon.

Pour the egg mixture over the sliced peaches, and bake for 40 to 50 minutes, or until lightly browned and bubbly. Serve warm.

Peanut Oatmeal Chewies

½ cup butter
1½ cups brown sugar
2 eggs
½ cup chunky peanut butter
1½ cups rolled oats
½ cup unbleached flour
½ cup whole-wheat flour

Preheat oven to 325 degrees F.

In medium mixing bowl, beat butter and brown sugar until light and fluffy. Add eggs and peanut butter, and beat until well incorporated. Then, gradually add oats and flour, and mix well.

Use a spatula to spread the dough into to a greased 9 x 13 inch baking pan, and bake for 35 minutes. Let cool to room temperature, and cut into squares before serving.

Plum Dumplings

"Schwäbische plum dumplings, or zwetschkenknödel, are ideal when served as an afternoon snack, with coffee or tea. It's important to use bluebird plums for this recipe. They're typically smaller, and have a deep blue/purple skin and amber colored fruit."

Dumpling Ingredients:
4 medium potatoes
1/3 cup butter, softened
2 eggs
½ teaspoon salt
1¼ teaspoons baking powder
2½ cups unbleached flour

Filling Ingredients:
12 bluebird plums, *halved and pitted*
12 teaspoons brown sugar

Streusel Ingredients:
¼ cup butter
¾ cup unseasoned bread crumbs
¼ cup brown sugar
1 tablespoon cinnamon

In a large pot or dutch oven, bring approximately 2 quarts water and 1 teaspoon salt to boil.

To prepare the potatoes, wash and peel the potatoes. Cut into 1 inch cubes, and place in a medium pot. Add 1 teaspoon salt and just enough water to cover. Bring to a boil over high heat. Then, reduce heat to medium low, and simmer until fork tender, about 25 minutes. Drain excess water, and let stand. *Once cool, mash the potatoes, cover, and set aside.*

To make the dumplings, combine the mashed potatoes, butter, eggs, salt, baking powder, and flour in a medium mixing bowl. On a lightly floured work surface, roll the dough into a 16 x 12 inch rectangle, and cut into 4 inch squares.

To prepare the filling, place 1 plum and 1 teaspoon brown sugar on each square. Moisten the edges with water, and pinch the corners together to seal the dough. Then, roll into a ball. Place the dumplings into the pot of boiling water. Cover, and simmer until dumplings are firm, about 8 to 10 minutes. Remove the dumplings with slotted spoon, and set aside.

To prepare the streusel, combine the butter and bread crumbs in a medium saucepan. Heat over a medium flame until light brown, stirring all the while. Then, roll the dumplings in the bread crumb mixture.

In a small mixing bowl, use a whisk to combine the brown sugar and cinnamon. Sprinkle over the dumplings, and serve.

Plum Kuchen

"Although my great-grandmother made apple kuchen far more often than plum kuchen, she typically added cherries to her plum kuchen. Since my great-grandfather cultivated bluebird plums and rainier cherries, that's what she used. I'm sure you can find a reasonable substitution though."

Dough Ingredients:
1 cup warm milk
1 package quick-rise yeast
2½ cups unbleached flour
¼ teaspoon salt
1/3 cup sugar
1 tablespoon vanilla sugar
1/3 cup butter, softened

Topping Ingredients:
8 bluebird plums, *pitted and cut into ½ inch pieces*
1½ pounds (*about 1 quart*) rainier cherries, *pitted and quartered*
½ cup unbleached flour
½ cup brown sugar
½ teaspoon cinnamon
¼ teaspoon nutmeg
¼ teaspoon salt
1/3 cup firm butter

To make the dough, in a medium mixing bowl, dissolve quick-rise yeast in milk. Then, add flour, salt, sugar, vanilla sugar, and butter. Mix gently, until lumps disappear. *Add a little more flour if necessary. Be sure not to over-mix!* Let the dough rest for a few minutes.

To make the topping, combine flour, brown sugar, cinnamon, nutmeg, and salt. Cut-in the butter until the mixture resembles coarse crumbs.

Gently press the dough into a greased 9 x 13 inch baking dish, and evenly distribute the plums and cherries on top. Then, sprinkle the streusel topping over the fruit. Set aside, and let rise in a warm place for about 30 minutes.

Preheat oven to 400 degrees F.

Bake for 30 to 35 minutes, or until golden brown.

Plum Puff Pudding

"Not to be confused with various plum puff pastries or christmas puddings; my great-grandmother's plum puff pudding is named such because of its soft, airy texture. It's also a great way to make use of plums that are so readily available from mid-summer to early fall."

8 large plums *(about 4 cups); peeled, pitted, and pureed*
1 tablespoon, + ¼ cup water
2 tablespoons quick-cooking tapioca*
¾ cup brown sugar
¼ teaspoon cardamom
½ teaspoon cinnamon
¼ teaspoon salt, divided
1 teaspoon vanilla extract

2 eggs, *separated*
1/3 cup sugar
¼ teaspoon cream of tartar
½ cup unbleached flour

Preheat oven to 325 degrees F.

Once the plums have been peeled and pitted, cut into ½ inch pieces. Combine the plums and 1 tablespoon water in a food processor, and puree. *Add a little more water if necessary.* Then, in a medium saucepan, combine plum puree, ¼ cup water, tapioca, brown sugar, cardamom, cinnamon, and 1/8 teaspoon salt. Bring to a boil, and cook for about 1 minute. Remove from heat, add vanilla extract, and spread the plum mixture into a greased 8 x 8 inch baking dish.

In a separate mixing bowl, beat *egg yolks* until light and foamy. Gradually add sugar, and set aside.

In a large mixing bowl, beat *egg whites*, remaining 1/8 teaspoon salt, and cream of tartar until stiff peaks form, at least 5 to 7 minutes.

Using a whisk, gently mix the egg yolk mixture into the egg whites. Gradually, add the flour, and spread over the plum mixture.

Bake for 50 minutes.

*If you prefer, you may substitute half as much cornstarch. However, cornstarch has a tendency to break down if it's mixed with acidic ingredients, cooked for a long time, frozen, or thawed.

Poppy Seed Cheesecake

Crust Ingredients:
1 2/3 cups unbleached flour
1 teaspoon baking powder
1/3 sugar
2 teaspoons vanilla sugar
2 eggs
¾ cup butter

Poppy Seed Layer:
1 cup poppy seeds
¾ cup milk
1/3 cup honey
½ cup brown sugar
2 tablespoons butter
½ cup sun dried raisins, chopped
1 teaspoon vanilla extract
1 teaspoon lemon juice
2 eggs, slightly beaten

Cream Cheese Layer:
2 egg whites
3 (8 ounce) packages cream cheese, softened
2/3 cup sugar
2 egg yolks
¼ teaspoon salt
Zest of ½ lemon
1/3 cup finely ground cornmeal
1/3 cup butter, melted

Blackberry Syrup:
3 tablespoons seedless blackberry jam
3 tablespoons water

Preheat oven to 375 degrees F. *To make the crust*, in a medium mixing bowl, combine flour, baking powder, sugar, and vanilla sugar. Add the eggs and cut-in the butter using a pastry blender. Mix just enough to blend well. Then, turn out the dough onto a well floured work surface. Knead until smooth, adding just enough flour to keep the dough from sticking.

To prepare the cream cheese layer, in a medium mixing bowl, beat egg whites until stiff peaks form, at least 5 to 7 minutes. Set aside. Now, in a separate mixing bowl, combine cream cheese, sugar, egg yolks, salt, lemon zest, cornmeal, and melted butter. Using a whisk, fold the egg whites into the cream cheese mixture.

To prepare the poppy seed layer, in a small saucepan, combine poppy seeds, milk, honey, butter, and raisins. Bring to boil over medium heat. Reduce heat, and let simmer for approximately 30 minutes (*stirring frequently*) until most of the liquid is absorbed. Remove from heat, and let stand 5 minutes. Then, add vanilla extract and lemon juice. In a separate bowl, beat egg, and slowly whisk into poppy seed mixture. Set aside to cool.

Gently press *two-thirds* of the dough into a greased 9 x 13 inch baking dish, spread the cream cheese mixture on top, followed by the poppy seed mixture. Roll out the remaining dough to about a ¼ inch thickness and cut into ½ inch strips. Then, arrange strips (on top of poppy seed layer) in a lattice pattern.

To prepare the syrup, in a small saucepan, combine blackberry jam and water. Bring to a boil, stirring constantly. Gently brush syrup over dough strips, bake for 50 minutes, and refrigerate overnight before serving.

Poppy Seed Coffee Cake

Filling Ingredients:
¾ cup poppy seed
¾ cup blanched almonds
½ cup sugar
1/3 cup milk
Zest of one lemon
3 tablespoon butter
1 tablespoon lemon juice

Coffee Cake Ingredients:
½ cup milk
¼ cup melted butter
1 egg
2½ cups unbleached flour
½ teaspoon salt
¼ cup sugar
1 package rapid-rise yeast

To make the filling:

In a food processor, combine poppy seed and blanched almonds. Mix until thoroughly incorporated.

In a small sauce pan, combine poppy seed and almond mixture with sugar, milk, lemon zest, butter, and lemon juice. Heat over low flame, stirring continuously for about 10 minutes. Set aside to cool.

To make the coffee cake:

In a medium mixing bowl, combine milk, butter, egg, flour, salt, sugar, and rapid-rise yeast. Cover loosely with greased plastic wrap, and set aside to rise half its size again. Anywhere from 45 to 60 minutes.

Turn-out the dough onto a floured work surface, and knead to release any air. Roll the dough into a 10 by 15 inch and ¼ inch thick rectangle. Then, carefully mark off two lines with your fingers to divide the dough into three equal lengthwise sections.

Spread filling lengthwise, down the center third of dough. With a sharp knife, cut 10 diagonal strips on each side. Overlap the strips, first from one side then the other, to create a braided appearance. Preheat oven to 350 degrees F.

Place on an un-greased baking sheet. Cover loosely with greased plastic wrap and let rise until doubled in size. Bake at 350 degrees F for 25-30 minutes or until golden brown.

Mom's Poppy Seed Roll

"One of my all time favorites! My mom's poppy seed roll, or potica, is made with a yeast dough, rather than a typical strudel dough. The recipe was handed down from my great-grandmother, and because I had a tendency to substitute chopped raisins, my mom was adamant that the maraschino cherries were an indispensable ingredient."

Poppy Seed Filling Ingredients:
1 cup poppy seeds
¾ cup milk
1/3 cup honey
½ cup brown sugar
2 tablespoons butter
1 teaspoon vanilla extract
1 teaspoon lemon juice
2 eggs, slightly beaten

Dough Ingredients:
1½ tablespoons quick-rise yeast
¼ cup warm water
¼ cup warm milk
½ teaspoon salt
¼ cup sugar
¼ cup melted butter
1 egg
2½ cups unbleached flour

Additional Ingredients:
¼ cup chopped maraschino cherries, *optional*

To prepare the poppy seed filling, in a medium saucepan, combine the poppy seeds, milk, honey, brown sugar, and butter. Bring to a boil over medium heat. Then, reduce heat, and let simmer for 30 minutes, or until most of the liquid is absorbed. Remove from heat, and let stand 15 minutes. Whisk in vanilla extract, lemon juice, and eggs. *Refrigerate for at least 2 hours.*

To prepare the dough, in a medium mixing bowl, dissolve the quick-rise yeast in warm water, with a pinch of sugar. Let stand for five minutes. Then, blend in the milk, salt, sugar, melted butter, and egg. Gradually add the flour, and beat to make a soft dough. Knead until smooth, place in greased bowl, and cover. *Allow mixture to double (about 1½ hours).*

On a lightly floured work surface, roll the dough into a rectangle, approximately 12" by 14". Spread the poppy seed filling onto the dough and dot with maraschino cherries, leaving about ½ inch between the filling and the edge of the dough. Now, tightly roll up the dough from the long end. Wet the edge/seam on bottom so it sticks to the roll, place on a greased jellyroll pan (*a baking pan with sides about ½ inch high*), cover, and *let rise for 45 minutes*. Preheat oven to 350 degrees F and bake for 30 to 35 minutes, or until golden brown.

Poppy Seed Squares

"It was during my first trip to Germany, when it seemed as though there was a bakery on every corner, that I tried mohnschnitte for the first time. Loosely translated as 'poppy seed squares' or 'poppy seed bars,' mohnschnitte soon became one of my favorite baked goods. My cousin, Marina, lives in Echzell, Germany and thankfully shared this recipe with me."

Dough Ingredients:
1 package quick-rise yeast
¼ cup warm water
¼ cup warm milk
½ teaspoon salt
¼ cup sugar
1 egg
¼ cup butter, melted
2½ cups unbleached flour

Streusel Ingredients:
1 cup unbleached flour
¾ cup sugar
¾ cup butter
1 teaspoon vanilla extract

Poppy Seed Mixture Ingredients:
2 cups poppy seeds
1½ cups milk
1 tablespoon honey
1/3 cup brown sugar
¼ cup butter
½ cup chopped raisins
¼ cup chopped walnuts
½ teaspoon cinnamon
Zest of one lemon
1 teaspoon vanilla extract
¼ cup amaretto liquor

Preparing the Dough:
In a medium mixing bowl, dissolve quick-rise yeast in ¼ cup warm water. Let stand for five minutes. Then, blend in milk, salt, sugar, butter, and egg. Add 2½ cups flour, and beat to make soft dough. Knead dough until smooth. Place in greased bowl, and cover. Allow mixture to double (about 1½ hours). On a lightly floured board, roll dough into a rectangle approximately 12" by 8".

Preparing the Poppy Seed Mixture:
In a medium saucepan, combine the poppy seeds, milk, honey, brown sugar, butter, raisins, walnuts, cinnamon, and lemon zest. Bring to boil over medium heat. Then, reduce heat and let simmer for approximately 30 minutes (*stirring frequently*) until most of the liquid is absorbed. Remove from heat, and let stand 5 minutes. Add vanilla extract and amaretto liquor. Set aside to cool.

Preparing the Streusel:
Preheat oven to 400 degrees F. In a medium mixing bowl, combine flour, sugar, butter, and vanilla extract. Mix by hand until the ingredients are evenly combined.

Spread dough in a greased 9 x 13 inch baking dish. Cover with poppy seed mixture, and sprinkle streusel on top. Bake for 30 to 40 minutes. *Refrigerate overnight, and cut into squares, and bring to room temperature before serving.*

Raisin-Date Bars

Filling Ingredients:
1½ cups water
¼ cup sugar
1½ cups sun dried raisins
1½ cups chopped dates
½ cup chopped walnuts

Dough Ingredients:
½ cup butter, softened
¼ cup shortening
1 cup packed brown sugar
½ teaspoon baking soda
1 teaspoon salt
1½ cups unbleached flour
1 cup quick-cooking oats

Preheat oven to 400 degrees F.

To prepare the filling, in a medium saucepan, combine water, sugar, raisins, and dates. Bring to a boil over low heat, stirring occasionally. Cook for 10 to 12 minutes or until mixture thickens, stirring occasionally. Stir-in chopped walnuts, remove from heat, and set aside.

To prepare the dough, in a separate mixing bowl, combine butter, shortening, and brown sugar. Gradually add baking soda, salt, flour, and oats, until the mixture resembles coarse crumbs.

Spread ½ the dough into a greased 9 x 13 inch baking dish, punching it down and pushing it into the corners. Then, spread the raisin-date filling over top, and sprinkle with the remaining dough mixture, pressing lightly.

Bake for 25 to 30 minutes, or until golden brown. Then, remove from oven and make a diagonal cut from one corner to another. Continue cutting, parallel to the first cut. Each cut should be about 1½ inches apart. Now, repeat; cutting in opposite direction. *Let cool to room temperature before serving.*

Raspberry Squares

"I prefer to use raspberry preserves with seeds, like my great-grandmother did. In order to keep the preserves from overflowing, be sure to work the edge of the dough with your fingers, pushing the dough up the side of the baking dish prior to spreading on the preserves."

Cake Ingredients:
1 cup unbleached flour
1 teaspoon baking powder
½ cup butter
1 egg
1 tablespoon milk
½ cup raspberry preserves

Topping Ingredients:
1 egg
½ cup brown sugar
1 teaspoon vanilla extract
¼ cup butter, melted
½ cup unsweetened coconut flakes

Preheat oven to 350 degrees F.

To make the cake, in a medium mixing bowl, combine flour and baking powder. Cut-in butter, add egg and milk, and mix well. Spread dough on bottom of a greased 8 x 8 inch baking dish, and cover with preserves.

To make the topping, in a separate mixing bowl, beat egg, brown sugar, vanilla extract, and melted butter together. Add coconut flakes, mix well, and spread on top of preserves.

Spread topping over cake, and bake for 30 minutes or until golden brown. *Refrigerate overnight, and cut into squares before serving.*

Raspberry Turnovers

1 (16 ounce) box frozen phyllo dough
½ cup raspberry preserves
2 tablespoons cornstarch
2 tablespoons brown sugar
½ teaspoon vanilla extract
½ teaspoon grated lemon rind
1 cup frozen raspberries, *thawed and drained*
¼ cup melted butter
Egg wash (*made by beating 1 egg white lightly, with 2 teaspoons water*)
2 tablespoons coarse granulated sugar

Allow phyllo dough to thaw in refrigerator overnight. Bring to room temperature before using.

Preheat oven to 375 degrees F.

Carefully unroll the phyllo sheets onto a smooth, dry surface. Divide the phyllo dough into equal parts, each consisting of approximately two or three sheets, and cut the dough into 6-inch squares.

In a medium mixing bowl, combine raspberry preserves, cornstarch, brown sugar, vanilla extract, and grated lemon rind. Gently fold-in the raspberries, and set aside.

Place the phyllo dough squares on an ungreased baking sheet, about 1 inch apart. Brush with melted butter, and place approximately 2 tablespoons of raspberry filling in the center of each square.

Then, brush the edges of each square with egg wash and fold in half, forming a triangle. Carefully press the edges together and use a fork to press down, sealing each turnover.

Lastly, brush the tops with remaining egg wash, and sprinkle coarse granulated sugar over top. Bake for 20 to 25 minutes, or until golden brown. Serve warm.

Rabarberkuchen

"This is my cousin (first cousin, twice removed actually), Katharina Diehlmann's rhubarb cake recipe. It's a family favorite, passed down to me by Katharina's granddaughter, Marina."

Cake Ingredients:
½ cup butter, softened
1/3 cup sugar
1 egg
2 tablespoons warm milk
1½ cups unbleached flour
2 teaspoons baking powder
¼ teaspoon salt

Rhubarb Mixture:
1 pound rhubarb, *thinly sliced*
¾ cup sugar
2 tablespoons unbleached flour

Topping Ingredients:
2 eggs
1½ cups sour cream
3 tablespoons sugar
½ teaspoon cinnamon
¼ cup chopped walnuts

Preheat oven to 350 degrees F.

To prepare the cake, in medium mixing bowl, beat butter and sugar until light and fluffy. Add egg and milk, and beat until well mixed. Then, gradually add flour, baking powder, and salt; until well combined.

Using a rubber spatula, spread the batter into a greased 9 x 9 inch baking dish. **Bake for 15 minutes.**

To prepare the rhubarb mixture, combine rhubarb, sugar, and flour. Place sliced rhubarb on top of cake. **Bake for 15 minutes.** Remove from oven, and let cool for 30 minutes.

To prepare the topping, in a separate mixing bowl, beat eggs, sour cream, sugar, and cinnamon together. Mix well, and spread on top of sliced rhubarb. Sprinkle with chopped walnuts.

Bake for an additional 20 to 25 minutes, or until golden brown. Let cool to room temperature before cutting into squares. Serve immediately.

Rhubarb Shortcake

"My mom had a patch of rhubarb on the side of the house, and every spring she made rhubarb shortcake. Without a doubt, this is one of my favorites!"

Cake Ingredients:
2 cups unbleached flour
1 tablespoon baking powder
1 teaspoon salt
½ cup sugar
¼ cup butter
1 egg
¾ cup milk
1 teaspoon vanilla extract
4 cups sliced rhubarb
1 (3 ounce) package of raspberry gelatin powder*

Topping Ingredients:
1/3 cup unbleached flour
1½ cups sugar
1/3 cup butter

Preheat oven to 375 degrees F.

To make the cake, in a large bowl, combine flour, baking powder, salt, and sugar. Cut-in butter until mixture resembles coarse crumbs.

In a small mixing bowl, combine egg, milk, and vanilla extract. Blend into flour mixture, and spread into a greased 9 x 13 inch baking dish. Top with sliced rhubarb, and sprinkle with raspberry gelatin powder.

To make the topping, combine flour, sugar, and butter. Sprinkle topping over top of rhubarb, and bake for 40 to 50 minutes.

Optional. My great-grandmother omitted the raspberry gelatin powder.

Rice Krispies Treats

"Snap! Crackle! Pop! My sister, Mary, used to be a member of the Girl Scouts and would make Rice Krispies marshmallow squares with her friends from time to time."

3 tablespoons butter
1 (10 ounce) package marshmallows
6 cups Rice Krispies toasted rice cereal

In a large saucepan, melt butter over low heat. Add marshmallows, and stir until completely melted. Remove from heat, and add Rice Krispies. Stir until well combined.

Using a greased spatula, press Rice Krispies mixture into a greased 9 x 13 inch baking dish. Let cool to room temperature, cut into squares, and serve immediately.

Slovenian Cream Nut Horns

"If you don't already have one, you'll need a set of cream horn molds for this recipe."

1 package quick-rise yeast
¼ cup warm milk
2½ cups unbleached flour
¼ teaspoon salt
1 cup butter, softened
3 egg yolks
1 cup sour cream
1 teaspoon vanilla extract

2 cups heavy cream
2 tablespoons powdered sugar
2 teaspoons cocoa powder
1 tablespoon coffee liqueur, cognac, or dark rum
1¼ cups ground walnuts
3 tablespoons brown sugar
1 teaspoon lemon zest
Egg wash (*made by beating 1 egg white lightly, with 2 teaspoons water*)

Dissolve quick-rise yeast in ¼ cup warm milk, and let stand for at least 5 minutes.

In a medium mixing bowl, combine flour and salt. Cut-in butter using a pastry blender. Add egg yolks, sour cream, vanilla extract, and yeast mixture. Mix well. Then, place in a greased bowl, and refrigerate for at least 2 hours.

In a separate mixing bowl, whip heavy cream until almost stiff. Beat-in powdered sugar, cocoa powder, and coffee liqueur. *Blend well and refrigerate.*

In a small mixing bowl, combine ground walnuts, brown sugar, and lemon zest. Set aside.

Preheat oven to 350 degrees F.

Turn-out the dough onto a lightly floured work surface, and knead to release any air. Roll out the dough to about 1/8 inch thickness, and cut into ½ inch wide strips. Beginning at the tip of a greased cream horn mold*, wrap a strip of dough around the mold, overlapping the strip slightly. Then, lightly brush the horn with egg wash, roll in walnut mixture, and arrange approximately 2 inches apart on a parchment paper-lined baking sheet. Repeat.

Bake for 25 minutes, or until golden brown. Remove from oven, and *let cool completely before removing the molds.* Then, use a pastry bag fitted with a star tip to fill each horn with cream. *Refrigerate for at least 30 minutes before serving.*

*If you don't have a set of cream horn molds, divide the dough into eight equal parts. Then, on a lightly floured work surface, roll each part into a 12 inch circle, and cut it into 12 equal pie-shaped wedges. Spread 1 teaspoon of cream onto each wedge, tuck in the edges, and roll up (toward the narrow part of the wedge).

Strawberry Shortcake

"This is my mom's strawberry shortcake recipe. It's another family favorite, and is made with fresh strawberries. Rather than cutting biscuit rounds, she preferred to drop the dough onto a baking sheet, using a large wooden spoon."

1 quart fresh strawberries, quartered
1 tablespoon powdered sugar
2 cups unbleached flour
1 tablespoon baking powder
2 tablespoons sugar
½ teaspoon salt
¼ cup shortening
¾ cup milk

Preheat oven to 425 degrees F.

In a small mixing bowl, combine strawberries and powdered sugar. Set aside.

In a separate, medium mixing bowl, combine flour, baking powder, sugar, and salt. Cut-in shortening. Add milk, and mix well.

On a floured work surface, knead the dough until smooth. Pat into ½ inch thick rounds (*or if you prefer, use a 2 inch biscuit cutter or drinking glass to cut rounds*) and place on a greased baking sheet.

Bake for 20 minutes. Top with fresh strawberries, and serve immediately.

Tapioca Pudding

"This is my great-grandmother's tapioca pudding recipe. Although it can also be made with tapioca flakes, I've always preferred tapioca pearls. Undoubtedly, this is my favorite pudding."

¼ cup tapioca pearls, or *1½ tablespoons minute tapioca**
2 cups milk, heated almost to boiling
1 egg, separated
1/3 cup sugar
¼ teaspoon salt
1 teaspoon vanilla extract

Soak tapioca pearls in cold water overnight. Drain. In a medium saucepan, heat milk until almost boiling, and cook over medium low heat until tapioca is transparent, about 1 hour.

Then, in a medium mixing bowl, combine egg yolk, sugar, and salt. Gradually, add 1½ cups tapioca mixture (about ½ cup at a time) to egg mixture. Return to saucepan, and cook until pudding thickens, stirring all the while.

Use a whisk to fold in the egg white (*beaten stiff*) and remove from heat. Refrigerate for at least 2 hours before serving.

**If minute tapioca is used, it need not be soaked.*

Walnut Frosties with Orange Butter Cream

Cake Ingredients:

Bottom Layer:

2 tablespoons powdered sugar
½ cup butter, softened
1 cup unbleached flour

Middle Layer:

2 eggs
1 cup brown sugar
2 tablespoons unbleached flour
½ teaspoon baking powder
1/8 teaspoon salt
1 cup walnuts, chopped
½ cup sweetened coconut flakes

Orange Butter Cream Ingredients:

2 tablespoons butter, melted
1 tablespoon orange juice
1¼ cups powdered sugar
1½ teaspoons grated orange rind

Preheat oven to 350 degrees F.

To make the bottom layer of the cake, in medium mixing bowl, beat powdered sugar, butter, and 1 cup flour until mixture resembles coarse crumbs. Gently knead the dough until smooth.

Spread the dough into the bottom of a greased 8 x 8 inch baking dish, using your fingertips to push it into the corners; creating a small ridge around the sides. Bake 10 minutes. Let cool for 10 to 15 minutes.

To make the middle layer of the cake, beat eggs, brown sugar, 2 tablespoons flour, baking powder, and salt together. Add chopped walnuts and coconut flakes, mix well, and spread on top of dough.

Bake for 25 minutes, or until top is firm. Let cool to room temperature.

To make the orange butter cream, in a medium mixing bowl, combine melted butter, orange juice, and powdered sugar. Add grated orange rind. Blend well. Frost with orange butter cream, and cut into squares.

Granny's Potica/Nut Roll

"Potica is a type of Slovenian yeast bread that's similar to strudel, but it's usually made with a walnut filling instead. My 2nd great-grandmother, Mary Kleindienst, was Slovenian. I'm pretty sure my great-grandmother learned how to make this walnut potica from her."

Walnut Filling Ingredients:
½ cup chopped sundried raisins
2 eggs, separated
¼ cup butter
½ cup honey
¼ cup heavy whipping cream
2 cups ground walnuts
1/3 cup brown sugar
½ teaspoon cinnamon
1/8 teaspoon ground cloves
½ teaspoon vanilla extract
1 teaspoon dark rum
½ teaspoon lemon juice

Dough Ingredients:
1 package quick-rise yeast
1 teaspoon sugar
¼ cup lukewarm water
2½ cups unbleached flour
2 tablespoons sugar
¼ teaspoon salt
¾ cup lukewarm milk
½ teaspoon vanilla extract
2 tablespoons melted butter
1 egg, slightly beaten

In a small bowl, combine the raisins with about ½ cup water. Set aside to soak. *To make the walnut filling*, in a medium mixing bowl, beat egg whites until stiff, about 5 to 7 minutes. In a medium saucepan, combine the butter, honey, and heavy whipping cream. Melt the butter over medium heat, stirring all the while. Remove from heat, and *let cool to room temperature*. Now, in a medium mixing bowl, combine ground walnuts, brown sugar, cinnamon, ground cloves, egg yolks, vanilla extract, rum, lemon juice, and *drained* raisins. Gradually, blend in the honey mixture, and use a whisk to fold-in the egg whites. It should be thick and a little milky. *Cover with plastic wrap and refrigerate for 1 hour.*

To make the dough, in a small bowl, dissolve quick-rise yeast and 1 teaspoon sugar in lukewarm water. Let stand for 5 minutes. Now, in a medium mixing bowl, use a whisk to combine flour, sugar, and salt. Add lukewarm milk, vanilla extract, melted butter, egg yolks, and yeast mixture. Mix just enough to blend well.

Then, turn out the dough onto a well floured work surface. Knead until smooth, *adding just enough flour to keep the dough from sticking*. Place in a greased bowl, Cover loosely with a clean kitchen towel or dish cloth, and let rise in a warm place for 1 to 1½ hours.

Roll out the dough to a ¼ inch thickness. Now, spread the walnut filling over approximately 2/3 of the dough, leaving about 1 inch between the filling and the edges of the dough.

Fold the edges of the dough over the filling. Then, use the table cloth to help roll the dough from the longer edge, starting with the filling. Roll tightly to maintain shape, and tuck-in the edges as you go. With the seam on the bottom, place on a greased baking sheet. Cover loosely with a clean kitchen towel, and let rise for 1 hour.

Preheat oven to 375 degrees F. Brush potica with egg yolks, and bake for 15 minutes. Then, reduce oven temperature to 300 degrees F and bake for an additional 30 to 40 minutes, or until golden brown.

Walnut Roll

"This delectable walnut roll is a log-shaped pastry made from yeast dough, ground walnuts, chopped raisins, sugar, butter, and cinnamon; typical of the Central and Eastern European variety."

Dough Ingredients:
1½ tablespoons quick-rise yeast
¼ cup warm water
¼ cup warm milk
½ teaspoon salt
¼ cup sugar
¼ cup melted butter
1 egg
2¾ cups unbleached flour

Filling Ingredients:
1 cup chopped sundried raisins
2/3 cup brown sugar
1/3 cup white sugar
1 teaspoon cinnamon
½ cup melted butter
2 cups ground walnuts
2 eggs, beaten

To prepare the dough, in a medium mixing bowl, dissolve the quick-rise yeast in warm water, with a pinch of sugar. Let stand for 15 minutes. Then, blend in the milk, salt, sugar, melted butter, and egg. Gradually add the flour, and beat to make a soft dough. Knead until smooth, place in greased bowl, and cover. *Allow mixture to double (about 1 hour)*.

In a small bowl, combine the chopped raisins with ½ cup dark rum or brandy. Set aside to soak.

To prepare the filling, in a medium mixing bowl, use a whisk to combine the brown sugar, white sugar, and cinnamon. Add the melted butter, ground walnuts, *drained* raisins, and eggs. *Cover with plastic wrap and refrigerate for 1 hour.*

On a lightly floured work surface, roll the dough into a rectangle, approximately 12" by 14". Spread a thin layer of filling onto the dough, leaving about ½ inch between the filling and the edge of the dough. Now, tightly roll up the dough from the long end. Wet the edge/seam on bottom so it sticks to the roll, place on a greased jellyroll pan (*a baking pan with sides about ½ inch high*), cover, and *let rise for 20 minutes*. Preheat oven to 325 degrees F. Bake for 15 minutes, *cover with foil*, and bake for an additional 25 minutes; or until golden brown.

Wedding Rings

"This is one of my great-grandmother's favorite recipes. Not to be confused with mexican wedding ring cookies though. The origin might be uncertain, but these wedding rings are tasty nevertheless!"

Chocolate Filling Ingredients:
3 eggs, separated
1 teaspoon almond extract
4 ounces baking chocolate, melted

Cake Ingredients:
5 large eggs, separated
½ cup sugar, divided
1 teaspoon vanilla extract
½ cup unbleached flour
2 tablespoons powdered sugar
1 (8 ounce) tub whipped topping

To make the chocolate filling, in a medium mixing bowl, beat egg whites until stiff peaks form, at least 5 to 7 minutes. In a medium mixing bowl, beat egg yolks until thick and creamy. Add almond extract and melted chocolate. Fold in egg whites, and beat until thick enough to spread. Set aside.

Preheat oven to 350 degrees F.

To make the cake, in a large mixing bowl, beat the egg whites until soft peaks form; at least 5 minutes. Add ¼ cup sugar, and continue beating until stiff peaks form.

In a separate bowl, beat egg yolks, vanilla extract, and remaining ¼ cup sugar until thick; about 5 to 7 minutes. Gradually add flour, mixing just enough to blend well.

Use a whisk to gently mix the egg yolk mixture into the egg whites. Spread the batter onto the bottom of a parchment paper-lined jelly-roll pan (*a baking sheet with sides that are about an inch deep*). Bake for 12 to 14 minutes, or until the top springs back when touched.

Sift the powdered sugar over a clean kitchen towel. Then, using a small knife, loosen the edges of the cake from the sides of the pan. Invert the cake onto a clean kitchen towel, and carefully peel off the parchment paper. Use the towel to help roll the cake like a jelly roll, beginning with the narrow end.

Immediately cut into 1 inch slices, quickly rolling into the shape of a ring by fastening the ends together with a toothpick. Then, place the rings on a sheet of wax paper, and use a pastry bag to fill each ring with chocolate filling.

Refrigerate for at least 2 hours. Then, use a pastry bag to pipe whipped topping over the chocolate filling before serving.

Soups

Cabbage Soup

¼ cup butter
2 medium onions, thinly sliced
1 medium celery stalks (*with leaves*), finely chopped
2 carrots, very thinly sliced
2 medium red potatoes, cut into ¼ inch cubes
3 cloves garlic, minced
2 teaspoons salt
½ teaspoon freshly ground black pepper
1 small head of cabbage, shredded
2 medium tomatoes, chopped
2 quarts chicken broth
1 small bunch fresh dill, finely chopped

In a large pot, melt butter over medium low heat. Sauté onions, celery, carrots, potatoes, garlic, salt, and pepper; about 3 to 5 minutes.

Add the shredded cabbage, and cook approximately 5 to 7 minutes longer, stirring occasionally. Then, add tomatoes and chicken broth.

Bring to a boil. Then, reduce heat to low, cover, and simmer, about 35 to 40 minutes. To serve, transfer soup to individual serving bowls, and top with fresh dill.

Cheddar Chowder

Chowder Ingredients:
2 tablespoons vegetable oil
1 medium onion, cut in half and very thinly sliced
1 medium carrot, peeled and very thinly sliced
1 medium celery stalk, finely chopped
1 red bell pepper, finely chopped
1 medium yukon gold or red potato, cut in ¼ inch pieces
Salt and freshly ground black pepper, to taste
2 tablespoons unbleached flour
1½ cups chicken stock
½ cup dry white wine
1 teaspoon worcestershire sauce
1 head fresh broccoli, cut into bite-size pieces
½ pound sharp cheddar cheese, grated

Croutons, Ingredients:
4 slices whole wheat bread, cut into ½ inch cubes
1 clove garlic, minced
3 tablespoons butter

To prepare the soup, heat the vegetable oil in a medium saucepan, over medium-high heat. Add the onion, carrot, celery, red bell pepper, and potato. Season with salt and freshly ground black pepper. Cook 5 to 7 minutes, add flour, and cook for an additional 3 minutes, stirring all the while. Then, add the chicken stock, white wine, worcestershire sauce, and broccoli. Cover, and let simmer for 10 to 15 minutes, or until broccoli and potatoes are tender. Remove from heat, and add grated cheddar cheese. Continue stirring until the cheese has completely melted. Serve immediately with croutons

To prepare the croutons, in a medium-sized frying pan, heat the butter over medium heat. Add the bread cubes and garlic, stirring occasionally, about 5 to 10 minutes or until golden brown. If the bread should soak up all the butter, simply add more.

Granny's Chicken Dumpling Soup

"This is my great-grandmother's chicken dumpling soup recipe. A bit different than my mom's...It's another economical, yet substantial dish though."

Chicken Broth:
1 medium, whole chicken
2 medium onions, chopped
3 medium celery stalks (*with leaves*), finely chopped
4 quarts cold water
2 teaspoons salt
½ teaspoon black pepper

Gravy Ingredients:
½ stick of butter
¼ cup unbleached flour
1½ cups warm chicken broth
½ cup milk
Salt and pepper, to taste
1 bunch fresh parsley, chopped

Dumpling Ingredients:
1½ cups unbleached flour
2 tablespoons baking powder
¾ teaspoon salt
¼ teaspoon nutmeg
3 tablespoons butter, softened
½ cup milk
¼ cup water

In a large pot, combine chicken, onions, celery, water, salt, and pepper. Bring to a boil. Then, reduce heat to low and simmer partially covered, until the chicken is tender; about 45 minutes.

Remove chicken, and set aside. When the chicken has cooled, remove meat from bones, and shred it into bite size pieces. Discard the skin and bones, strain broth, and discard the vegetables. *Be sure to reserve the broth, however.*

To prepare the dumplings, in a medium mixing bowl, use a whisk to combine the flour, baking powder, salt, and nutmeg. Then, in a small saucepan, over low heat, bring butter, milk, and water to a simmer. Gradually add to dry mixture, stirring just enough to blend well.

Bring remaining chicken broth to a boil. Then, drop dumplings by tablespoon into boiling water. Cover, and cook for 10 to 12 minutes, or until dumplings rise to the surface. Transfer to paper towel to drain.

To prepare the gravy, in a saucepan, melt butter over medium-high heat. Use a whisk to mix-in the flour. Then, add the chicken broth and milk, season with salt and pepper, and let simmer; stirring continuously until it thickens.

Place the chicken, dumplings, and broth in serving bowls, top with gravy and fresh parsley, and serve immediately.

Mom's Chicken Dumpling Soup

"Whenever my mom would roast a chicken, she'd remove the meat from the bones and freeze the carcass so she could make soup with it. I have many childhood memories of being pampered by my mom when I was sick. She'd make all kinds of soups that could soothe a sore throat, clear up congestion, and well, just make you feel better. You can also use this recipe to make chicken noodle soup, simply by preparing a package of thin egg noodles instead of making dumplings."

Soup Ingredients:
1 large chicken carcass (neck, back, wings and bones)
5 to 6 quarts cold water
1 onion, coarsely chopped
3 stalks celery (including celery leaves), quartered
2 whole carrots, peeled and quartered
1 parsnip, peeled and quartered
1 bunch fresh parsley, chopped
4 teaspoons salt
1 teaspoon black pepper

Dumpling Ingredients:
1 cup milk
½ cup butter
½ teaspoon salt
½ teaspoon nutmeg
1 cup unbleached flour
3 eggs
½ small onion, grated
½ teaspoon parsley

To make the soup, place the chicken carcass in a large pot, and add enough cold water to cover, about 5 to 6 quarts. Add onion, celery, carrots, parsnip, salt, and pepper.

Bring to a boil. Then reduce heat to medium low, and simmer covered for approximately 4 hours, using a large wooden spoon to skim any excess fat that rises to the surface.

Discard chicken carcass, onion, celery, carrots, and parsnip. Strain the broth. Remove 3 to 4 quarts of broth and, if you prefer, refrigerate or freeze for later use. Cover the remaining broth, and let simmer.

To make the dumplings, in a medium saucepan, bring the milk and butter to a boil. Add salt and nutmeg, and remove from heat. Immediately add flour, stirring until the mixture leaves the sides of the pan. Add the eggs, 1 at a time, to form a sticky dough.

Add tablespoon-sized balls of dough, and let simmer until dumplings rise to the surface.

To serve, transfer soup and dumplings to individual serving bowls, and top with fresh parsley.

Corn Chowder

"Whenever I have corn chowder, I'm reminded of an elementary school field trip to the Little Red Schoolhouse in Willoughby. It's just a small, one-room, red brick schoolhouse that was built in 1901 but the Little Red Schoolhouse was always a favorite outing for school children. Although I was eliminated from the spelling bee that day for misspelling the word 'sadness' (s-a-d-d-n-e-s-s?), I thoroughly enjoyed the corn chowder they served for lunch. If I'm not mistaken, the kids brown bag it nowadays. Too bad."

2 tablespoons vegetable oil
2 slices bacon, chopped
1 medium onion, chopped
2 cloves garlic, minced
2 ribs celery with leaves, chopped
1 medium carrot, finely chopped
1 teaspoon thyme
Salt and freshly ground black pepper, to taste
2 tablespoons unbleached flour
2 cups milk
2 cups chicken stock
2 medium potatoes, peeled and grated
1 (16 ounce) package frozen corn, thawed*

Heat vegetable oil in a medium saucepan, over medium-high heat. Add bacon, onion, garlic, celery, carrot, and thyme. Season with salt, and freshly ground black pepper. Cook 5 to 7 minutes, add flour, and cook 1 minute more.

Add milk and chicken stock, and bring to a boil. Stir-in shredded potatoes and corn. Return to boil, then reduce heat and simmer for 15 minutes, or until potatoes are fully cooked and soup has thickened enough to coat the back of a wooden spoon.

*Substitute 2 (10 ounce) cans of whole baby clams for clam chowder; or 2 pounds of cod, haddock, or halibut, cut into bite sized pieces for fish chowder.

Cream of Asparagus Soup

1 pound fresh asparagus
1 medium onion, chopped
1 tablespoon butter
3 cups chicken stock
1 medium potato, peeled and diced
1 celery rib, finely chopped
1 sprig fresh thyme
1 cup heavy cream
Salt and pepper, to taste

Remove 1 inch from the top of each asparagus spear, and trim the tough root ends. Cut into 2 inch lengths, reserving the middle portion of the stalks.

In a large saucepan, melt the butter and sauté the chopped onion, over medium heat, for 3 to 5 minutes. Add chicken stock, asparagus, potato, celery, thyme, salt, and pepper.

Bring to a boil, over high heat. Then, reduce heat to medium low, and simmer for 12 to 15 minutes. Remove from heat, and let cool.

Remove asparagus tips, and set aside. Then, place the soup in a food processor. Cover, and grind until smooth.

Pass through a fine mesh strainer, and return soup to saucepan. Add reserved asparagus tips and cream, and heat for an additional 10 to 12 minutes.

Cream of Mushroom Soup

¼ cup butter
1 medium onion, cut in half and thinly sliced
4 cloves garlic, minced
1 teaspoon parsley
½ teaspoon thyme
1 teaspoon salt
¼ teaspoon freshly ground black pepper
8 ounces mushrooms, sliced
3 tablespoons unbleached flour
4 cups chicken broth
½ cup milk
1 teaspoon port or sherry

In a medium saucepan, heat the butter over a medium-high flame. Add the onion and cook, stirring occasionally, until tender; about 5 minutes. Then add the garlic, parsley, thyme, salt, freshly ground black pepper, and mushrooms; and cook for an additional 3 minutes. Stir in the flour and cook for 2 minutes more.

Add the chicken broth and bring to a boil, stirring frequently. Then, lower the heat and let simmer for 10 minutes. Add the milk and port, remove from heat, and allow to cool. Divide among soup bowls, and serve immediately.

Farina Dumpling Soup

"My great-grandmother used to cook farina fairly often. Although my mother enjoyed it, my grandmother couldn't stand it. Perhaps farina's an acquired taste."

Dumpling Ingredients:
2 eggs, separated
¼ teaspoon nutmeg
¼ teaspoon salt
1 cup farina *or cream of wheat*

Soup Ingredients:
3 tablespoons extra-virgin olive oil
1 onion, cut in half and thinly sliced
2 cloves garlic, minced
1 carrot, very thinly sliced
1 young, tender bulbs kohlrabi, peeled and cut into ¼ inch cubes
2 medium red potatoes, cut into ¼ inch cubes
Salt and freshly ground black pepper, to taste
2 quarts chicken broth
1 bunch fresh parsley, chopped

To make the dumplings, beat egg whites until stiff, at least 5 to 7 minutes. Gently fold-in egg yolks, nutmeg, and salt. Gradually add farina, to make a stiff paste. Set aside.

To make the soup, in a large pot, heat olive oil over medium-high heat. Sauté onion, garlic, carrot, kohlrabi, potatoes, salt, and pepper for approximately 5 to 7 minutes. Add chicken broth, and bring to a boil. Then, reduce heat to low, cover, and simmer 35 to 40 minutes.

Drop tablespoon-sized balls of farina mixture into boiling soup, and let simmer until dumplings rise to the surface, about 15 minutes.

To serve, transfer soup and dumplings to individual serving bowls, and top with fresh parsley.

French Onion Soup

"My mom's french onion soup is a much like the traditional onion and beef broth soup, but is served with a loaf of crusty french bread on the side."

2 tablespoons vegetable oil
6 medium onions, *cut in half and thinly sliced*
2 teaspoons brown sugar
3 cloves garlic, minced
¼ teaspoon thyme
Salt and freshly ground black pepper, to taste
6 cups beef broth
½ cup dry white wine
1 bay leaf

Heat the vegetable oil in a medium saucepan, over medium heat. Add the onions, and cook for about 15 minutes, stirring frequently.

Now, add the brown sugar, and cook for an additional 30 to 45 minutes, until the onions have caramelized.

Add the garlic, thyme, salt, and freshly ground black pepper, and cook for approximately 1 minute. Add the beef broth, white wine, and bay leaf. Cover partially, and let simmer for 30 minutes. Remove and discard the bay leaf, and serve with a loaf of crusty french bread.

Gazpacho

1 seedless cucumber, peeled and diced
1 small red onion, diced
2 cloves garlic, minced
3 large tomatoes, diced
1 red bell pepper, diced
2 cups tomato juice
1½ cups chicken broth
¼ cup red wine vinegar
1 teaspoon oregano
1 teaspoon basil
¼ teaspoon hot sauce
½ teaspoon salt
¼ teaspoon freshly ground black pepper

In a large mixing bowl, combine cucumber, red onion, garlic, tomatoes, red bell pepper, tomato juice, chicken broth, red wine vinegar, oregano, basil, hot sauce, salt, and freshly ground black pepper. Mix well, and refrigerate overnight. Serve cold.

Italian Wedding Soup

"'Wedding Soup' is a bit of a misnomer... The Italian 'Minestra Maritata,' actually means 'Married Soup,' and is a reference to the fact that the assorted ingredients go so well together. Of course, I don't think anyone will complain if you serve it at your wedding. My son, Matthew, loves it!"

1 pound ground beef and pork mixture
¼ cup unseasoned bread crumbs
1 tablespoon parsley
½ teaspoon basil
¼ teaspoon garlic powder
½ teaspoon salt
¼ teaspoon freshly ground black pepper
1 egg
8 cups chicken stock
16 ounces frozen chopped spinach, *thawed and drained*
2 teaspoons chicken bouillon
¼ teaspoon garlic powder
½ teaspoon marjoram
½ teaspoon savory
1 cup orzo or other soup pasta
¼ cup freshly grated parmesan cheese

Preheat oven to 350 degrees F.

In a medium mixing bowl, combine the ground beef and pork mixture, bread crumbs, parsley, basil, garlic powder, salt, freshly ground black pepper, and egg. Gently mix with your hands, just enough to combine. Then, shape mixture into tiny meatballs (about 1½ teaspoons), arrange on an ungreased baking sheet, and bake for 30 minutes.

In a medium saucepan, combine the chicken stock, chopped spinach, chicken bouillon, garlic powder, marjoram, and savory. Bring to a boil. Then, add the meatballs, and return to boil. Now, add the orzo and cook until tender, about 10 minutes. Stir in the parmesan cheese, and serve immediately.

Kohlrabi Soup

3 tablespoons vegetable oil
1 onion, cut in half and thinly sliced
4 young, tender bulbs kohlrabi, peeled and cut into ½ inch cubes
2 cloves garlic, minced
Salt and freshly ground black pepper, to taste
1 quart chicken broth
¾ cup heavy cream
½ pound cooked bratwurst, cut in ¼ inch pieces
1 bunch fresh parsley, chopped

In a large pot, heat vegetable oil over medium-high heat. Sauté onion and kohlrabi for approximately 3 to 5 minutes. Add garlic, salt, pepper, and chicken broth. Bring to a boil. Then, reduce heat to low, cover, and simmer until the kohlrabi is tender, about 35 to 40 minutes.

Using a handheld blender, puree the soup. Add heavy cream, return to stove, and slowly heat to simmer (*do not boil*). Add cooked bratwurst and fresh parsley. Serve immediately.

Lentil Soup

2 tablespoons vegetable oil
1 medium onion, cut in half and very thinly sliced
2 medium carrots, very thinly sliced
1 medium celery stalk, thinly sliced
2 cloves garlic, minced
1 tablespoon curry powder
1 (14 ounce) can diced tomatoes
2 teaspoons lemon juice
1 bay leaf
1 (16 ounce) package dried lentils, *rinsed, picked over, and drained*
6 cups beef broth
1 (10 ounce) packages frozen chopped spinach, *thawed and drained*
Salt and freshly ground black pepper, to taste

Heat the vegetable oil in a medium saucepan, over medium-high heat. Add the onion, carrots, and celery. Cook 5 to 7 minutes, or until tender. Add the garlic and curry powder, and cook for one minute more.

Add the diced tomatoes (*with juice*), lemon juice, bay leaf, lentils, and beef stock. Bring to a boil over medium-high heat. Then, cover, reduce heat, and let simmer until lentils are tender, about 30 minutes.

Remove and discard the bay leaf. Add the spinach, and cook for an additional 3 to 5 minutes. Season with salt and freshly ground black pepper, and serve immediately.

Pasta Fagioli

"Pasta Fagioli is a traditional italian soup made with cannellini beans and pasta. If I'm not mistaken, you don't actually pronounce the 'i' at the end of Fagioli."

1 tablespoon extra-virgin olive oil
1 medium onion, thinly sliced
3 cloves garlic, minced
1 medium celery stalk, finely chopped
1 medium carrot, peeled and finely chopped
1 teaspoon basil
½ teaspoon oregano
¼ teaspoon crushed red pepper flakes
1 (14.5 ounce) stewed tomatoes, quartered
3 cups chicken stock
1 (15 ounce) can cannellini beans, drained and rinsed
1 cup soup pasta (*such as ditalini, stortini, tubetti, or elbow macaroni*)
¼ cup fresh parsley, chopped
Freshly grated parmesan cheese, for garnish

In a large pot, heat the olive oil over a medium-high flame. Sauté the onion for 2 to 3 minutes, or until tender. Then, add the garlic, celery, carrot, basil, oregano, and crushed red pepper flakes. Cook for approximately 3 to 5 minutes. Add the stewed tomatoes and chicken stock, and bring to a boil. Reduce the heat to low, and let simmer for 30 minutes. Add the cannellini beans and pasta. Let simmer for 6 to 8 minutes, or until tender. Stir in the parsley, and serve hot with freshly grated parmesan cheese.

Potato & Leek Soup

2 tablespoons vegetable oil
1 onion, cut in half and thinly sliced
6 potatoes, peeled and cut into ½ inch cubes
2 cloves garlic, minced
Salt and freshly ground black pepper, to taste
2 cups chicken broth
2 tablespoons butter
2 leeks, chopped
1½ cups heavy cream

In a large pot, heat vegetable oil over medium-high heat. Sauté onion and potatoes for approximately 3 to 5 minutes.

Add garlic, salt, pepper, and chicken broth. Bring to a boil. Then, reduce heat to low and simmer until tender, about 20 to 25 minutes.

In a medium skillet, heat butter over medium flame. Sauté leeks for approximately 5 to 7 minutes, or until tender.

Using a handheld blender, puree the potatoes. Then, add the leeks and heavy cream, and serve immediately.

Pumpkin Soup

3 tablespoons butter
1 medium onion, chopped
2 cloves garlic, chopped
1 large carrot, peeled and chopped
2 stalks celery (including celery leaves), chopped
7 cups vegetable broth
1½ cups pure pumpkin puree
¼ teaspoon cinnamon
¼ teaspoon allspice
¼ teaspoon ginger
¼ teaspoon nutmeg
2 tablespoons honey
Salt and freshly ground black pepper, to taste
¼ cup sour cream

In a medium saucepan, melt the butter over medium heat. Add the onion, garlic, carrot and celery, and cook until soft, about 3 to 5 minutes.

Add the vegetable broth, and bring to a boil. Then, reduce the heat and let simmer for 20 to 30 minutes. *Strain the broth and discard the onion, garlic, carrot, and celery.*

Add the pumpkin puree, cinnamon, allspice, ginger, nutmeg, and honey. Bring to a simmer, and cook for another 15 to 20 minutes.

Remove from heat, season with salt and pepper, and add the sour cream. Serve immediately.

Red Bean Soup

Soup Ingredients:
1½ cups dried red beans, *soaked overnight in cold water*
2 tablespoons vegetable oil
1 onion, cut in half and thinly sliced
3 cloves garlic, minced
2 medium celery stalks, finely chopped
2 medium carrots, very thinly sliced
2 teaspoons parsley
2 teaspoons oregano
2 teaspoons thyme
Salt and freshly ground black pepper, to taste
1 teaspoon hot sauce
1 (14.5 ounce) can diced tomatoes, *with juice*
1 smoked ham hock, *weighing about 1 pound*
6 cups chicken stock
2 cups water
2 bay leaves
½ cup sour cream

Chicken Ingredients:
3 tablespoons paprika
½ teaspoon cayenne
½ teaspoon garlic powder
1 teaspoon oregano
½ teaspoon salt
½ teaspoon freshly ground black pepper
2 tablespoons vegetable oil
5 boneless, skinless chicken breast halves

Place the beans in a medium saucepan. Add enough water to cover by approximately 2 inches, and soak overnight. Drain, rinse thoroughly, and set aside.

To prepare the soup, in a large pot, heat the vegetable oil over a medium-high flame. Sauté the onion, garlic, celery, and carrots for 3 to 5 minutes, or until tender. Add the parsley, oregano, thyme, salt, freshly ground black pepper, and hot sauce, and cook for an additional 3 minutes. Now, add the diced tomatoes, ham hock, chicken stock, water, bay leaves, and red beans, and bring to a boil. Reduce flame to medium-low, and let simmer 1 to 1½ hours, or until the beans are soft.

To prepare the chicken, in a small mixing bowl, use a whisk to combine the paprika, cayenne, garlic powder, oregano, salt, and freshly ground black pepper. Now, in a large heavy skillet, heat the vegetable oil over medium-high heat. Season the chicken with the prepared seasoning, and sear the chicken until browned, about 3 to 4 minutes per side. Remove from skillet, let cool, and cut into bite-size pieces.

When the beans are tender, add the chicken and cook for an additional 5 minutes. Remove bay leaves, ladle into soup bowls, and top with a generous portion of sour cream.

Sausage Bean Soup

"My mom would typically make this soup for dinner on a cold winter's evening. It's simple to make, but very enjoyable. She used two different types of beans; black beans and butter beans. We prefer using corn and black beans, however."

¾ pound Italian sausage, *cut in ¼ inch pieces*
1 medium onion, chopped
2 cloves garlic, minced
1 teaspoon basil
1 (15 ounce) can butter beans, *rinsed and drained*
1 (16 ounce) package frozen whole kernel corn, *thawed*
1 (15 ounces) can black beans, *rinsed and drained*
1 (14.5 ounce) can diced tomatoes, *(do not drain)*
1 (14.5 ounce) can beef broth
¼ cup freshly grated parmesan cheese

In a large saucepan, cook sausage, onion, garlic, and basil until lightly browned, about 3 to 5 minutes. Then, drain any excess fat, and add the corn, black beans, diced tomatoes, and beef broth. Bring to a boil over high heat. Then reduce heat to medium low, and simmer for 10 to 15 minutes. To serve, top each bowlful of soup with freshly grated parmesan cheese.

Sour Cherry Soup

1½ teaspoons cornstarch
½ cup cold water
1 (16 ounce) can pitted sour cherries, drained and halved (*reserve juice*)
1 tablespoon sugar
¼ teaspoon cinnamon
2 tablespoons red wine
¼ cup heavy cream
¾ cup sour cream

In a small mixing bowl, combine cornstarch and cold water. Mix well and set aside.

In a medium saucepan, combine cornstarch mixture and reserved cherry juice. Bring to a boil over high heat. Then reduce the heat to medium low and simmer for approximately 5 minutes, stirring all the while. Add sugar, cinnamon, and red wine. Remove from heat.

Let cool to room temperature before adding the heavy cream, sour cream, and cherries. Refrigerate at least 2 hours before serving.

Split Pea Soup

2 teaspoons vegetable oil
1 medium onion, finely chopped
1 pound dried split peas
1 ham bone
Salt and freshly ground black pepper, to taste

In a large pot, heat the vegetable oil over medium-high heat, and sauté the onion for 3 to 5 minutes, or until tender. Add the split peas, ham bone, salt, freshly ground black pepper, and just enough water to cover.

Bring to a boil over high heat. Then, reduce heat to low, cover, and let simmer until peas are soft, about 2 hours. Remove from heat, and let stand 15 minutes before serving.

Swiss Chard Soup

1 (8 ounce) package capellini
2 tablespoons extra-virgin olive oil
2 medium onions, cut in half and very thinly sliced
2 carrots, peeled and very thinly sliced
1 small bunch swiss chard
6 cups chicken stock
1 (15 ounce) can cannellini beans, drained and rinsed
1 large tomato, chopped
¼ cup fresh basil leaves, chopped
3 cloves garlic, minced
¼ cup fresh parsley, chopped
Salt and freshly ground black pepper, to taste
½ cup freshly grated parmesan cheese

To prepare the swiss chard, separate the leaves from stalks and cut both into thin strips, crosswise.

Bring a medium pot of water to boil. Cook the capellini according to package directions. Drain in colander, and rinse with cool water.

Heat the extra-virgin olive oil in a medium saucepan, over medium-high heat. Add the onions, carrots, and swiss chard, and cook until tender, about 5 to 7 minutes.

Add the chicken stock, cannellini beans, tomato, basil, and garlic. Let simmer, partially covered, for about 10 minutes or until the beans are tender. Use a handheld blender to puree the soup.

Then, and add the cooked capellini and fresh parsley. Season with salt and freshly ground black pepper, and cook for an additional 3 minutes.

To serve, ladle the soup into individual serving bowls, and garnish with freshly grated parmesan cheese. Serve immediately.

Tomato & Corn Soup

2 tablespoons vegetable oil
2 medium onions, cut in half and very thinly sliced
4 large tomatoes, chopped
2 tablespoons unbleached flour
1 (16 ounce) package frozen whole kernel corn, thawed
½ cup fresh basil leaves, coarsely chopped
1 tablespoon tomato paste
3 cups chicken stock
Salt and freshly ground black pepper, to taste

Heat the vegetable oil in a medium saucepan, over medium-high heat. Add the onions and tomatoes, and cook until tender, about 3 to 5 minutes.

Add the flour and cook for an additional 2 minutes, stirring continuously. Next, add the corn, basil, tomato paste, and chicken stock. Bring to a boil over high heat. Then, reduce the heat to medium low, and simmer for 25 minutes, stirring occasionally.

Using a handheld blender, puree the soup. Pass through a fine mesh strainer, season with salt and pepper, and refrigerate for at least 4 hours. Serve chilled.

Silvia's Smoky Tomato Bisque

"This recipe was inspired by the Blue Point Grille's roasted tomato bisque, which is actually served with crumbled gorgonzola and sourdough croutons. Located in the Warehouse District, at the corner of West Sixth and Saint Clair, the Blue Point Grille arguably serves the best seafood in Cleveland. Though, I prefer Silvia's take on their tomato bisque."

Tomato Bisque Ingredients:
1 (6 ounce) can tomato paste
1 (10 ounce) can tomato sauce
1 (10.75 ounce) can tomato puree
1½ cups water
1 teaspoon chicken soup base
1/8 cup brown sugar
1½ tablespoons basil
1 tablespoon oregano
1 teaspoon garlic powder
1 cup heavy cream
¼ teaspoon liquid smoke flavoring
Salt and freshly ground black pepper, to taste
½ cup mozzarella cheese, shredded

In a medium saucepan, combine the tomato paste, tomato sauce, tomato puree, water, chicken soup base, and brown sugar. Bring to a boil over high heat. Then, reduce to low heat and let simmer, *stirring frequently*. Add the basil, oregano, and garlic powder, heavy cream and liquid smoke flavoring. Season with salt and freshly ground black pepper, heat gently, and stir until smooth, but *do not boil!*

Crouton Ingredients:
3 tablespoons butter
4 slices whole wheat bread, cut into ½ inch cubes
1 clove garlic, minced

In a medium frying pan, heat the butter over medium heat. Cook the bread cubes and garlic (*stirring periodically*) for 5 to 10 minutes, or until golden brown.

If the bread should soak up the butter, simply add more. Remove the croutons from the frying pan and set aside.

Serve tomato bisque and croutons in a bowl, and a top with shredded mozzarella cheese.

Turnip Soup

"It's best to use turnips that are small, but feel relatively heavy for their size. If you prefer, you can substitute kohlrabi, rutabaga, or parsnips in place of turnips."

1/3 cup butter
3 medium onions, very thinly sliced
3 pounds turnips, peeled and thinly sliced
2 pounds potatoes, peeled and thinly sliced
¼ teaspoon nutmeg
Salt and freshly ground black pepper, to taste
6 cups chicken broth
¼ cup fresh basil leaves, chopped

In a large pot, melt the butter over medium heat. Sauté onions until tender, about 3 to 5 minutes. Add turnips, potatoes, nutmeg, salt, and freshly ground black pepper. Cook over medium-low heat until tender, stirring occasionally, for 15 to 20 minutes.

Add chicken broth, and bring to a boil. Then, reduce heat to low, cover, and let simmer for 30 to 40 minutes, or until tender. Using a handheld blender, puree the soup. Add fresh basil, and serve immediately.

Tuscan Tomato Soup

8 slices of crusty french bread
2 tablespoons extra-virgin olive oil
1 medium onion, cut in half and very thinly sliced
3 cloves garlic, minced
4 large tomatoes, chopped
4 cups chicken stock
½ cup fresh basil leaves, coarsely chopped
Salt and freshly ground black pepper, to taste
½ cup freshly grated parmesan cheese

Preheat oven to 300 degrees F.

Place the bread on a baking sheet, and bake until lightly browned, about 5 to 7 minutes per side.

Now, heat the extra-virgin olive oil in a large pot, over medium heat. Add the onion, garlic, and tomatoes, and cook until tender, about 3 to 5 minutes. Add the chicken stock, and bring to a boil over high heat. Then, reduce the heat to medium low, and simmer for 30 minutes, stirring occasionally.

Using a handheld blender, puree the soup. Add the chopped basil, and season with salt and freshly ground black pepper. To serve, place a slice of toasted french bread in the bottom of each bowl. Sprinkle with parmesan cheese, and ladle the soup over top.

Vegetable Barley Soup

¼ cup barley, rinsed and drained
4 medium carrots, very thinly sliced
1 medium yukon gold or red potato, cut in ¼ inch pieces
1 (14.5 ounce) can diced tomatoes, with juice
1 (16 ounce) package frozen whole kernel corn, thawed
2 quarts (8 cups) vegetable stock
1 (16 ounce) can green beans, rinsed and drained
Salt and freshly ground black pepper, to taste

In a medium pot, combine the barley, carrots, potato, diced tomatoes, corn, and vegetable stock. Bring to a boil over high heat. Then, reduce heat to medium low, and simmer for 30 minutes, stirring occasionally.

Add the green beans, and cook for an additional 15 minutes, or until the potatoes are tender and the barley is soft. Season with salt and freshly ground black pepper, and serve immediately.

Zucchini Soup

1 cup chicken broth
2 cups grated zucchini
1/8 teaspoon basil
1/8 teaspoon thyme
1/8 teaspoon marjoram
Salt and freshly ground black pepper, to taste
2 cups milk

In a medium saucepan, add the chicken broth and zucchini. Bring to a boil. Then cover, reduce heat, and simmer until zucchini is tender, about 10 to 15 minutes.

Add the basil, thyme, marjoram, salt, and pepper. Puree the soup in an electric blender or food processor until smooth.

Return the soup to saucepan and stir in the milk. Continue cooking over medium heat, stirring occasionally, until heated throughout. *Do not boil!*

Index

A

Almond Biscotti · 358
Almonds, Roasted · 270
American Flag Cake · 68
Apple Cinnamon Cake · 69
Apple Cinnamon Muffins · 276
Apple Date Squares · 359
Apple Dumplings · 360
Apple Fritters, Helen's · 361
Apple Kuchen, Granny's · 362
Apple Oatmeal Cookies · 106
Apple Pie · 287
Apple Squares · 363
Apple Strudel · 364
Applesauce · 297
Austrian Nut Butter Cookies · 107

B

Babka · 162
Bacon Bread · 30
Baked Beans · 298
Banana Bread · 31
Banana Cake · 70
Banana Oatmeal Cookies · 108
Bannock · 350
Bavarian Dumplings with Vanilla Glaze · 365
Bean Salad, Curried · 309
Bee Sting Cake · 71
Beef Chow Mein · 187
Beef Stroganoff & Egg Noodles · 188
Beets · 300
Biscuits, Granny's Homemade · 32
Black Bean Chili · 189
Black Bean Salad · 301
Black Walnut Cookies · 109
Black-Eyed Peas · 302
Blarney Stones · 171
Blueberry Muffins · 277
Blueberry Pie · 288
Blueberry Scones · 351
Boxty · 190
Bran Muffins · 278
Bratwurst & Kraut Sandwich · 336
Brazil Nut Sticks · 110
Bread Pudding, Porgie's · 366
Bread Stuffing · 176
Bread, White · 54
Broccoli Salad · 303
Brown Betty · 367
Brown Bread · 33
Brownies · 368
Brunswick Stew · 191
Buckeyes · 111
Butter Tea · 261

C

Cabbage & Bacon · 192
Cabbage & Noodles · 193
Cabbage Soup · 409
Carrot Cake · 72
Catfish, Fried · 194
Chai Tea · 262
Cheddar Chowder · 410
Cheese Biscuits · 34
Cheese Scones · 352
Cheese Spaetzle · 6
Cheese Strudel · 369
Cheeseburger · 337
Cheesecakes, Mini · 131
Cherry Pie · 289
Cherry Winks · 112
Chicken & Rice, Baked · 201
Chicken & Vegetables, Roast · 205
Chicken Breast, Honeyed · 195
Chicken Curry · 196
Chicken Dumpling Soup, Granny's · 411
Chicken Dumpling Soup, Mom's · 412
Chicken Fried Rice · 197
Chicken Puffs · 7
Chicken Salad · 338
Chicken Salad Casserole · 8
Chicken Soft Tacos · 198
Chicken Tandoori · 199
Chicken Wings · 9
Chicken with Sun dried Tomatoes & Basil · 200
Chicken, Della's Almost BBQ · 202
Chicken, Fried · 203
Chicken, Jerk with Rice & Peas · 204
Chili, Kathy's Classic · 206
Chocolate Biscotti · 370
Chocolate Cake, Aunt Mary's · 73
Chocolate Chip Cookies · 113
Chocolate Fudge Cake · 74
Chocolate Layer Cake, Butter Cream · 75
Cleaning Lady's Cake, Hilda's · 371
Cockles and Mussels · 207
Coconut Cake · 76
Colcannon · 10
Coleslaw · 304
Compote · 305
Corn Chowder · 413
Corn Pudding · 12
Corn Pudding with Cheese · 11
Corn, Herbed · 177
Cornbread · 35
Cornbread Stuffing · 178
Corned Beef & Cabbage · 172
Cornmeal Rolls · 36
Crab Cakes · 208
Cranberry Sauce · 179
Cream Cake, Old Fashioned · 77
Cream Cheese Cookie Tarts · 372
Cream of Asparagus Soup · 414
Cream of Mushroom Soup · 415
Crescent Cookies, Filled · 115
Crescent Cookies, Vanilla · 116
Crescent Roll Cheesecake, Junior's · 373
Cucumber Salad · 308
Curry Noodles, Singapore-Style · 209
Custard Frosting · 263

D

Dandelion Salad, Creamy · 311
Dandelion Salad, Vinegar & Oil Dressing · 310
Date Balls, Frosted · 117
Date Bread · 37
Date Coffee Cake · 78
Date Drop Cookies · 118
Date Nut Bars · 374
Date Nut Torte · 79
Date Oatmeal Cookies · 119
Date Oatmeal Squares · 375
Date Pudding · 376
Date Raisin Nut Cookies · 120
Date Sticks · 377
Deviled Eggs · 13
Dobos Torte · 80
Dublin Coddle · 210
Duchess Potatoes · 14

E

Easter Bread · 164
Easy Fudge Icing · 264
Egg Noodles, Potatoes & Cucumber Salad · 211
Egg Salad · 339
Eggplant & Beef Stew · 212
Eggplant Caviar · 38
Eggplant Farfalle · 213
Eggplant Lasagna · 214
Eggplant Moussaka · 215
Eggplant Parmesan · 216
Eggplant Spread · 39
Eggplant with Steamed Rice, Chinese · 217
Enchilada Casserole · 218

F

Face Soap · 265
Farina Dumpling Soup · 416
Fettuccine Alfredo · 219
Fish & Chips · 220
Fish Fry, Granny's Battered · 221
Fish Pie · 222
Fish Tacos · 223
Frankfurter Kranz · 81
French Onion Soup · 417
French Toast · 59
Fried Dough (Krapfen) · 40
Fried Eggplant Sandwich with Pesto Sauce · 340
Fried Green Tomatoes · 312
Fruit Nut Bars · 378
Fruitcake · 151
Fudge Icing · 264

G

Garlic Butter · 41
Gazpacho · 418
German Apple Cake · 82
German Potato Salad · 313
German Wreath Cake · 165
Gingerbread Hearts · 379

Gingerbread Men · 152
Gingersnaps · 121
Goulash · 224
Green Beans, Company · 314
Green Beans, Dutch-Style · 315
Green Beans, Sweet & Sour with Bacon · 316
Green Beans, Sweet & Sour with Pimentos · 317
Guacamole Dip, Five Layer · 15

H

Ham Roll Ups · 16
Ham Salad · 341
Ham, Baked · 163
Hawaiian Cake · 83
Hershey's Kiss Cookies · 122
Honey Drops · 123
Hot Cross Buns · 166
Hot Toddy · 266
Hungarian Nut Torten · 84
Hurricane · 208
Hush Puppies · 17

I

Ice Cream Cone Cupcakes · 279
Icebox Cookies, Brazil Nut · 124
Icebox Cookies, Granny's Sour Cream · 125
Icebox Cookies, Walnut · 126
Indian Pudding · 380
Irish Cream Cheesecake · 173
Irish Soda Scones · 356
Israeli Nut Cookies · 127
Italian Sausage · 225

K

Key Lime Pie · 290
Kimmel · 267
Kipfels · 128
Kohlrabi & Dill · 318
Kohlrabi Soup · 420
Kolachky Cookies, Poppy Seed · 140

L

Lasagna, Kathy's Legendary · 226
Lebkuchen · 153
Lemon Cheese Filling · 268
Lemon Poppy Seed Muffins · 280
Lemon Poppy Seed Scones · 353
Lentil Soup · 421
Linzer Cookies · 154
Lobster Rolls · 342

M

Macaroni & Cheese · 227
Macaroons · 129
Maple Cookies · 130

Maple Glaze · 130
Maple Nut Chews · 381
Maple Walnut Cupcakes · 281
Maple Walnut Scones · 354
Marshmallow Cream Frosting, Whipped · 274
Marzipan Stollen · 155
Mashed Potatoes · 180
Meat Pie · 228
Meatloaf, Kathy's Magnificent · 229
Mince Pie · 156
Molasses Cookies · 132
Monkey Bread · 42
Morning Glory Muffins · 282
Muesli · 60
Mulberry Pie · 291
Mushroom Risotto & Tomatoes · 230
Mushy Peas · 319

N

Nachos Grande, Trina's · 18
Nut Queens · 383

O

Oatmeal · 61
Oatmeal Cookies · 133
Olive Bread, Kalamata · 43
Omelette, Kalamata · 62
Orange Date Squares · 384
Orange Marmalade Bread Pudding · 385

P

Palatschinken · 63
Pancakes, Blueberry · 58
Pancakes, Pumpkin · 64
Pancakes, Zucchini · 66
Paprikash · 231
Parsnips, Creamed · 306
Pasta Fagioli · 422
Pasta Salad · 320
Peach Kuchen · 386
Peach Pie · 292
Peanut Butter Cookies · 134
Peanut Butter Cupcakes · 283
Peanut Butter Roundup Cookies · 135
Peanut Cookies · 136
Peanut Oatmeal Chewies · 387
Peanuttiest Cookies · 137
Pear Butter · 102
Pfeffernüsse · 157
Pickles, Sliced Cucumber · 104
Pierogies · 232
Pigs in a Blanket · 19
Pine Nut Cookies · 138
Pistachio Pudding Cake · 85
Plum Dumplings · 388
Plum Kuchen · 389
Plum Puff Pudding · 390
Polenta with Spinach & Feta Cheese · 233
Popovers · 284
Poppy Seed Bread · 44

Poppy Seed Cheesecake · 391
Poppy Seed Coffee Cake · 392
Poppy Seed Coffee Ring Cake · 86
Poppy Seed Cookies · 139
Poppy Seed Custard Pie · 293
Poppy Seed Filling · 269
Poppy Seed Roll, Mom's · 393
Poppy Seed Squares · 394
Pork Roast · 168
Pork, Pulled · 234
Portobello Burgers with Pesto Sauce · 343
Potato & Leek Soup · 423
Potato Dumplings · 235
Potato Pancakes · 20
Potato Rolls, Three Hour · 45
Potato Salad · 321
Potica/Nut Roll, Granny's · 405
Pretzels, Soft · 25
Pumpernickel · 46
Pumpkin Bread · 47
Pumpkin Cake · 87
Pumpkin Pie · 181
Pumpkin Scones · 355
Pumpkin Seeds, Roasted · 299
Pumpkin Soup · 424
Pumpkin, Baked · 299
Puppy Cookies · 141

R

Rabarberkuchen (Rhubarb Cake) · 398
Raisin Bread · 48
Raisin-Date Bars · 395
Raspberry Squares · 396
Raspberry Turnovers · 397
Red Bean Soup · 425
Red Beans & Rice · 236
Red Cabbage · 322
Red Velvet Cake, Silvia's · 88
Relish, Crisp Sweet · 98
Relish, Cucumber · 99
Relish, Green Tomato · 100
Relish, Peach · 101
Relish, Rhubarb · 103
Reuben Sandwich · 344
Rhubarb Custard Pie · 294
Rhubarb Shortcake · 399
Rice Krispies Treats · 400
Rice Sausage & Sauerkraut, Slovenian · 237
Roast Beef with Yorkshire Puddings · 239
Rock Cookies · 142
Root Beer · 271
Rosemary and Sage Butter · 183
Royal Icing (No Egg Whites) · 272
Rum Balls · 143
Rum Cake · 89
Rutabaga, Mashed · 323
Rye Bread · 49

S

Saffron Rice · 21
Salmon Patties & Creamed Peas · 241
Salmon with Dill Sauce · 242
Salsa, Tomatillo · 27

Sauerbraten · 243
Sauerkraut · 23
Sauerkraut Balls · 169
Sausage Bean Soup · 426
Scalloped Potatoes · 24
Schmarren · 65
Seafood Gumbo · 244
Shamrock Cookies · 174
Shepherd's Pie · 245
Shortbread Cookies · 144
Sloppy Joes · 345
Soda Bread · 50
Sour Cherry Soup · 427
Sour Cream Cookies · 145
Sour Cream Sugar Cookies, Granny's · 146
Spaghetti & Italian Sausage · 246
Spaghetti & Meatballs · 247
Spaghetti Squash · 324
Spanish Rice · 248
Special Occasion Cake · 90
Spice Cake, Anna Beer's · 91
Spinach Marie · 325
Spinach Pie, Ricotta & Feta · 238
Spinach, Creamed · 307
Split Pea Soup · 428
Springerle Cookies · 158
Spritz Cookies · 159
Squash, Stuffed · 326
Strawberry Pie · 295
Strawberry Shortcake · 402
Stuffed Cabbage · 249
Stuffed Peppers · 250
Sugar Cookies, Classic Christmas · 160
Summer Squash · 327
Sunflower Seed Rolls · 51
Sweet Potatoes with Maple Syrup & Marshmallows · 184
Swiss Chard Soup · 429
Swiss Chard with Cream Sauce · 328

T

Tabouleh · 26
Tapenade · 52
Tapioca Pudding · 403
Three Bean Salad, Beaner's Favorite · 329
Three Beans & Rice · 251
Three Sisters Stew · 252
Thumbprints · 147
Thumbprints, Coconut · 114
Tilapia, Baked · 253
Tiramisu Cake · 92
Tomato & Corn Soup · 430
Tomato Bisque, Silvia's Smoky · 431
Tomato Butter · 53
Tomato Salad · 330

Tomato Salsa · 22
Tomato Sauce · 273
Tomato Soup, Tuscan · 433
Tuna Casserole · 254
Tuna Salad · 346
Turkey Brine · 185
Turkey Burgers · 347
Turkey, Roast · 182
Turnip Soup · 432

V

Vanilla Cheesecake · 93
Veal Parmesan · 255
Vegetable Barley Soup · 434
Vegetable Beef Casserole · 256
Vegetarian Chili · 257
Vegetarian Lasagna · 258
Veggie Burgers · 348
Veggie Burgers, Black Bean · 335

W

Walnut Cream Cake · 94
Walnut Frosties with Orange Butter Cream · 404
Walnut Roll · 406
Wedding Rings · 407
Wedding Soup · 419
Whiskey Cake · 95
Whiskey Cakes, Aunt Mary's Mini- · 382
White Bean & Tomato Rotini · 240
White Layer Cake · 96
Wiener Schnitzel · 259
Wilted Lettuce Salad · 331
Wine Cookies · 148
Wurst Salad · 332

Y

Yeast Dough, Aunt Dorothy's · 55
Yorkshire Puddings · 239

Z

Zucchini & Potato Pancakes · 28
Zucchini Bread · 56
Zucchini Cookies · 149
Zucchini Muffins · 285
Zucchini Soup · 435
Zucchini, Mother's · 333

Made in the USA
Columbia, SC
13 May 2025